Soaring Where Christ Has Led

Innovative Worship Ideas
For The 21st Century

Richard Avery

and

Don Marsh

CSS Publishing Company, Inc., Lima, Ohio

SOARING WHERE CHRIST HAS LED

Copyright © 2002 by
CSS Publishing Company, Inc.
Lima, Ohio

Library of Congress Cataloging-in-Publication Data

Avery, Richard K. (Richard Kinsey), 1934-
  Soaring where Christ has led : innovative worship ideas for the 21st century / Richard Avery and Don Marsh.
    p. cm.
ISBN 0-7880-1906-6 (pbk. : alk. paper)
1. Public worship. 2. Church year. I. Marsh, Don. II. Title.
BV30 .A95 2002
264—dc21   2002004389

For more information about CSS Publishing Company resources, visit our website at www.csspub.com or e-mail us at custserv@csspub.com or call (800) 241-4056.

ISBN 0-7880-1906-6   PRINTED IN U.S.A.

Table Of Contents

Introduction

What language shall I borrow
To thank Thee, dearest friend,
For this, Thy dying sorrow,
Thy pity without end?

These words are sung in the great passion chorale "O Sacred Head Now Wounded" by Bach. They explain the reason for this book. The wonder of God's love revealed in the life, teachings, death, and resurrection of Jesus; the power of God's justice and compassion revealed in our world right now; the splendor of God's creation; and the love we experience in the church and other relationships all move us to worship God as *creatively and with as much energy and feeling* as possible.

What languages *can* we borrow? What forms of human expression can we claim and adapt for the church's communications with God and God's communications with us? How can we effectively share the gospel with our contemporary world in ways that people can really understand?

For some ten years we had the privilege of seeking answers to these questions in a monthly CSS publication called *In the Worship Workshop with Avery and Marsh*. In a newsletter format we shared ideas and experiences emerging from our work as pastor and music and arts director, respectively, in an ordinary church in a small, industrial, middle-class town. We continue to honor the congregation of the First Presbyterian Church of Port Jervis, New York, for their creativity, their willingness to learn new vocabularies for their weekly encounters with God, and their capacity for laughter and tears as we struggled together to learn how to be the people of God in the modern world.

Now we are grateful to editor Stan Purdum and to CSS for the opportunity to share material selected from those 500 issues of *In the Worship Workshop* that may continue to be helpful in this new century.

Through our forty years of collaboration in ministry in Port Jervis, as well as through workshops, conferences, and assemblies we have led in 46 states and many denominations of the church, we have tried to submit to the leadership of the Holy Spirit in several particular directions. One of these was in **bringing all generations of people together in worship**. Many congregations have discovered that as children, young people, and adults of all ages gather to worship *together,* that services become more exciting, more significant in people's lives and more genuine in relation to the real world. Therefore, many of the ideas in this book are attempts to engage folks of all ages in receiving the Word in scripture and expressing our needs and hopes to God in intergenerational unity.

Another mission expressed in these pages is to encourage active **participation** by the whole church body in the liturgy. As we look back on our ministries, among our strongest and fondest memories are of things that ordinary church members did in leading parts of worship, and of acts of the congregation which "took off" beyond what we as leaders expected or controlled. We found that services were much more significant in people's lives when the people themselves had active roles in planning and leading acts of worship in a variety of "languages" of the Spirit.

A third purpose in our exploration: To engage **all senses, human capacities, and talents** in worship. Vital worship must move beyond the leaders' treatment of the congregation as a *sedentary* *and passive audience* that moves only to hold hymnals and reach to their pockets for their offerings. Drama, movement and dance, and the use of light, fabric, color, and other physical sensations have major roles in the history of worship, and the Holy Spirit has moved people to reclaim them for our own services in our time. The reading of printed words in a bulletin and passive attention to the voices of leaders are not enough to experience or express the glory and wonder of God's power and grace.

It seems that there is currently a new and dramatic recognition among churches of all kinds of the **power of music** to shape our lives. Yes, music has been an essential part of worship through the centuries, but we have come to fresh realization of its importance in worship in recent years. So the claiming of *all kinds of musical forms and styles* for the glory of God is a major emphasis in these pages, along with suggestions for greater creativity in using old and familiar music.

Finally, we hope that readers recognize in these articles that one central mission of the church must always be to **let the Bible come alive**. In some churches we have observed that the Bible actually gains little attention and interest in worship, and many members have little knowledge of the book's contents. Therefore, through drama, music, and other means, we have sought new ways to recover the liveliness and power of scripture to shape and guide our corporate and individual Christian lives.

In all of these pages we offer both respect for vital traditions of worship and the recognition that *the Holy Spirit continues to move among us.* As we write these words the Western world is coping with new feelings of insecurity and tension, and scenes of violence around the world are crowding into our homes through the television news. There are also many signs of spiritual hunger among the nations. We cannot worship God in isolation from this changing world, nor can we fail to offer the Good News of God's love and comfort in vital and vigorous ways, proclaiming ancient truths in fresh forms and, by God's grace, even discovering new truths along the way.

Richard Avery and Donald Marsh
Santa Fe, New Mexico

The Church At Worship

The cars pull in the driveway and squeeze into parking places around the yards, and — there's cousin Randy and his new wife! And her younger brother is with them, the one who was in that bad accident. And old uncle Howard, still lamenting his wife's death a few months ago, holds the door and greets the youngest nieces and nephews with obvious delight. Meanwhile, the grandmas and the grandpas are inside welcoming everybody with warm embraces, and meeting new members of the family and finding a place for them. The little kids are already scurrying about, but nobody seems to mind; everybody seems to love the children, and they take turns holding the little ones and asking the older ones about their schoolwork and activities. Good news about family members, their adventures, and projects is shared by everybody — and the bad news, too ... then, soon, all the people here for this family reunion begin to anticipate the meal which draws us all together, young and old, new members and old members, in all our variety.

Worship as a family reunion

For some of us in recent years, the Sunday morning service has come to be more and more conceived of and experienced as a family reunion, the gathering of a scattered household. This has not been a choice of ours so much as, we believe, the unfolding of God's patterns of grace for us.

Or think of a slightly different description: the gathering of friends, friends coming together, not because of their own friendship with each other first of all, but because of a mutual Friend they all have in common — one who is the best Friend of all of them, through whom they are becoming friends of each other, just as a large family is bound first of all by a common ancestry before the present members of the family find other things in common. But assume that the common friendship or common ancestry carries with it great meaning, powerful meaning, a strong sense of identity — as the descendants of an unusual historic personage must know, or as friends of a colorful leader of an earth-shaking contemporary movement might discover when they gather together.

A song of ours expresses this concept of worship this way:

> Sweet is the friendship of the friends of Jesus,
> Bound by the power of his affection.
> With laughter and tears and strong embraces
> We share our joys, our labors, our woe.
> Praise God from whom all blessings flow.
>
> Sweet is the friendship of the friends of Jesus,
> Drawn by the cost of his devotion.
> With struggle and prayer we stay together,
> And by God's grace our circle will grow.
> Praise God from whom all blessings flow.
>   (From *Songs For All Seasons*)

What we are talking about, of course, are analogies of, or variations on, the New Testament model of the church. Early Christians, as described in Acts and portrayed between the lines of other New Testament passages, gathered in homes as a table fellowship, a "household of faith." And they often came there, undoubtedly, to share both inspiring stories of God's acts in their lives and their history and to share harrowing tales of persecution. For Jewish Christians, this intimate apostolic fellowship was complemented often by the rituals of the temple, just as we gather in our large "temples" of awesome dimensions and stately proceedings.

But today we have widely lost the intimacy, the feeling of friendship and relatedness and the urgency of those primitive gatherings and we have only the temple experience — missing often its "corporateness."

With these understandings of worship in mind, we acknowledge that for us the Sunday service is *an experience to share rather than a routine to get through, or an agenda to complete.* Most worship we have seen in other places during our lives, at least until recently, seemed to be "worship by agenda" — a sequence of events that were themselves the point of our gathering. The order of worship as printed was itself the subject of the meeting. Not the people and their lives and experiences — except in the sermon, perhaps, and not even the presence of God or God's involvement with us at this time and place.

Of course there is a natural order to what we do, just as there is to the family gathering where we come, we greet each other, we share good news and bad news, we respond to that news, we have a meal, we have certain messages from elders and leaders of the family about the family history and tradition, we make plans. But the order is not the essence of the household gathering. Nor is the place. It is helpful at the family reunion that the place be conducive to our gathering, with sufficient space, enough chairs, and room for moving around, etc.; and it is great when the place has itself an identification with the family's history, with pictures and furnishings which remind us who we are — just like Grandpa's house used to. Still the place is not usually the crucial factor.

Shape and style

The shaping of the Sunday service as a household gathering begins with our entrance into the gathering-space, where the emphasis is on people and our common relationship as God's people, rather than on solemn, quiet, individual piety. Just as at a happy gathering of friends or relatives in our homes we expect to be greeted at the door and then to exchange news about our lives since we have last been together — rather than having to walk in and sit down and be quiet and immediately listen to a musical performance, so there is an emphasis in our church on greetings and conversation as people gather, rather than on silence and the organ prelude. We come as relatives and friends with Good News (what God has been doing in our lives) and bad news (perhaps what the Devil has been doing in our lives), news to share immediately. Then we come to God, the divine Host, the Parent, with our gathered-up lives, uniting to relate as friends and relatives, a human community, to God.

In the service itself, we continue to recall and submit to God the actual experiences of our lives, rather than relating to abstractions. Just as the household fellowship at home involves all our lives and respects our real experiences — often with humor as well as solemnity. Perhaps that is one of the distinctions in the emerging shape of worship — that there is more laughter; and there is also more weeping, since we are allowed and encouraged to feel as well as — well, to read words and get through the agenda.

One interesting thing about worship in our church that is probably true about worship in all churches: The more we have done together during the week, the richer and more energetic is our worship on Sunday, just as the early, persecuted church was vital in its meetings. This kind of feeling is experienced to some degree, as we give more energy to the announcements about group life and the congregation's mission by more lay leaders, turn the spotlight of our attention on people who give unusual service, are quite candid about our struggles and feelings of joy and sadness among the church members, and enjoy that initial time of friendship before we begin to sing and pray together.

Another result of the conception of worship as an experience of the household of God rather than as a routine or agenda is that the clock becomes less important. The enslaving, trivializing concept of worship as necessarily confined within one hour on Sunday is new in the history of the church, and speaks more about the patterns of our culture and of human manipulation of sacred realities than about faithfulness to God. The persistent pressure that lay people put upon clergy and clergy put on themselves to be "finished by noon" is one of the more obviously silly things we see in the life of the church. It becomes all the more amazing when laid alongside facts about long hours spent sitting stiffly before inane television programs, in tedious meetings, or at tables in stuffy restaurants making dull conversation. Black churches, "charismatic" churches, and Orthodox churches of the world have somehow found that the experience of God and of human communion in Jesus' name is not subject to the clock, that worship can be exciting, moving, and participatory to the point where the clock is actually irrelevant to what is going on.

Yet another important implication of this understanding of worship is that all the household is welcome and present, not just the older members. Do you recall family reunions from your childhood? If there were such events, it is unlikely that you were left home while the parents all gathered for the Thanksgiving dinner at Grandpa's and Grandma's house. You were there, and you were there for the whole day's activities, including the meal, the "Communion" of the family.

As we traveled around the land leading workshops we were amazed and appalled at the number of churches in which the children were not welcome at worship, or were welcome for just the opening of worship — not the family prayers, not the reading of "messages" from former leaders of the family (like Isaiah and Paul), not the meal — *not even the meal!* The scheduling of Sunday school classes at the same time continues to be a major problem in the churches of America, since it means that most children never attend a whole service until out of school, and the vital ministry of children is lost to the rest of the congregation in that most important hour of the week for the church. No! Let all ages gather together!

One of the characteristics of the congregation-household, as we conceive of ourselves as a gathering of family members or as friends of all generations bound in friendship, is a certain *gracious tolerance* of one another and our disparate tastes and styles. It is not expected in a large household that all members of all ages will dress alike, think alike, act alike, and like the same things. But there is a bit of pleasure in the family in diversity. At the family gathering, we rejoice in the energy of children — unlike church. Furthermore, bizarre styles of dress among some members are sources of amusement and amazement to others — but there is no excommunication from the family! At the golden anniversary of Grandma and Grandpa, all kinds of music are played by the band for the large gathering, so members of all ages and tastes can have a good time. In the same way more and more churches are becoming quite open and eclectic in their choice of music and in their use of other worship materials — a richness often recommended in the pages of this periodical ever since its founding.

Perhaps this understanding of worship is nowhere more obvious and exciting than in connection with the style of the sacraments. Holy Communion and baptism in many churches are no longer cool, quiet, stiff-upper-lip ceremonies to be watched with detachment. Nor are they usually somber. Nor are they done with an emphasis on delicacy, refinement — or with haste, as if to be gotten through as quickly and painlessly as possible. They are household celebrations — like Christmas morning, or birthday parties, or farewell gatherings, with laughter, tears, applause, and many other kinds of participation. The Eucharist is more like a festive meal shared by good friends than a solemn, individualistic experience of piety. Baptism is more like a victory celebration or a "Welcome Home" party than a "nice" and incidental religious ritual.

As more and more churches choose to celebrate Holy Communion more often, some moving to once-a-month from quarterly celebrations and others going to weekly observances, worship every Sunday — even when the Sacrament is not celebrated — is more centered in the Table as well as the Word. Thus our concept of worship as household gathering will become more common, with the "household meal" being the normative form of worship effecting all else we do. Some churches are blessed with architecture that emphasizes this idea; more churches can be, with simple moving of furniture or redesigning of lighting to center on the Table as well as pulpit and lectern and choir loft.

Dangers

Ah yes, there are always dangers with any reconceptualizing of worship. And there are certainly perversions of the new image of the Sunday service across this land. Moreover, we ourselves wish to be clearly understood. It is always possible for worship leaders to get too chummy and folksy, first of all. And maybe it's not so much a danger of becoming too relaxed and friendly in the way we worship as it is that we can get sloppy in our planning, careless and thoughtless in the way we do things. Though our own church has something of the quality of friendship that we have been describing, and though there is much spontaneous participation, the service is carefully planned and organized, designed to relate to issues of the church year or world history or other sequences and events. Uncle Joe's speech to the large gathering at the family reunion may be very carefully prepared for weeks in advance ... and the song presented by little Cousin Susie may have been rehearsed for long hours ... not to mention the preparation of the big dinner and the arrangement of the house in which we come together.

But another danger in the emerging new shape of Christian worship is that of domesticating God. It is a common theological issue of our time — that for millions of Christians in the U.S.A., the holy and transcendent and almighty God is always "the Lord" who is ready to "give us a blessing" as we come "just to praise the Lord." Without being disdainful of sincere and often vital forms of pious language and personal commitment, we must yet confess our nervousness about the easy and casual and too-automatic assumption of God's support of our interests and God's involvement in our most incidental and trivial concerns and projects. In worship this can, of course, lead to the absence of any sense of the majesty of God, any sense of God's judgment over our nation and all nations, any sense of the ultimate mystery of God's plans and purposes in this vast universe.

Tough-minded Christianity is not inconsistent with the concept of the church as a household, a loving company of the friends of Jesus. Nor is humility before God impossible as we come joyfully and enthusiastically together on Sunday morning. There can be both much laughter and long silences in worship, and both are natural and essential responses to the acts of God and God's revelations of our human nature.

The final danger we shall mention is also readily avoidable, that of the church becoming centered on itself. The household, after all, gathers in response to a Word from beyond itself — and that Word, along with the lively sacraments, must be central and lively as the source of the household's meaning, just as the friends who gather in friendship in the church are there first of all just because they have that mutual Friend who invites us to his dining table. Furthermore, we have found that the lively church, the enthusiastic and loving church is more likely than the calm, austere, and unfriendly church to be concerned about the real world and the mission of Christ in the world, because people are excited about the Gospel and the reconciliation they have experienced.

Worship as a learning experience

The Sunday service should be a learning experience for the congregation, a time to get information they don't have.

"What did you learn in church today?" is not only a good question to ask about the children's Sunday school experience; is also a good question to ask about the service of worship. More members gather at that service than will come to classes in the church, some people only come to the Sunday service and not to other activities, and we all need tools for decision-making and for functioning as Christians in the world.

First, in every service people should learn something *about* the Bible and even something *in* the Bible they didn't know before: Where to find an important passage, the history of some biblical people, the meaning of Hebrew or Greek words or phrases, a key to understanding a story or book of the Bible. This education can be done with brief introductions to the scripture readings, and in the sermon, of course. It can best be accomplished when the congregation has Bibles in their own hands to look at. One Sunday in our church Dick-the-preacher explained the weight of the words "he sat down" (ex *cathedra,* professor's "chair," etc.) and "he opened his mouth and taught them" (Matthew 5) in ancient culture and the Greek language, as he began a series on the Sermon on the Mount.

Second, let there be theological education, training about issues of belief. Many people in our church are now interested in movements in theology and in theologians present and past, what they teach and have written. Bombarded as many people are these days with television preaching and teaching, they need to be helped *beyond gullibility.* Recently, this preacher spoke of the phrase "born again" with references to contemporary teachers of Bible and theology, so that term can be rescued from trivialization and politicization.

Third, let there be education about the church, what it is doing near and far, and about its history. Perhaps with knowledge of the church's past errors we can be saved from repeating a few of them. Conflicts of the past may also shed light on conflicts of the present. Let people also enjoy knowing who church leaders are today, and about their courage and their skill. The congregation does *not* need to know all about petty controversies that may not affect them, it seems to us. Some conflicts in the church become major conflicts just because preachers talk about them as such, instead of talking about "the great things God has done."

Fourth, assume that the congregation knows little about the world and its people — by which we mean races and other religions and world need. Most people don't read the grim facts and figures, and most people don't watch documentaries about suffering or hunger in the world. One Sunday, this preacher gave many rather startling facts about races and colors in the world, about world population growth and, to many people's amazement, the size of other religious groups. It put world mission in context and encouraged a certain humility among us white Christians.

11

Think about it: Beyond inspiration, what did your congregation *learn* in worship last Sunday that they did not know before? What new information to inform their thinking, their news-viewing, their decision-making during the week?

Worship planning

How do we plan for worship? What are the best ways to plan for creative worship that honors God and relates to the real needs of the congregation? How can we do it so this planning does not consume all the hours of the week? When we were conducting worship workshops in various parts of the country, we were often asked, "How do you plan your weekly worship in Port Jervis? Do you go week by week, year by year, or how? Does the music always go along with the sermon, and how do you do that? Do you use the Worshipbook? Do you have an order of worship that is the same each week? Or do you just wing it?"

We believe that careful planning is an essential part of being creative and of simple survival in the maelstrom of church life. An article in an issue of that delightful and irritating magazine, *The Door*, bears the complaint of the author that too much "contemporary worship" is attempted without planning, and that without the hard work of preparation it is often frivolous and insignificant. The author seems to hold the opinion that this is a problem uniquely characteristic of the present scene. We protest: There is, in our experience, no less hard work being done in connection with so-called contemporary worship than with so-called traditional worship. We have been in many very conventional services in which there seemed to be an absence of thematic development, constant reliance on religious clichés, no relating of music with anything else that happens, and much rambling. Perhaps the same thing is widely true of innovative services, but we haven't seen it. Nevertheless, the author of that article is right in insisting that there is no substitute for the careful, earnest planning of worship.

Accordingly, as pastor and choirmaster, here are the things we urge:

1. Plan general and particular themes as far ahead as possible *for each season of the church year.* If there are particular or overarching symbols or concepts to be put forth by the preacher, the choirmaster knows about these generally several weeks in advance; or the choirmaster may indeed suggest these ideas to the pastor and we mutually discuss their development.

2. If the pastor uses the Revised Common Lectionary (the calendar of Old Testament, Epistle, and Gospel readings shared by several denominations) for the basis of preaching, make sure the choirmaster has a copy of this lectionary and studies it in advance of the season along with the pastor. The choirmaster should choose music in keeping with the lectionary readings as often as possible — or at least have possibilities in mind when the two confer together about services for, say, the next three or four weeks.

3. Strive for common understandings about the purpose of worship and what might be accomplished in a service, especially among the pastor, choirmaster, and organist.

4. Have a list of traditions, a file on significant local rituals, special ceremonies and events, and large and small liturgical customs that have emerged over the years. The list provides hooks on which to hang one's need for security and continuity in worship life.

5. Make sure all parts of the service are planned before the service begins. All parts. An obvious idea? Not really, because it is easy for all leaders of worship to go careening into the hour of worship without thinking ahead on what the Call to Worship is to be in relation to themes of the day, what the Prayers of Intercession are to be about and how concerns should be actually articulated, how each hymn should be introduced beyond the announcing of a number, what spoken responses or silences should follow anthems or solos, etc. Where such planning does not happen we fall back on empty slogans, superficial remarks, or meaningless routine. Dick admits that the best leading of prayers he does on Sundays is when he has the most time getting ready — carefully outlining or writing out the key sentences, even planning the silences. There is always room for inspiration and spontaneity — but first comes the planning.

6. Several parts of the service are looked at often with this question in mind: *Who can best do this?* It is not true that the pastor should do everything always. While Dick usually does most parts of the service, he often steps aside to let other people's perceptions of God's reality be expressed. Some people can do some kinds of liturgical acts *better* than the pastor or with greater personal involvement. And thus the pastor's voice is made less routine.

7. There is candid evaluation of worship services among members of the staff — and by quite a few members of the congregation as well. We are free to be analytical and critical, without rancor, and without feeling threatened or in danger of losing favor. If some music doesn't work, doesn't reach people, isn't intelligible or just doesn't fit the service, the pastor can tell the choirmaster his honest opinion. If the sermon doesn't make it, prayers ramble too long, or if the scripture reading is dull as dishwater, the choirmaster or others can tell the preacher without his getting suicidal — or homicidal. Our belief is that *we all are servants,* not masters! And we all work for a gracious and forgiving God who has already saved us and who is himself our "ego strength." Evaluation is an essential part of planning. Along the same lines, this pastor keeps a file of his own frank and sometimes merciless evaluations of each year's major services for use in planning next year's events. These evaluations are written right after the service has happened. They save us from the repetition of dumb mistakes and from persistent illusions.

8. A season of services is from time to time assigned to a committee of members and officers for planning with the staff. The committee includes all kinds of people. They study and discuss texts and/or main themes of the season and are encouraged to respond creatively to those motifs or stories. The staff retains some final authority about putting the service together in line with the concerns of the whole liturgical year and with the needs of the present congregation.

9. Though we rarely print an order of worship, there is a three-part structure to the service within which a variety of things happen from week to week. All music, drama, speeches from the congregation, readings — all things happen *where they make sense* within that structure. (For example, a penitential anthem will go in the opening "Liturgy of Praise and Penitence," not just before the sermon or the offering!)

10. Every service is designed to contain emotional anchors: Moments of rest, of reassurance, of falling back on the tradition, for those who come in need of such support. Every service is also designed to have a moment or more of stretching, of adventure, in word, song, movement, or relating among the flock.

11. We use many traditional forms and many of the prayers and the rituals from our denominational worship book. But we don't use it for the general content of the regular service because it is too *verbal*: it is a book of many words. And worship needs to involve much more than words. Moreover, some members of our congregation don't read well. The use of many words in a book excludes many children, many people of limited sight, and people of little or no education.

The authentic leader

One of the most important keys to the quality of worship is clearly the personal attitudes and level of understanding of the pastor, music leader, or lay leader. Worship will doubtless be done better — i.e., will be a more significant, life-transforming experience for more people — when it is led by an authentic, sincere straightforward person at a level of deep involvement. And at the risk of belaboring the obvious, we must say that loyalty to the way of Christ demands leadership of worship that is without pretense, deception, or condescension. Jesus spoke of faithful worship as being "in spirit and in truth."

We bring this up for two reasons: First, some leadership of worship and music we see is so terribly impersonal, bogged down with postures and clichés; second, some conversations and reports that we hear among clergy and church musicians indicate that — would you believe? — many professional church leaders would not themselves attend worship regularly, if they were not paid to!

This has led us to ask ourselves critical questions: How do I feel about worship for me? Does the worship I help plan and lead really speak for me and to me, and is it essential to my existence? Could I happily live without it? Is it genuine, at the level of my real decision-making and self-understanding? Do I care about the people with whom I worship each week?

Taking this line of thinking one step further: Do I (pastor, lay planner, choir leader, organist, officer) really expect anything to happen in the Sunday morning worship hour? Do I truly believe that God will speak to us, heal us, direct us to new mission, give us peace? Will we be different? Lloyd Ogilvie, author and zealous pastor, insists that, in one sense, we get what we expect, and we don't get exactly what we don't anticipate in the service we lead. Such a teaching surely drives us back to examine our own basic faith and the content of our praying.

The leadership of worship involves us personally in two ways: First, we are enablers, representing and guiding others as they bring hopes, needs, beliefs, problems, and possibilities to God. Second, we are ourselves bringing our hopes, needs, beliefs, problems, and possibilities to God. Part of the time the first happens through the second. Rarely should there be a conflict between the two. Indeed, when we try to be something other than who we really are, then the phony and distracting things happen, the inauthentic personality gets in the way of worship. To best illustrate what we mean we offer rules for the preservation of authenticity, rules for ourselves that might help you:

- **Pray real prayers.** Don't just voice words to be filling a space indicated on the bulletin. Decide ahead of time what you want to thank God for, what you want to ask for — and then try to figure out what four specific and diverse people in the congregation might thank God for and ask for. If on Sunday you are reading a traditional prayer, take time during the week to see if its words can relate to any events or situations in your own experience. Then read the prayer with those in mind (which means you'll read it more slowly and reflectively or passionately than you would otherwise).

- **Practice reading scripture aloud as if it were actually written just for you.** Then practice reading it as if it were specifically and personally for the congregation in front of you. Then read it on Sunday combining feelings and techniques that have emerged from both ways of reading.
- **Music leaders, choose music which actually voices your feelings — or those of some specific persons in your congregation.** Choir leaders, explain to the choir what each anthem means to you, what it accomplishes, why it is worth doing. (Beyond "This is an example of eighteenth century developments in harmonization....")
- **In preaching and all parts of the service, let the language spoken be the native language of the congregation** free of pious clichés and religious jargon, though that language be spoken correctly — and intelligently. Let clarity have priority over eloquence, and, in music, meaning over "impressiveness." (Thus a simple, unison anthem done by a small group with passion and good diction can be more truly worshipful than a big, six-part piece done with detachment and garbled lyrics.)
- **Let leaders be themselves, without affectation or self-exaltation.** And let them say only what they believe. Be uncompromising and honest in your faith, with all its empty spaces and questions. Don't pretend to accept doctrines you don't hold. If you respect a doctrine and feel that your skepticism is your problem rather than the doctrine's, then explain the doctrine as one which is important in history or precious to others, without claiming it as your own.
- **Finally, as you lead worship, let love and good will show.** Let the appreciation you feel spill over in words, laughter, tears. Don't force your feelings on others, but be honest as you lead them and care about them. Then, when worship is done, live out what you preach, pray, sing, or play. If you can't, examine what you've done in that sacred hour. And examine yourself. If you don't want to, take a leave of absence to think and pray.

Worship standards

To have or not to have, that is the question (to paraphrase Hamlet). Whether 'tis nobler to accept any and everything that is given, said, done, written, drawn, sewn, cooked, thought, etc., etc., to and for the church in the name of the Holy Spirit and face the slings and arrows of "those who know" OR to set up standards against a sea of mediocrity, bad lyrics and rhymes, poor theology, unsingable or mundane tunes, etc., etc., and by proclaiming those standards face the slings and arrows of those who claim guidance by the unseen spirit and say it is a gift from Heaven and is therefore free for the church to use ... Ay, there's the rub! We get it in the neck both ways!

However, let's risk a bit the slings and arrows from both sides and suggest that when we bake a pie, we work to make it edible; that when we knit a sweater, we work to make it fit; that when we clean the house, we work to make it livable. So we ask, how about trying to make the song singable, the dance danceable, the sermon relevant, the banner communicative, the services of worship worshipful, the prayers manageable, etc., etc.?

This radical idea is presented with the knowledge that first and foremost in the leaders' minds must be a working knowledge of where their congregations are. Abstract poetry forced on an ill-read congregation is at least an insensitivity if not a sin from the pulpit. Doggerel fed to an intellectual congregation is likewise an indication that the leaders know not their constituency. But both are possible if they are used with explanations and with belief that both are worth using. It's so difficult to be all-embracing, to be allowed to know and love jazz as well as Franck, "Letters to God by Children" and Barth, finger painting and Rembrandt, home movies and "Close Encounters." But this is what we are asking for and trying for ourselves. And because we believe in all kinds of material and all kinds of communications, all methods and media, we study content and technique and work at trying to figure out how best to present each thing to the worshiping congregation, this particular one. (Note, we are not talking about "taste," not pushing snobbery and elitism. We're urging standards, self-criticism.)

Casting

Except in crisis situations, don't have the blind judge the art show, don't let the dumb preach the sermon, don't let the deaf lead the choir nor the lame person the dance group — until *after* the miracle has happened (see Isaiah 53). Don't let the blues anthem be done by a singer with an operatic wobble; don't let the melismatic aria be done by a singer who always sings slowly; don't let the person who dislikes country music sing the Country & Western anthem or solo. Let each thing be done as *well as possible,* which means having the right person doing it.

Casting is the first major job of the worship leader, choir director, choreographer, banner designer, program leader. This is all so obvious that we need reminding of it because we in the church are often guided by sentimentality rather than reality. Once in our own church, most of the members-at-large on the very important nominating committee who were chosen lived so far from the church that a winter of bad weather almost kept the needed quorum from ever being present. Or we think of Mr. So-and-so, for whom a place on the nominating committee would be so nice, until someone remembers that he is in a wheelchair with no one to drive him anywhere, wears a hearing aid that is often on the blink, and has been away from the church for so long that he doesn't know any of the new members of the last five years. Statistics have indicated that sentimental choices have formed weak committees, poor choirs, etc., etc. (Find other service Mr. So-and-so can really do in his way.)

Perhaps the covered-dish supper model is right: Everyone brings what he or she makes *best.* Let's *glorify* the Lord, not *test* the Lord nor the Lord's Creation — namely, you and me.

Principles and priorities

Let's review some standards relevant to the planning and conducting of worship that we have found significant:

1. Worship takes its point of departure from scripture and provides an encounter with scripture. Things that are said and sung as well as why we do what we do must emerge from the Bible or be true to biblical teachings. This means that we will not do just any "religious song" that is popular or pleases somebody. If its message is essentially pagan we won't do it. With one exception: If it's a song that asks a question or poses a point of view contrary to the Bible, we may recognize that, answer it, or respond to it critically. Ultimately, obedience to the Word is the final test of worship's validity.

2. Every service of worship must contain, in some form, the Good News. This means that every theme of worship must offer a word of hope, a statement of God's love and grace, an offer of help from God, to which response can be made. Not just judgment, not just criticism, not just penitence, not just a challenge to compassion or work, but also, as clearly as possible, the offer and the promises.

3. Every service should evidence both spontaneity and order. Order and spontaneity. Worship, for us, could hardly ever be just a "what-do-you-folks-feel-like-doing-today?" experience. Simply because we move from biblical sources and because we need to move corporately, we go at things in an orderly way, in patterns which are true to our sources and our deepest needs. At the same time, as in any liturgical order or pattern, there must be opportunities for the Spirit to move beyond our expectations. There must be opportunity for spontaneous sharing, for surprising gestures of grace and excitement, and expressions of need or suffering. This means leaders must be flexible and aware of feelings and impulses.

4. The order must make sense. We don't just do something in an hour of worship because we enjoy that thing, because "it would be nice," because it's impressive, because it's ready. We don't do a thing in the order of worship where it does not fit. On this subject we have three hang-ups: (a) Hymns that do not relate in any way to the thematic or emotional context of the part of worship in which they're sung — e.g., a rousing hymn of praise just before a quiet time of prayer; (b) the "anthem slot," in which every Sunday the anthem is done at the same point regardless of what it's about — e.g., performing Williams' "In the Year That King Uzziah Died" just before a sermon on "the Unfaithful Steward" (with no attempt in the sermon to use the anthem's text); (c) separating the scripture readings from the sermon with announcements, "pastoral prayers," and the offering in between, thus destroying a natural continuity.

5. The order and content of worship must make emotional sense. At a recent ordination service in our community, the opening and second hymns were both so long, slow, and demanding of energy that we were all very tired before we got to the actual ordination ceremony. One aspect of this standard is simply a concern for *attention*. Are people interested in what's going on? Is anybody listening? We have been in major meetings and services where the leaders seemed quite unaware or else uncaring about the fact that at least half of the congregation was quite obviously not paying attention, not interested at all in what was going on, and even showing many signs of wanting to leave!

6. Most of what happens in a Sunday service must interest all ages. Yes, there will be some points when we pray specifically for a concern of the small children — or the retired adults; and the rock-style anthem *may* appeal more to those under 35. But most of the praying, the songs, the sermon illustrations, and the readings should be done so as to interest all ages. Moreover, we insist that all age groups must have their special moments in just about every service — illustrations and "props" which apply directly to them, a prayer which voices their unique concern, a point of relevance (made explicit) in at least one hymn. Difficult? Yes. But an essential standard.

Rehearsing

Recognizing that "re" means again, Don has for years (as actor and director in the professional theater) wondered what the "hearse" part of the word meant. Did it mean dragging it off again by hearse because it (the performance or whatever) didn't have a chance to live? Of course, he made all sorts of bad use (mostly puns) of that possibility. So we finally decided to look it up in that forgotten book called the dictionary. The *American Heritage Dictionary of the English Language* says: "1. To practice in preparation for a public performance. 2. To perfect. Or cause to perfect (an action) by repetition. 3. To retell (OF *rehercer*, to repeat)." Not very exciting, but it gives us our point of departure about the necessity of rehearsing and also the amount of rehearsing. Two end results will be held in mind: perfection and spontaneity.

Perfection, of course, takes lots of repetition. When there is a script to learn and say correctly in the words of the author, when there is a routine outlined by the choreographer or ice skating director or the swimming ballet instructor, when there is a score of definite notes for specific instruments and voices, repeating (almost endlessly) is essential. When Don was coaching singers for concerts or stage or night club performances he used to say that they needed to go through being *bored* with the song or routine before they could perform it most tellingly.

We feel the main reason for aiming toward perfection of this kind of material is to make the listener/viewer/worshiper comfortable, free from worry and distraction. It is much easier to listen to content when the performer exudes confidence. Therefore, a layperson needs to read in the pulpit the lesson or Psalm he or she is going to lead in Sunday's worship, not just at home. Doing it in the room and in the spot where it will be done is important. The acoustics are different; the space feeling is different; the fact that the sanctuary is a room with a living history makes it different. It is often easier to memorize lines for a play in the set, as one moves around becoming more used to the place and sometimes going through the action as well. If you plan to do a frieze or a pantomime, it is essential for the performers to know where in space they are going to do it. Practice there.

Rehearsals for most professional actors, dancers, singers, instrumentalists are the most exciting part of their work. It is in rehearsals that some of the great performances happen, before no one but the performer and the teacher or director. It is there where the depths are plumbed, where motivations and other considerations are talked about and tried on for size, where possibilities are examined and where finally choices are made. There is a terrible tendency to just go through the notes without any commitment to content for worship services. As if we were counting on God to be gracious and understanding when our efforts are not what they could or should be. There is a tendency to walk through or dry run a dance or pantomime because we are all so busy doing other things, or we're tired today. This can lead to casualness and eventually callousness. And there is a huge difference between casualness and spontaneity.

Spontaneity depends on vast resources in the performer. Actors, fledgling ones, like to say they have to try everything in life in order to become better actors (usually as defense for doing something that someone they worry about will think is naughty or a no-no). This is partially true. True to the extent that the more we have experienced (which includes reading about it), the more we have to offer in that special moment when something bigger/deeper can add further content to a performance. The good ad-libber is someone who has heard thousands of lines/jokes and carefully stored them.

Spontaneity depends a great deal also upon the taste of the performer. Knowing when to stop; knowing that one more thing will distort; knowing when something is appropriate and particularly when it would be inappropriate. And very often these moments of spontaneity are next to impossible to repeat in exactly the same way (even in the same or a repeated context).

Risk is terribly important in spontaneity. A sermon that is read by the writer from the pulpit has a harder time to strike sparks than one that is done without the written script. Children listen to remembered stories in sermons when they recognize the speaker has moved from the script to personal experience. The best spontaneous sermon is one that has been thought about a great deal but just not committed to paper. And that kind of sermon is risky. The preacher must be able to put the listener at ease by exuding security of technique. The technique is one of being able to set up a situation in which the vast (or limited) resources of the person can be called on and used.

Improvisations and other forms of role playing are occasions in which experience and resources are the very lifeblood of the medium. And here, in improvisations, rehearsing must not be over-done. The more often you go over (rehearse) an improvisation, the more certain lines begin to sound like a written script and the spontaneity is lost. This happens partially because if a funny line happens in the first rehearsal, we try to repeat it when the other actor has not set up the possibility for the same line or the exact situation. Many excellent improvisers are rotten playwrights.

One of our favorite things to do in choir rehearsals is rehearse an anthem or response in a number of different tempos, pointing out the change in weight of tone and texture, and then telling the choir we don't know which tempo we will use come Sunday, but we will have to wait and see what Sunday brings to the anthem. This is one way to make an anthem sound almost spontaneous. A number of times we have improvised anthems using biblical texts. The rehearsal is a time when we work out resources and signals that call upon them. Here is an almost limitless area if we are willing to risk (our throats and the congregation's ears).

We would like to say that we feel everything should be rehearsed: all the music, the readings, yea, even the announcements, the prayers (particularly if being done by someone who is not used to praying in public), the sermon, the benediction. Our benediction is: "Have a great rehearsal!" It's like having lots of small resurrections!

The anthem

Since we are devoting an entire chapter of this book to music, we have not said much about it in this chapter. But because the choir's anthems are so much a "regular" part of worship, we offer a few general suggestions here.

One basic conviction we hold about the songs offered by the choirs is that they should happen *where they fit*, where their lyrics and the impact of the music make sense within the order for that particular day. No "anthem slot!" If it's an anthem of praise, do it in the part of the service given to the praise of God. If it relates to the lections very nicely, do it before or after those readings from scripture. If it voices penitence, calling out for mercy, do it with the Prayer of Confession. The same principle applies for youth choir music as for the "big choir," and for solos, too. Of course this means that there must be planning, and communication among members of the staff so music somehow does make sense within that order of worship! But when there is this kind of planning and the resulting mobility of anthems for the greatest meaning, attention, and responsiveness to worship as a total experience (beyond "Nice sermon, Reverend") will follow.

A second thing about the anthem: Pastors should often introduce the choral music with a few well-chosen words, even mentioning who the composer is or was, where the piece was written, and, more important, *why* the choir is singing it today. Perhaps the congregation may learn that the music actually grows out of someone's personal experience and may be heard as a word of witness.

And a third conviction about anthems: They take on greater meaning when they are heard and studied by the preacher before he preaches, so the lyrics can be used in the sermon or prayers. This enhances the understanding of the anthems and also reinforces important ideas within the con-sciousness of the people, especially those who sing the lyrics. Along with the preacher's discipline regarding the anthem, let the choirs themselves learn in the rehearsal why the anthem is done on the particular Sunday, what it relates to in the service, and what it's about.

A final thought about doing anthems effectively: It should be unnecessary to mention this idea, but sad to say, it is not. Many choirs are not trained for good diction, and, moreover, the emphasis in rehearsal time is on singing the music and not on singing the *words*. Let the words be understood! Don't just depend on printing the words in the bulletin, so people can read what they cannot hear. Let rehearsal times stress the ideas, in the songs as well as the harmonies, tunes and rhythms, and then let those ideas be clearly enunciated for the congregation on Sunday.

Laity participation

As most people know, the word "liturgy" comes from two Greek words that combine to mean "the work of the people," "the action of the congregation." What a challenging word to represent the work of the Christian church! Perhaps the most essential element of renewed and vital worship is the participation of the whole people of God.

Participation is much more than a set of gimmicks to please people, more than fun and games. Participatory worship, as we are going to describe it, can be more real — an act related to real feelings, to real life, and the real world. It can also simply be done better, when more people are bringing their abilities, insights, and ideas into the service, more than just a few professional leaders. Still another reason it is essential: It is hard to be casual and uninvolved about something in which you yourself have a vital part. Participation encourages concentration, thought, alertness — more than sitting back as a spectator. And worship that is easy and casual can have little to do with our biblical faith. Participatory worship is not just another way "to get more people out." It probably won't work that way: When worship demands something of people, some stay home.

Here we offer and present a list of participatory acts or forms which have been meaningful and fruitful in the life of our congregation. Some of these are quite simple, some more complex and hard to describe. Some we have mentioned before, but this is an attempt to "put it all together," or at least some of it.

1. Let officers and representative members read a responsive reading, scripture readings, or certain formal prayers Sunday after Sunday. This is a formal and humble way to begin involving non-clergy types "up front." The use of lay people to read the sacred scripture is an ancient practice, and it can be used as a way to honor and identify the Session, the Vestry, the Council, the Board of Deacons, the Consistory, the Angelic Leaders, or whatever you call it in your church.

2. From time to time, invite the members of the congregation to suggest concerns as points of departure for the Prayers of Intercession or the Pastoral Prayer. In our church, Dick makes this request down on a level near the congregation. For this to work the leader must have patience, a readiness to wait as people think, and the ability to extemporize in the prayers that follow. Congregations get better at this, making more honest and thoughtful suggestions as weeks go by.

3. The singing of an Introit or musical Call to Worship by everybody. A song like our own "We're Here to be Happy" can be quickly learned by the congregation after hearing the choir sing it. The same is true of choral responses to the benediction and to other prayers in the service.

4. If you have announcements in the service, let people other than the pastor make them; namely, the leaders of those activities. Let them be visual as well as verbal. We believe that announcements done with feeling and imagination can be a significant part of the celebration by the people of God, especially when representative members do them.

5. If you have Bibles in the pews, don't just have the congregation follow along as the pastor or lay leader reads. (a) Have the congregation read alternate paragraphs of the lesson. (b) Have the congregation read all words in quotation marks as the leader reads the narrative lines. (c) Divide the congregation in half for lines of a scriptural dialogue (as between Jesus and Peter or Pilate and the crowd).

6. If you don't have Bibles in the pews, ask the congregation simply to repeat words or phrases from the scripture reading that are repeated by the reader. Ask them to try to express the emotional content of those phrases as they repeat them. A simple device, but remarkably effective for us.

7. Invite the congregation to wear a specific color for a special day: red for Pentecost, purple for the first Sunday of Advent, green for a Sunday in Epiphany, etc.

8. Have a "Ceremony of Gratitude," a participatory offering of praise, from time to time. Invite members to stand where they are to tell one thing ("no long speeches, please, just a word or a phrase") for which they are grateful on this particular day. Suggest a point of departure for their thinking: something that's happened in the past week, something happening in the world of nations, gifts of God to you personally, what God gave you for Christmas, good things that are happening in our town, etc. Limiting the range of possibilities makes for more thoughtful offerings from people. After each person speaks, respond with an echoed line from the Psalms: "It is good to give thanks to the Lord," "See the great things God has done," "Make a joyful noise to the Lord, all the lands," or some other line which seems particularly appropriate to the subject at hand. Once again, the leader must be patient, friendly, and not pompous.

9. Let the preacher ask for illustrations and examples in his sermon from members of the congregation. Instead of his or her recounting what people have done or said, let them do it themselves. Usually, they should be warned of such a request so they can be prepared to speak clearly and succinctly.

10. Have different people, male and female, of all ages, prepare their own prayers of gratitude, petition, or intercession for specific occasions. Occasions like the opening of school — a teacher, a parent, a young pupil, a university student; or Labor Sunday — a factory worker, a merchant, an artist, a housewife, a civil servant; a summer Sunday — people of different ages expressing hopes to God about the summer.

11. A simple matter of posture, or physical position: For longer prayers, the times of silent prayer or led intercessions or petitions, invite the congregation to sit forward in a comfortable position, to put both feet on the floor, and to rest their hands, palms upward and open, on their thighs. This is a position that encourages and enables alertness and openness, so that prayers are not passive experiences for the congregation.

12. Encourage participation in hymn singing, including dividing stanzas between parts of the congregation, or between soloists or choirs and congregation; reading certain stanzas aloud before singing them; asking particular people to explain the hymn's personal meaning before everyone joins to sing it; having conversations with the whole congregation about key phrases ("How can you illustrate the ideal 'in Christ now meet both East and West'?" "What does it mean (in 'Joy to the World') 'and makes the nations prove the wonders of his righteousness'?"), etc.

Other ideas

1. Introduce choir members

Early this autumn, formally introduce the individual members of the choir in a Sunday service before they do the anthem of the day. Have them emerge from the congregation one by one as their names are called. Tell which part they sing, so that people will understand what a choir consists of (not everybody does). Ritualize this experience a bit, perhaps with quiet background playing by organ or piano or a hymn like "O For A Thousand Tongues To Sing," or "Praise Ye the Lord." Don't assume that people in your church know the names of even the people who stand before them each Sunday. Moreover, why not recognize and honor members of the group that probably meets most and may work hardest in the life of the congregation?

Or, have the choir enter and stand at the foot of the stairs to the loft, or at the entrance to the choir rows or some such place and enter their section as their names are called by the pastor or lay leader, section by section, then let the choir explode into a strong, exultant introit.

2. Commune with bread from different ovens

Many churches now call upon bakers of the congregation to provide the bread for Holy Communion — not professional bakers, but men and women who make the bread in their own kitchens and bring it to the church. Have the family or individual who baked the bread bring it forward as an offering in the service before the celebration of the sacrament; or at least announce to the rest of the congregation each time who baked the loaf. And encourage the people to bake different kinds of bread through the year, perhaps with recipes from the lands or regions of their ancestry. Thus the church household shares and enjoys the offerings of the many households within the congregation.

3. Pray about friendship

We all need help from God in being friends, good friends representing to each other the friendship of Christ. Children need to have early help in growing up as faithful and thoughtful and loving friends to others. Invite three people of different ages to pray about friendship one Sunday. An anthem to precede this time of prayer: Gilbert Martin's beautiful (and not difficult) setting of "What a Friend We Have in Jesus," using a folk melody that helps the words come alive again (publisher: Hinshaw Music).

4. Celebrate the anniversaries of baptism

Check your church records. What children were baptized five years ago this season? What young people were baptized twelve years ago and are now facing the threshold of adolescence and teen years? Phone them, invite them to be ready to come forward on an appropriate Sunday, then pray for them — and for all Christians — that they may "live out their baptisms" and continue to grow in discipleship. Make it a celebration of growth, of God's continuing grace, and an honoring of God's providence.

5. Promote the Christian year

We have discovered that making as much use as possible of the Christian year is an exciting Christian education experience, whether done in worship or in special program or in church school program. And the pushing of the colors of the days and seasons can be most stimulating. It is very much like a liturgical scrapbook. There is so much to remember about Jesus than anchoring events in the appropriate seasons is very helpful. Here are four suggestions:

- **Banners.** Make banners for each season, large and colorful. This could be a project for a single person or a group, an adult group of a youth group, an art group, or a crafts group. Put the banners on poles and on the first Sunday of each season announce the name of the season and give a short description of it as the banner is carried forward with a flourish and placed in a standard down in front where it can be seen best. Make this very clear by saying: "Bring forward the banner for Advent (or whatever)!" and let a drum roll begin or a short trumpet fanfare. Do it up big. Explain the symbols that have been incorporated in the design.

- **Visitors books.** With paper available in a wide variety of colors, put together a sheaf to be used for visitors to sign in the rear of the church, labeling each day or season on paper of the appropriate color. Such as, purple for Advent. Then try to get another shade of purple for Lent. At the end of the year put them all together and display the list of people who visited during the seasons of that specific year.

- **Robes.** Our Adult Choir has robes of red and of green and of purple mixed together in the loft. Poncho-shaped, they go well over any of the lovely or weird things that choir singers are likely to wear on an average Sunday. They are of different lengths, all made of polyester that is marvelously washable and wrinkle-free. And since people here made them in a simple design, they were inexpensive. We now call ourselves God's "gumdrops" because we look so merry in the choir loft. On occasion we wear just the purple ones, or just the red ones. (On Easter, we wear our own festive clothes like everybody else in the congregation. Why should we hide our "lilies could not be more beautiful" arrays under the robes the people have enjoyed all during the year?)

- **A line-up.** As the church year comes to an end and Advent is about to start again, have a line-up across the front of the chancel. Have different people wearing robes or clothing of the different colors to remind the congregation of the variety of the liturgical year. Perhaps a child in purple for Advent, or even a baby in purple being held by a mother in white and a father in green, showing how Advent goes into Christmas and the Epiphany. Show off the variety of ages and types as well as colors. Variety is the spice of it all!

6. Start a collection of chalices

We have in our church on our Communion table now sixteen chalices from different countries. The church started off with one. Then a high school student went to Florida for college. He came back at Christmas with a beautiful pewter chalice as a gift for the church. Now many people from our congregation have brought or sent chalices from countries they have visited. We have them from Korea, Haiti, Germany, the Holy Land, Spain ... in wood, crystal, pottery, brass, and other materials. Thus we have symbolized the world-wide and international nature of our Communion.

7. Display a variety of crosses

Dick did it himself in our church, but anybody in the congregation or pastorate of a church could do the same thing. Dick went to the marvelous gift shop and got ten crosses in different styles that he presented to the church on his tenth anniversary. They are displayed on a huge piece of acrylic on a rear wall in the church. The collection includes very ornate crosses and very simple ones, very modern and very old, relatively large and small, with different symbolic shapes and decorations.

8. Use a hymn as a prayer

Take an unfamiliar hymn with a good text for a prayer, especially a hymn which you would like to use in worship sometime. Have the congregation simply read the hymn's words as an invocation or prayer of petition in the service. (Perhaps the leader of worship should read the first stanza to help the people get tuned in to the hymn's ideas and mood.) Use the hymn this way two or three times in a few months, then sing the hymn some Sunday. The tune will, if it's a good tune, enhance the now-familiar lyrics, and people will sing with greater interest because they have used the words in worship.

9. Evaluate the end

It's important to look rather often at how the service of worship ends and to evaluate that part of the service. Think on these things: How do people usually feel at the end of your time of worship? (No, they don't have to feel happy every Sunday, or even "ready to roll," but they should properly feel something other than glad it's over or tired or gloomy. Nor should they feel the *same* every Sunday.) Is the sequence of parts of worship at the close of the time really significant or just a winding-down? After the benediction, or other last thing you do, is there opportunity and encouragement for the church family to greet each other and share friendship? Or does the organ drown out all natural conversation? Is there a "rush toward the exits"? If there is, what does this say about the feelings generated in the service? Are the final few minutes of worship a time of spirited participation, as if something important is happening? Does the ending undercut any motivation given to Christian living earlier in the hour?

10. Surround the greetings with song

We hear around the country that the "Time of Greeting" or "Passing of the Peace" in some churches often lacks meaning and is unpopular with some members. Some people feel that this social element is an intrusion into the mood of worship. Honesty requires us to admit that the exchange of greetings is widely little more than a "Hi, how are ya?" experience, often just a repeat of what happened when people greeted each other on the front steps. We suggest that the worship leader *tell people what to say* some Sundays: "Now reach out to those around you and say, 'Welcome to the House of God' "; or, another time, "Grace and peace" or "Happy Easter" or "You are the salt of the earth." But another idea is to formalize the greeting within a song. Sing a hymn's first two stanzas and then do the greeting and sing the latter two stanzas, with the organ playing as people shake hands and speak to one another. The point is to make the greeting a *liturgical* act, not just a social, chummy gesture.

For example, sing two stanzas of "Come, Christians, join to sing" and tell people to keep their fingers in the hymnals and reach out with the other hand and say "God's love never ends" (inspired by words of the hymn). Or sing "He's got the whole world in his hands" and say at some point

"You're in the hands of God." Or sing, "My hope is built" and tell each other "Always have hope!" One result of this practice is that the hymns take on new meaning as a continuing expression of the basis of our fellowship. (And people may *sing better,* too, with voices encouraged by the experience of community.)

11. Repeat the most important passages

Since biblical illiteracy is a major problem among many churches in our era, and since that lack of knowledge of scriptures includes unfamiliarity with even the most important and crucial parts of passages, use them often in the services of your church. For example, instead of always using the Psalms for responsive readings, have a simple but strong reading of the "Beatitudes" from Matthew 5 — and do it several times during the year. First Corinthians 13 breaks up nicely as a responsive reading and could often precede, for instance, the intercessory prayers. Jesus' quotation from Isaiah 61 in the synagogue of Nazareth can be a strong and profound "statement of purpose" with which to conclude worship — and frequent repetition could impress the congregation with a special sense of mission. With liturgical use of such basic scripture passages, worship can be grounded in the Bible whether the preacher is a "biblical preacher" or not! And certain lines of scripture deserve to be deeply imbedded in our consciousness. Repetition will help.

12. Search for new ways to make announcements

Many members are already doing as much as they can in the church program and they do not need to know alternatives or be seduced into taking on "one more thing." But others don't really know what the continuing life of the congregation has to offer. They read in the bulletin about the choirs, gatherings, small groups, marriage encounter weekend, and so forth, but they often don't really know what goes on at the meetings. So we suggest you try different means of giving the flavor of whatever each group does. Not many people know what goes on at a choir rehearsal (in many cases that's a good thing) but if you are trying to recruit people into the choir it might be very interesting to show in two minutes what happens so that an untrained singer who can't read music but has a pretty nice voice can become a member of the group that is most noticeable Sunday mornings in worship.

As Dick was starting to make announcements in a service (we make them verbally; since we don't have a bulletin, most of the time we are not just repeating something that the congregation has just read), a nine-year-old boy named Billy walked down the aisle. He was wearing a Presbyterian Camp & Conference T-shirt, a rain hat, a bright orange pack filled with clothes, a canteen, a fishing pole, two pans and a cup and a fork and spook and knife tied together and hung around his neck, a yellow slicker half on. He clanked all the way to the front of the church and then said, "Last year I wanted to go to church camp but I didn't have enough money to send off my registration. The church came through and gave me the money, but the one I wanted to go to was already filled up and I was too late. This year I'm ready to go. Does anybody know when it starts?" That information was then given, and we had more inquiries about camp at the end of the service than we ever have had before.

13. Make announcements count

Oh, how many of us worship leaders are rather ashamed and embarrassed about making announcements in worship, with the lurking belief that they are a distraction from the main purposes of worship, and interruption of the "mood of worship." We don't believe this. Announcements, which are part of "the Sharing of Concerns" in our services in Port Jervis, are both times of fellowship and moments

25

when we lift up the action of the church as a studying and working community. Yes, like other parts of the service, the announcements should be succinct and articulately presented, but they should also be offered with appropriate passion: The happy announcements should sound happy, the sad announcements should be sad and thoughtful, the urgent ones and challenging ones properly urgent and challenging, all as celebrations of life together.

Furthermore, let these announcements be made by different people, persons prepared to step forward and speak on behalf of their groups, or to speak simply because they know what's happening. Another thing we have found to be of special importance in this part of our service is the sharing of news about people in crisis. While a large church could not take time to speak of all the persons in crucial situations, most of our churches can share a few major events in the lives of our people without making undue demands on time and attention.

Ah, time! There's the issue! If we really share our human and communal concerns, if we really take our crises seriously, if we really deal with the work and fellowship of the church earnestly, we may not get through by noon! But let's face it, friends, the churches in the world and in history which seemed to make a difference, the Christian groups we look to with admiration, were not just one-hour-on-Sunday experiences, nor did they accomplish what they did or remain true under threat as they did because they managed to confine their "fellowship of the Holy Spirit" within one hour. While we must be sensitive to spans of attention, we find that if the service is interesting and participatory, and if all parts have personal meaning to many people, attention is not a problem and people do not worry about time. (Our services are usually about one hour and twelve minutes long, and sometimes closer to an hour and a half, but complaints are rare, and complaints only come when the parts of the service are poorly planned or represent bits of self-indulgence by us leaders, or when ideas in the service just don't relate to the real lives of the people.)

14. Translate worship words

Don't assume that people know what Latin and other foreign words for parts of the service or for the Church Year mean. Church professionals can become very parochial and hoity-toity with their use of technical jargon. "Sursum corda" and "Magnificat" and "Quinquagesima" and even "Sanctus" and "Introit" and names for church furniture are often "Greek" to laypersons. And clever use of the terms wins no special brownie points with the God of heaven and earth. Translate. Interpret. Publish a simple glossary. Don't leave anyone out of the church family with a special language. And don't separate the church from reality.

15. Invite new members to lead

In large churches where a "new members" class may include forty or fifty people, this would be impossible, but many of us don't have such problems; we rejoice at receiving six or seven folks in a season. One way to get the new members known before the congregation and at the same time inspire greater interest in the processes and content of the service by the new folks themselves is to invite them to share in leading worship on the Sundays after they are received. Have each one take a turn reading the scripture, offering a prayer of their composition and based on their occupation or age or experience, or doing some other part of worship as their skills suggest. Some new members will reject such an opportunity or not be able to do it for one reason or another. Fine. But for others it will work very well. Take time to train each person and to inspire his or her best efforts. And in the service offer a brief personal introduction of the new member before he or she steps forward, and show your gratitude and delight for their participation in your church.

16. Draw greeters from many groups

There are many possibilities of using members of the congregation to greet other members and visitors on an average Sunday morning as well as on special days.

- Have all the members of a family be greeters.
- Have the children's choir do the greeting.
- Have the adult choir do the greeting before the processional.
- Pick greeters from all the different organizations in the church as you have in the suggestion on offerings.
- Have the new members who joined the previous week be greeters.
- Have members of the confirmation class do it.
- On different Sundays have members of the different boards of the church do the greeting.
- Let the professional staff be the greeters. The preaching pastor very often meets people at the door *after* the worship; try reversing the procedure and have him greeting them before. Also have the organist, the choir director, the custodian, and any other staff people.
- Have the church school faculty be the greeters.
- On pledge Sunday have members of the budget committee do the greeting and introduce themselves to the people coming in.

17. Invite a variety of responses

We all are aware that our hymnals contain a series of responses, usually to be read or to be sung by either the choir or congregation. It might be an expanding experience to ask the congregation or a group outside of the actual worship experience to make a list of natural responses to illumination. It would include things like:

"Ah!"
"Oh!"
"Aha!"
"Right!"
"Of course!"
"Wow!"
"I see!"
"Now I understand!"
Applause

18. Sing that introit at the door as people come in

Instead of having the usual greeters at the doors of the sanctuary, or regular members of the congregation who are not otherwise involved, have the choir be the greeters. One of our songs is particularly appropriate of this: "Come, let's get together" from "Hooray for God, #2" It is quite short, but don't do it four or five times. Wait until the bulk of the people are in and seated, then sing out. Let the singers remain in the rear of the church (or wherever the doors are) through the call to worship and then process into the choir loft as they sing the first hymn.

19. Let people be seen

A simple-minded but necessary suggestion (so simple it took us several years to think of it). When baptizing and when receiving new members or confirming or installing officers before the congregation, turn the person or persons being received, baptized or installed to face the congregation, with the presiding pastor turned away — rather than the other way around. The congregation sees the pastor all the time, and the others they want to see are face-to-face on this occasion.

20. Include the unordained staff in leadership

A telecast from a big and famous New York church a few years back included a bit of narration by one man who was apparently the custodian of the church. Marvelous! Have the janitor of the church and secretaries and other staff members offer prayers or readings from time to time, especially as these express their own concerns or reasons of gratitude. A receptionist in the church has a very crucial role and may be moved to pray for the ability of the church to relate to strangers with the love of Christ. A janitor may have a peculiar sense of the beauty and historicity of a building, just as he or she may also be keenly aware of many kinds of problems in the church — human problems as well as breakdowns in plumbing. If such people hesitate to speak before the congregation, they might at least stand as a part of a visual presentation, for example, as "living statues" in a frieze showing forms of service or types of persons that constitute the church.

21. Use prayers of intercession instead of the "long prayer"

The so-called Pastoral Prayer can lull people to lethargy and become repetitious and cliché-ridden. The problem with such prayers is often that they are just not specific enough, that they don't cover enough subjects of concern over a period of weeks, and that they get short shrift in the pastor's planning. Growing in popularity these days is the practice of having several paragraph-long and specific Prayers of Intercession. Of course this practice has been traditional in many kinds of churches for centuries, but not in others. These prayers can be led by people who have the most knowledge of the subject or feel most keenly about it — the teacher praying about school problems, the nurse about ministry to the sick, the policeman about increase in crime, etc.

Along with such prayers, let there be silence, time for people to share their feelings of need, their sense of dependence on God's grace, in silent prayer. And, once again, we plead for muzak-free silence, prayer without sweet nothings from the organ, so that the Holy Spirit can move among us as he chooses, unlimited by "mood music."

Regarding the practice of the pastor leading prayers, the challenge we hold before you is to plan this part of the service *as carefully as the sermon.* Let the pastor keep lists of concerns, real concerns out of the life of the town and the world and the lives of the particular congregation, lists which are the sources of subjects for this time of intercession as the weeks go by. The bad reputation of "the long prayer" is the result of lack of planning and evaluation, and perhaps also the fact that the pastor too rarely shares his deepest personal feelings in these prayers, the concerns he truly feels about the life of the church, copping out instead with habitual phrases, warmed over clichés recalled from the old prayerbook, and the mentioning of points omitted from the sermon.

22. Integrate the ushering teams

Communicate a new image in your church about jobs and positions formerly thought to be "masculine" or "for adults only." Women can pass plates for the offering as well as men! So can young people and children! Use male and female, young and old, family groups of two and three generations as ushers on Sunday morning. And let one of them offer the Prayer of Dedication, instead of the pastor, when the offerings are presented.

23. List the most important hymns

At the beginning of this fall season have the church staff (including musicians, of course) and three or four representatives of different age groups in the congregation make a list of 25 important hymns — hymns that everybody should know in your church. Let these be hymns on a wide variety of themes, hymns in a variety of styles, new songs as well as old, hymns that most adults in your congregation already know and that newcomers and children should know in order to participate fully in the church's worship. Practice these hymns in church school worship, in senior citizens' groups, in choir rehearsals, in men's and women's organizations throughout the year. Post the list (with page numbers) in big letters in a prominent place or two through the year.

24. Examine the role of guest preachers

Do you have many guest preachers during the year? What kind? What do they represent as they come before your people? Does their very presence broaden the congregation's understanding of the church's life and work? Plan carefully your selection of guest preachers so that the congregation is exposed to the ministry and mission of the wider church in some variety and richness. Have women as well as men, old and young, people who do things for the church which most folks don't know about — institutional chaplains, media experts, theologians. Plan also to have *enough* guests preaching in your church during the year to make the resident preacher's voice and style something a bit special.

25. Pray about commonplace paper

Invite five members of your congregation — male and female, young and old — to prepare brief prayers about five paper objects (one each). Then on a Sunday have the five people offer their prayers as they hold the objects, as if considering the meaning of that thing and the people or issues it represents. Here are five things: a local phone directory, a monthly bill for heat and light, a copy of *People Magazine* or some other gossipy magazine about famous people, a letter from a son or daughter far away from home, a copy of *TV Guide*. Let the objects be identified by the one who introduces the sequence of prayers; let the one who prays also identify the object being held and let the thing be held high enough for people to see and leafed through or moved in the appropriate way as the prayer begins.

26. Start the autumn with a bang

Plan immediately to begin your autumn series of services with excitement and the involvement of as many people as possible. Yes, you are working on getting everybody back from the summer doldrums or summer travels — "back to church" in September, but that isn't all we are talking about. It's partly a matter of the attitudes of the leaders. Pray and plan with high expectations, and then set a style of keen participation and interest in the first service of the season. Involve as many people "up front" of as many ages as possible; get the choirs to do an anthem which speaks to as many people as possible (not just one the choir director likes); let sermons and prayers and readings be carefully prepared and, where possible, put on their feet, dramatized or made visual and vigorous. And advertise the service, letting the people of the community know about your joy in worshiping together.

27. Share questions

One Sunday, let the leader of worship — one who is known well and trusted by the people — come to the level of the congregation and ask people to stand and identify simply their deepest and persistent questions about life. Introduce this time of sharing as a preparation for prayer and continuing fellowship; don't promise that someone is going to answer all questions before the service is over! Perhaps the leader should be prepared to begin by sharing his or her own deep question — about God, about death, about meaning, about people. Then have a time of prayer, asking God's help and offering thought and time to help each other with these questions. Pray also for those who have left the church because some questions upset them too long and too profoundly.

28. Share new discoveries

Invite people to stand and share, as an act of gratitude, the things they have discovered about God and about their own lives in recent months: New ideas, new assurances, new meanings. Lead the congregation in responding after every two or three statements with a line from the Psalms, such as "The Lord is good! His love lasts forever!"

29. Share initial experiences of faith

Sometimes faith is renewed and warmed by the recollection of early, inspiring encounters with Christ, those moments of insight and transformation that turned life around. Some Sunday invite members of the congregation to think back and, in silence, to thank God for those first experiences. Or, if the people are ready, invite them to stand and share these experiences with everyone, or to share them with a neighbor. Be careful not to put pressure on people, and don't let this go on too long or get too sentimental. But don't dismiss the idea too readily either.

30. Call to prayer with the oldest and the youngest together

Invite your oldest member present to come forward and simply hold or sit beside the youngest child present; then lead an eyes-open prayer about our pilgrimage from birth to age, about the meaning of the unfolding years, or about time and change. Keep it a simple, thoughtful, and honest prayer, being careful not to characterize old age negatively. The best years for many people are the last years. Maybe that idea should be in a prayer.

31. Call Sunday "the Lord's Day"

With the steadfast encroachment on Sunday by all kinds of interests, let's use the traditional term from time to time and remind people that God did ordain one day as special. Some churches use this heading for their orders of worship: "Service for the Lord's Day." Let's reclaim Sunday for worship and rest and fellowship.

32. Make sure people hear

Frequently check the audibility of parts of the service. Leaders can get into habits of speech that make them hard to hear, and P.A. systems can be improperly tuned for the space and the people. And acoustical properties do change with other changes in the space. And people get harder of hearing with age.

33. Unite with other churches for a Sunday service

An end-of-the-summer-start-of-the-fall "Celebration of Unity" service was held recently here, bringing together our Presbyterian congregation, a neighboring United Methodist church, and a nearby Reformed congregation. It was not a "summer union service" scheduled to accommodate vacations and diminished congregations but an attempt to show our oneness in Christ. All three pastors participated and musicians from all three churches (soloists and ensembles rather than choirs, since choirs had not reassembled for the Fall), including instrumentalists, shared leadership. It was the first time such a thing had happened on a Sunday morning in our city in many years, and yet seemed such a natural kind of gathering it will happen again soon, probably on Epiphany. One obvious feature of this event was that all three pastors are good friends and enjoyed being together. And friends from the different churches got to sit together for the first time in worship to God, as did families where members are in different congregations. Think about such a service with your neighboring churches or with churches of similar heritage in your city.

34. Take "A minute to share the Gospel"

Many Presbyterian churches have each Sunday something called "A Minute for Mission." Other denominations have similar things — times in services for brief descriptions of the church at work in many places. We suggest that there also (or instead) be a short time in the service — perhaps through a season of the year — for lay members to tell "What Jesus Means to Me" or perhaps "What God Has Done for Me" or "The Difference God Makes in My Life." Insist on brevity: A statement, not a sermon or lecture. Insist on a personal statement of faith, not moralizing. Use people of different ages and lifestyles and races. Follow it with an invitation to commitment and membership, or just with silent prayer in which each person of the church can try to express personal gratitude for the difference God has made in his or her life.

Designate a section for silence

In our church we have some folks who like to enter a silent room and sit quietly before worship formally begins on Sunday and other folks who like to greet others and talk and share experiences before the service — often noisily. What to do? Put a sign on one side: "Sit in this section if you want a time of silence before the prelude." This may remind the talking folks to hold it down a bit.

The Advantage Of Music

It was 4:25 in the afternoon. The last of the nine choirs of children had sung our song, "Thank You, Thank You." The whole congregation of over 250 had finished singing and dancing our song, "David Danced." The laughter and applause had subsided. Don then asked the ministers for the nine churches whose choirs had sung in this, the Sixth Annual Youth Choirs Festival, to stand up and be recognized. Don then pointed to the banner for the Second Helvetic Confession that Dick and Don had designed for the United Presbyterian Book of Creeds and Confessions. "In the creed represented by this off-white banner with a slim, blue cross on it there is the following statement: 'Some churches do not have *the advantage of music.*' " Don then swept his arms around including all of the pastors and said, "Gentlemen, you are rich." The pastors immediately started applauding their choirs and choir directors. It was a most exciting moment for all of us.

Pastors, cherish your music program. Nurture it. Cultivate it. Applaud it. Enlarge it. Support it. Remember that they often are the most important link between the Word you preach and the congregations absorbing it. Church music is not time out, a part of the service to do something else, nor a pretty sentimental moment. Nor is it a moment for the musical sophisticates or dropouts to speak or sing their piece.

Nor is it a moment to "elevate the taste" of the congregation. Or to lower it. It's as essential as "Then they sang a hymn and went out to the Mount of Olives," Mark's description of the transition from the Lord's Supper to the desperate moment in Gethsemane. Praise God with music! Praise God FOR music!

The way we do music

To alter a well-known poem "How do we tell the story? Let me count the ways." Here are some ways, some distinctive patterns, in which we present THE story and our church's nature in music.

1. The music of our choirs is almost always exciting. Having heard a great teacher of music say that every piece of music in worship should be a "show-piece," a production number, we try very hard to follow that suggestion. We take a number of pieces of music a bit faster than some churches do, but not so fast that the words will not be understood. If the choirs are gasping with the momentum of the music, the congregation will be also, and probably paying attention. If we do a slow song or anthem, we do it in a very heavy way, emphasizing the beat, underscoring the intensity; if we do a quiet number we do it so softly that the people have to sit forward to hear it. Most other composers like the way we do their works. There is the feeling in the air that something important. is happening. As we have previously explained, some anthems are *staged* simply.

2. The adult choir and the Genesis Singers (fourth through eighth grade) both sing every Sunday. This allows for music that will appeal to peer groups as well as people who like all kinds of music, each week. This also plants the message that music and worship are not just for the adults. Both choirs hold copies of music most of the time. If the adults don't have to memorize each anthem, why should the children's choir?

3. We sing the scriptures. Our congregation, more often than many others, gets to hear the Sunday lessons sung rather than just read. We find anthem settings of the lections for the Sundays, we sometimes improvise anthems using the words of the Bible, or we line out verses of scripture. So scripture looms larger in the fabric of the service, claiming attention, involving emotions.

4. The adult choir sings all kinds of music. There is no one type of writing, no one sound, no one style of pronunciation that is uniquely holy or even most appropriate for worship. And so we use them all. One year, the choir sang a British folk tune with whistling, a conventional anthem by Jane Marshall, a soft and gently swinging jazz "Kyrie," a number of works by Eugene Butler (who led our "At Home" workshop with us), a throbbing early-American Shaker song, Brahms' "How Lovely" from the Requiem, a driving pseudo-jazz Avery and Marsh carol, and Britten's "Ceremony of Carols." And we tried to have each one be true to its own style and way of sounding.

5. We use lots of guest singers and instrumentalists. Flute players have played in anthems, but more often Offertories or Preludes. We have trumpets and horns with hymns, anthems, or alone. Also clarinet, piano, and guitar. A new person in our community, a historian, plays twelve-string guitar and sings folk hymns and spirituals most movingly, and he has enriched our services. We have also included young students playing their instruments as they are learning them, using them in ways that make the students sound good and feel good about sharing that part of their lives with the church family.

6. Our song, "This Room," has helped us share our own life stories as Christians, moving people to think about sacred places and holy times in their lives.

The servant attitude

Don once had to rehearse two singers in music they were performing at a wedding. He was presented with a pop song, Malotte's "Lord's Prayer", and the Avery and Marsh song, "Shines There Such a Light." He went over the music two or three times with them. At one point, the young woman said to him: "It is a real pleasure to work with you. You didn't give us a hard time about any of the music, you gave us suggestions, and you were certainly less condescending than the last organist who played for us. He had to come in from sailing a boat somewhere and was terribly put out with us although he had set the time. And he was more than half an hour late."

It occurred to us as we were talking about the experience afterwards that this is not an unusual experience in the church, the condescension and so forth. As organist/pianists and choir directors we need to take stock of ourselves. Since the Son of God came to be the *servant* of people, we need to rethink our positions in the church.

First of all, we need to recognize that most of us are far too strong. We control the tempo and the emotional climate and mood of each worship service. If we are annoyed, the music will show it. If we are overexcited, the music will show it. We get away with being the hardest person on the church staff to deal with. And nobody checks us until the patterns of power are established and really difficult to change. We need to be reminded or remind ourselves through reading of the Bible, for one thing, that our servanthood in worship is on the line each time we play.

Secondly, we are arbiters of taste and we need to be humble, open, and willing to listen and learn as well as to musically pontificate. Don, as choir director, has been so lucky the 23 years he has spent in Port Jervis because every single organist was willing to try any kind of music and try to do it well. There has been no condescension. As servants of the members of the church, as well as of outsiders who come in for weddings and funerals, we need to be ready to accommodate anything that comes up. Musicians have a real ability to put other people down.

Perhaps it is because it has taken a certain amount of time and discipline on our parts to develop the ability to play and we want to be treated with respect. We should feel humble and grateful that we were given the gift in the first place, and the supportive families that allowed us to develop them. There are books, which we will not recommend, with marvelously funny snobbish putdowns said by great, and not-so-great, musicians through the years. Christian musicians should take Advent as a time to wipe our slates clean and start over.

Thirdly, as we have said often before: "It is not our responsibility to elevate the musical taste of the congregation to the point at which we have *stopped*." And many musical schools stop us. They are usually run by musical elitists, the kind of people Jesus may discuss unflatteringly when he grows up. Our experience is always limited, which is not at all what we mean when we start a sentence with the phrase: "Now it's my experience that...." We mean to imply a great breadth of experience that is more often than not just not true. So we need to hear the needs and musical desires of each person in the congregation and find time to use each style in our worship ... together. After all, worshiping is doing it together. So let's take time to stir ourselves up, try new things, open our ears, and learn to love, humbly and naively again.

To come at this from another direction, here are a few things for us musicians to think long about ourselves and for us pastors as shapers if not hirers of the church staff (namely, the musicians) to think about.

A. The following is a suggested advertisement to put in the local paper, a church magazine, the official AGO magazine, and in letters to schools that are training church musicians:

> Organist/pianist/accompanist needed for the congregation. If you can't play everything or won't play everything from Bach to rock and Bacharach and Bock and Rachmaninoff, do not apply for the job. Instead apply yourself to learning what's needed in your job as *servant to the church!*

B. In the problem of tempo, choose the one that does most for the singers, the congregation. Too slow will bore the people and put them in an unreceptive mood to hear the Word and the exposition. Do you accept that responsibility? On whose authority? Music, by its very nature, colors and shapes a context of whatever follows it. If you are in charge of picking and presenting the music in the worship, you must be terrifyingly aware of the whole service and what is desired by the other leaders. If the pastor does not know what she desires, then it is your job to point out the possibilities. Too fast will leave people breathless, with a feeling of "where are we now" which will also interfere with the pastor's job in the rest of the service. Too loud will overwhelm them and leave them frustrated; too soft will expose them and leave them embarrassed.

Some suggestions for you:
- Practice a hymn as fast as you can play it, as written.
- Practice the same hymn faster by improvising your own rhythmic pattern.
- Practice it slowly and heavily.
- Drag it.

- Try it on organ; try it on piano; all the ways mentioned above and other ways you come up with.
- Practice each verse at a different tempo.
- Dance it. See how the body moves to it.
- Check with your pastor and see which tempo he wants.

C. Take time to talk to your pastor and worship committee and explain your position as a person who wants to serve in the service in the most responsible way you can, and as one who needs help in knowing what she wants to accomplish within that one hour. Perhaps you will need to tell what the possibilities are and how well you can reach them. Most of all, get together in order to get it all together for God.

D. We close with a quote from a dear friend of ours who may want to remain nameless: "The (Synod) school is flat, dead, so uninspired that everyone is saying, 'When will it start — when will things begin to mo-o-ove!?' It won't — I knew it after the first hymn Monday morn, in chapel. Can you imagine my shock when this group of 400 singing Christians began to vigorously sing one of the great old hymns of the church and the *organist slowed them all down* to a dragging pace! I was sitting third row from the front and felt shock waves washing between the singers and the organist; he won as he thunderously plodded on and the school died right there.... Well — it's over — Nothing left to do but bury it!"

If the church dies, could it ever be the fault of the organist/pianist/accompanist? An accompanist by definition should go down in flames *with* the rest of the people.

Musical preferences

The trouble with seminaries, many of them, and with at least some graduate programs in Church Music is that they don't prepare people for musical leadership in real churches. They don't take into account where people really are. The same can be said of some music conferences. Too often in our observation, schools and training conferences get people ready to lead great (according to some tastes) older works, mostly in the "classical" repertoire for choirs, and to play the same kind of organ works. But the congregation may actually not particularly respond to Bach or Handel of Purcell — at least not a majority of people. What can the church musician do to reach those who most prefer jazz or country music or rock or Broadway music, with the best in those styles and with texts that are theologically sound and relevant?

We too often see young church musicians at sea in their first jobs, not knowing how to cope with the interests of their choirs, congregations, and pastors. Often these musicians feel superior to those with whom and for whom they work, feeling that the others are just not sophisticated enough, not up to their own standards. The issue, however, may be that the others have a broader background in music than the trained musician, knowing and appreciating more kinds of music and knowing that God speaks in a variety of forms. They may be quite confident that the Holy Spirit kept on working in the present century, inspiring new lyrics and tunes, while the recent graduate appears to believe the Spirit retired in 1899. Or, even though young musicians may agree with their interests and share their desire to do a variety of kinds of music and contemporary works, they may not know any good things to do. And they may find themselves directing some work of questionable theological content and schmaltzy-and-cutesy musical style because they know nothing better to do.

May we not look to the seminaries and graduate music schools for leadership in this area, for preparation of real leaders with a breadth of knowledge as well as technical skill? We ourselves have had good experiences on certain campuses, responding to a desire of the professors to acquaint students with what's being written for churches now. And doubtless other contemporary composers have also, but from what we hear, such occasions are rather rare. Perhaps some letters from alumni should go to these schools, some pressure be applied by pastors and other church leaders, some questions asked.

Introducing new hymns

So often the traditional hymns of worship are just items on the agenda to *get through*; or devices to get people up on their feet after they have been sitting; or pleasant but rather meaningless activity, bearing little fruit. And often dull, dreary, lifeless. Along with the "Service of Hymns" idea, here are a few ways we have found helpful for rediscovering the beauty, vitality, rhythmic interest and message of some hymns, that they may live and through them God's Spirit may breathe life into us. Why not try them?

- Simply pause in the singing of a hymn to *read a stanza* — everybody, aloud. The leader of worship may need to announce before the hymn something like "Let us sing the first two stanzas of Hymn 312, and then pause with our books open." Some lyrics need looking at apart from the singing of them.

- Let people *discuss the words* before singing the hymn, or after singing it once and before singing it a second time. For example, when singing "This Is the Day the Lord has Made," come down toward the people and ask, "What days are the second and third stanzas about? They refer to events that happened on Sunday; what events?" Or, when singing "All Hail the Power," ask, before the stanza containing the words, a hard and provocative question: "What does it mean, 'spread your trophies at his feet'? Bowling trophies? Golf trophies? What trophies?" OR simply ask before any familiar hymn for mental pictures the hymn provokes. Let the congregation suggest pictures in their heads as they sing "All Hail the Power" or "A Mighty Fortress" or "For the Beauty of the Earth" or "How Firm a Foundation." OR ask from people short explanations of a time or situation to which the words relate in their experience or thinking. "Can you think of an event in your life this hymn speaks to?" Don't let this go on long, just enough to get people thinking about the hymn.

- Have a *dramatic reading* of the words of the whole hymn by someone who can read with great understanding. A simple, but thoughtful and sensitive, reading or recitation, with a bit of staging, perhaps. For example, "Beneath the Cross of Jesus" by a person standing beneath the big cross in your church, if you have one. "O Jesus, I Have Promised" by a solitary person standing and walking in an attitude of lonely prayer. "Lead, Kindly Light" by someone holding one candle in a darkened church. The words of a good Communion hymn by someone walking up to the altar or table and just looking at and picking up the bread and chalice slowly, thoughtfully. Caution: No sing-song recitations! And don't let the words sound sentimental and sweet, even though dear and familiar.

37

- *Whistle the tune* before singing the words. Everybody. Outlandish? No, not really, not if we truly believe in the joyful quality of the Christian life. Right now, before going on to read, whistle the tune of "For the Beauty of the Earth" at a rather fast tempo and with a bounce. It brings out the feeling of affection the poet had for the creation and for the Creator, doesn't it? Now try the tune of "O Sing a Song of Bethlehem" singing just "La, la, la" on the notes. Or, if you don't know that, "Take My Life and Let It Be" or "O for a Thousand Tongues." Some melodies, done in a not-too-slow free, bouncy, or soaring style — as we leave behind the ponderous mood of most churchly singing — are delightful to whistle or "La, la" and we can thus discover their meaning all over again.

- *Divide the congregation to sing the lines responsively*, as in a Responsive Reading. "Watchman, Tell Us of the Night" can be an interesting dialog this way. St. Francis' "All Creatures of Our God and King" takes on new excitement as the lines and the "O praise Him's" are separated across the aisle. Many other songs divide naturally in this way.

- *Introduce new music in the fellowship hall.* Some people have an uphill fight introducing any new materials into the Sunday service — new songs, new forms of participation, etc. Of course, we must evaluate carefully the style in which we introduce new things to find out whether we ourselves may be the reason they are not accepted or enjoyed. But if you know that's not the problem, try introducing the material at a church Family Night, while people are gathered around the tables in a relaxed and friendly mood. Include a new song in a "hymn sing"; do the new form of participatory worship in an after-dinner time of celebration. Do this a number of times until people become comfortable with whatever it is, then do the same thing — without apology or clue to your clever strategy — on a Sunday morning.

Organizing music

We recently got a brochure from a business management company with a marvelous picture of a desk piled high with messy, messy paperwork and a man's hand disappearing as he drowned in his unfiled material. This immediately spoke to us, as the amount of paper used by must churches is phenomenal!

As we consider planning in relation to the music program of the church, the first thing to consider is where you are going to store all the music *that you haven't used yet*! Most choir directors get lots of free copies of music from major publishers, complete octavo anthems or sizable reproductions. After we have gone through the music (as it arrives, of course, ha ha!) and marked some to order specifically and marked some to reconsider and others to put on hold, we start making piles since there is no place to store it. And it must be kept at all costs if you want to have an exciting and relevant music program. That music is valuable because you never know what weird subject is going to be brought up in the lectionary readings for which you will have to find a related anthem, solo, small group work, or instrumental.

You mean you don't always relate the music to the rest of the worship? Gosh, we thought everybody was over the "pick a few anthems that are nice and do them whenever you choose to" syndrome. The discipline of planning music that is fitting for each specific service seems to us to be essential. Many of the songs that we have written were written simply because we could not find music that was appropriate to an occasion, to a day, to a theme. If you have most of our music, now is your chance to look through it again and make a theme and scripture list of the words to help you in picking songs, hymns, and anthems.

For example, our anthem, "The Water Is Rising" deals with (1) being too late, (2) refusing to listen, (3) the necessity to eventually face facts, among other things. If the pastor is preaching on Noah and the Flood, the anthem is a natural, with a new twist since it is being sung by people who did not heed Noah and are now in the attic waiting to drown. It is funny and ironic and ghoulish and real. But if the pastor is preaching on how to listen to present-day prophets, you might not necessarily think of that particular anthem. With your list at hand, your job of choosing music that fits but says something different about the pastor's theme is made simpler. Don had his secretary keep a list of themes, major themes such as loneliness and love and death, and music, including pop and folk songs that relate to them. A faithful friend of the church went through Don's music files and reorganized them. After the filing was in shape, the friend and Don made a similar list of anthem themes. It is great fun to find a new context for an anthem you have done a number of times, one that the congregation likes and asks for.

Long-range planning

Long-range planning is helped immeasurably if the lections are adhered to. We have a choir director friend who sets his whole year's schedule of music in September! We can't imagine that, not because of the work it would take but because it doesn't seem to allow for new compositions or special surprise events that need to be dealt with in worship, events both good and bad. In the past we have commiserated with pastors and choirmasters who have a printed bulletin each Sunday that must be at the printers by Tuesday, locking out the actions of the Holy Spirit from Tuesday to Sunday. However, having the three lessons or a sermon series theme for a month or a season ahead is tremendously helpful. It sends Don to his files of anthems, collections that the children's choir sing from, solos of religious music, and also folk songs and gospel songs and contemporary church songs of the Broadway or rock type.

Then comes the tricky planning. As each piece of music that seems appropriate is considered, we ask ourselves these questions:

1. Who will this speak to? Because of the type of music it is, who will not listen to it or at most give it a perfunctory hearing? Does the music get in the way of the words or does it amplify it? And so forth.
2. Who does this kind of music best? Can the whole adult choir handle this? Should we do it with a small group? Would it be more effective, in that people will listen to it more readily or more surprisingly, sung by the children or the teenage choir?
3. Where should we do it, where in the sanctuary? The choir loft? Scattered through the congregation? The balcony? In front? In back?
4. Should it be danced? or pantomimed? or staged? or should props be used?
5. Will that special soloist be here and available (if healthy) on that day?
6. Do we have a choice of performers?
7. Will it take some special rehearsing?
8. When can we schedule this?

Long, long range planning can be fun. We hear a piece of music and love it. After lots of thought, we get copies. Then we start thinking up possible occasions in the distant future. Ours is not the kind of situation in which the congregation will accept or the choir be capable of producing a major work each month, or each week as some churches can, or even each season. So we work on five-year plans (or variations thereof). A special service of Psalms is being rehearsed for slowly, one that will include Bernstein's "Chichister Psalms" and possibly Stravinsky's "Symphony of Psalms" as well as hymns based on the Psalms (done in a variety of ways) and improvised Psalms as we are known for doing. Some will be danced, staged, pantomimed by special people or the congregation as a whole. A line from Psalm 63 comes to mind: "As I lie in bed I think of you." This is true, so true, of those of us who are trying to be creative in worship. We spend hours of sleepless nights working on movements, figuring props, staging fragments. There is always pencil and paper by the bed. Because planning goes on and on and when we least expect it an idea comes and it must be kept. The Psalm service may turn out to be a special ecumenical service that we schedule, a service in which our Jewish friends can come and worship comfortably, and be amazed to hear us singing the words in the original Hebrew. Oops, we just got an idea! Who moved my pencil and paper?

Evaluating music

We have seen several articles containing sweeping criticism of current trends in liturgical change, including the rejection of new church music. Most of these articles were not of the crackpot or hateful or even "whatever-it-is-I'm-agin-it" types, but were rather serious and well-written and, at points, had a scholarly sound. A couple of them, in fact, came from people of some prominence.

Listening to criticisms gives us a way to think about evaluating music, so here are some random reflections on recent criticisms, offered not defensively, but confidently, yet with a measure of humility, since we are all servants groping for patterns of faithfulness.

1. When people say that a lot of new liturgical forms and new church music is *trivial, superficial, foolish and unbiblical,* they are probably right. We've heard and seen a lot like that. We all need to be highly selective and use our heads as we plan creative worship and education. But we also know about some great things being done in all kinds of churches, some beautiful and thought-provoking and inspiring things. We wonder how broad and diverse the experience of some critics may be when they make broad, negative generalizations. What are they talking about? Where have they been? An academic community, as we all know, can be a pretty insular place, a sheltered world; and big-city church worship can be very unimaginative and ineptly done, with innovations often awkwardly introduced into traditionally stuffy patterns.

2. While there is some pretty bad music coming off the presses these days, *a lot of old, traditional hymns don't stand up well under close evaluation,* either. Musically, many of the solid old favorites of both congregations and erudite directors are musically repetitious, laden with clichés of their periods or just hard to sing. Often the words and music don't fit together well at all. Speaking of the words, some hymns in the hymnal just don't say anything of much significance. Some are unbiblical in their textual content, even well-nigh heretical: They emphasize Jesus' divinity in odd ways ("veiled in flesh the godhead see"), they push perfectionist ideas of history ("These things shall be: a loftier race"), they exalt patronizing and imperialistic views of mission ("Can we to men benighted the lamp of life deny?"), they confuse the gospel with morality ("He died to make us good/That we might go at last to heaven") and stress over and over again, more than the Bible does by far, the salvation of the individual soul and the bliss of life after death.

This is not to mention the purely literary embarrassments of the hymnals. (What small hymnals we would have without the constant use of inversions of predicates and adjectives in poetic lines to obtain the rhymes! "Let us all Thy life receive" instead of "Let us all receive Thy life" — to rhyme with "Never more Thy Temples leave"!) Yes, some of these less-than-perfect old hymns have found important places in our lives, they are beloved to thousands, including us. Fine, but let's not pretend that the words of the past are automatically superior to those of the present!

3. Few churches we know about are throwing out all old forms, all the classics and all the traditions, and *just using new stuff*. Many churches are seeking a creative combination of old and new. Yet some critics speak as if there was a widespread renunciation of vital traditions and great music from the past.

4. Some writers put down new worship materials and new music by saying *"it won't last,"* it's "ephemeral." Goodness, so were all the things written through the centuries; they were written for a time and place, in response to feelings, issues, events of their times, in the language and artistic or literary forms of their times. Who knows what will last? (It's amazing to us that "Mary, Mary," written for a specific Christmas program in 1959, is being sung around the world years later!)

5. It has been written with some passion that current innovations *neglect the transcendent quality* of truly Christian worship, that things are too "chummy" and that there is too much emphasis on the congregation and its good feeling, rather than awe and reverence before God. Once again, we might agree — to a point. But we must hasten to say three things about this issue.

First: The feelings of transcendence some people miss often seem purely aesthetic responses (matters of architecture and volume and lighting) and escapist in effect (a desire for leaving the real, nitty-gritty world in the vestibule). Behold, the Gothic experience is not a biblical norm for all Christian worship forever and ever, nor is the style (in English language, note) of the *Book of Common Prayer*, nor is the musical form of the eighteenth-century chorale!

Second: Frankly, many of the people who insist on awe and reverence and "formality" as highest values are, in our experience, often desiring separateness from other people. Or else they are hurting, overwhelmed by changes in their lives. Or else they are threatened by a loss of personal power in church and society. Related to this observation, we find that worship leaders everywhere are trying to make up for lost time in recovering the ethical dimensions of worship, that is, the personal, incarnational dimensions; they are stressing God's will for reconciled, loving, caring, New Testament-style community — in sermons, in songs, in ceremonies, in many ways. This is itself a desire for transcendence of a rare kind, a "going beyond" ourselves, a "rising above" our sinful, self-centered, self-protective patterns of living. Formerly, it was possible to go to awesome, reverent services in a church for thirty years and never have to relate to another human being. That's much harder to do these days, thank God.

Third: It's true that not much new church music is about the "otherness" of God, about his majesty and glory in an abstract sense. Rather than be discouraged by critics' condemnation of the use of less "exalting" music and the old "uplifting" hymns, let composers and poets be encouraged to write strong hymns of praise and adoration in modern terms, in modern language and about present experiences.

6. Some new music has been accused of being *imitative* of current popular styles. Of course. Church music has always been written in the styles of the period when it was written. And when the music was for congregations to sing and relate immediately to their experience, the music was in the pop styles of the time. Sadly, a disdainful sneer can be detected in some of the putdowns of new music when it is thus criticized; and what's revealed is a rather narrow and merely aesthetic preference for "classical" music over folk, jazz, ballad, or rock-styles of today. That preference is fine — to each his own — until it is expressed with a self-righteous tone, as if such matters of taste were actually matters of piety or theology.

We insist on (a) a variety of styles for the variety in the congregation; (b) music for the ordinary people to sing that is natural and accessible to them (namely, "popular" styles for the populace, who couldn't sing Penderecki or Stravinsky or eight-part Vaughan Williams or other complex "serious" music now any more than they could handle Handel back in his time); (c) Christian ideas in the music, whatever its style, or genuine expressions of feelings and needs in the world to which Christians relate.

7. Another kind of criticism suggests that the more "eloquent" prayers of the prayerbooks, the more "formal" (sedate, solemn, confined) styles of liturgical leadership up front and the traditional hymns and anthems inspire *more profound feelings, deeper internal attitudes*, than the new forms. "Reverence" rather than "glad to be here"; "joy" rather than "fun"; "penitence and reflection" rather than "fellowship," etc., etc.

In our experience, this is assuming a lot on behalf of the older forms that may or may not be true. A lot of people may be moved to deep, inner joy while listening to the old Elizabethan-style prayers and some of the old and stately hymns of joy, but a lot of people may just be going through the motions — and often look to be. The professor who claims folks find such deep and quiet joy in solemn moments may be bringing his own personal associations to the worship experience — possibly of a rather elite variety, and he may be doing some wishful thinking about others! We find a lot of people are bored, lulled to a sleepy state of noninvolvement, or merely settling into a comfortable feeling of nostalgia and easy security when the music of the "joyful" old hymn begins.

On the other hand, the "fun" of some of the new music represents, or can become an experience of obvious joy and excitement when interpreted and shared. (Thus "We Are the Church" and its gestures and relating to neighbors can be fun, but when thought about for a moment in the service or done in quiet reflection and slower tempo later on, or when recalled in a moment of tension or crisis in the church can be truly joyful, in a profound sense. Or so it has been for us and, apparently, for many others.)

Perhaps some of our responses to criticism reflect our impatience. We are increasingly impatient with liturgical patterns and church music that doesn't conspicuously change anybody or any situation, or even have that purpose. There is a lot of great old music and beautiful old prayers and majestic this and that which seem to have no purpose but to entertain people, to make them feel nice or proud or relaxed. One more Messiah at Christmas time, even bigger and louder and with more orchestra, is not going to produce much more concern for justice or the feeding of the hungry or one's alcoholic neighbor. Or if it does, it will be because of fresh, innovative, and imaginative presentations — not just another "get through it" performance so another church can boast "WE did the Messiah!"

Too much impressive and "exalting" church music is really just concertizing for the upper classes in the community. There may be a place for this, but let's not pretend it's the highest form of communication of the Gospel. It may indeed be one form of evangelism, but no more so than a country-and-western concert with biblically-inspired words.

Let the criticisms of contemporary trends challenge us to think carefully about what we are doing and to do what we do better. But let's not be overwhelmed by them.

Ways to attract singers

Some years ago, we were privileged to share in the leadership of a Church Music Institute for leaders of music in American military base chapels of Europe, an institute sponsored by the U.S. chaplains and held at Berchtesgaden in West Germany. One of the workshops at that conference, led by Chaplain John Kays, an outstanding musician and director as well as military pastor, was on the subject "Ways to Attract Singers to the Chapel Choir." The workshop group compiled an impressive list of ideas which has implications for all kinds of church programs and for the worship of the local church as well as for "the Chapel Choir." We would like to cite some of these ideas and "bounce off" them, with hearty thanks to Chaplain Kays and the Berchtesgaden workshop. So here are "Ways to Attract" — for you choir leaders, but for all the rest of us as well.

1. *"The director should exude confidence and enthusiasm."* Which is to say, the Christian leader should show Christian faith and vigor and hope, rather than cynicism, constant disappointment, ho-hum indifference, and fatigue. How many services may die on their feet each Sunday across our land — not to mention choir rehearsals and group meetings — because of a negative attitude on the part of the director/pastor/president/chairperson.

2. *"Proper timing: Make sure rehearsals begin and end on time as scheduled."* While we have probably tried to "clock the Holy Spirit" on Sunday mornings for far too long, the allowance for interest spans, for emotional process within the service of worship, for definite beginnings and endings is a valid concern. And regarding rehearsals and other church meetings, how often we communicate a "this is not really important" attitude for disrespect for the schedule. Many struggling choir programs are really "done in" by directors who fail to get the rehearsals going with vigor and concentration *on time.*

3. *"Give proper recognition to singers."* The honoring of faithful sopranos, faithful Sunday school teachers, faithful board members, faithful pastors — such recognition encourages other people to know Christian service is important. Yes, the work is done for God's glory, but the scriptures teach us to honor each other and to be grateful as we serve together. Moreover, the members of the congregation need to know who the choir members are who sing up there in front (or behind them) each Sunday as part of their community, and who the officers are and what they are doing. Take time every few months to introduce each choir member by name, each board member by name, each staff member by name — with honor and gratitude.

4. *"Allow for fun,"* says the Berchtesgaden workshop of chapel music directors. And allow for fellowship to grow among members of all working groups in the church. Play together, eat together, allow real time for conversation (not just snatched time during discussion or when everyone should be following the director.) Enjoy the humor of rehearsals, and of times of worship as well. Fun is an essential element of the Christian life, often a form of joy, and an expression of love.

5. *"Establish a plan to reach young service people early in their assignment."* Now this idea for attracting people may seem rather limited to military base situations, but let's think again. The mobility of people within the United States and the picture of young teachers, young businessmen and women, students, retiring senior citizens moving in and out of our parishes should inspire us to take this idea seriously. Devise strategies for reaching people soon after they come to town — before they get into a rut of non-participation — for special interest groups in the church, for performing groups, for contribution of new ideas to the worship planning of the church.

6. *"Flexibility of Chaplain, Choir Director, and Accompanist — a crucial area."* The issue here, as expressed by the workshop, was the recognition of problems and willingness to deal with them, even if *leaders must change.* Sometimes, what's wrong with a church's program is *us*, our style, our biases, our plans. What the congregation or group actually needs may not be provided for in our designs, just as the preacher may preach brilliantly about issues which have nothing whatever to do with the life of this particular congregation at this time. "Flexibility" is the word, or call it openness to the Spirit.

7. *"Remember to be courteous."* Courtesy toward choir members, yes, and to board members, and fellow staff members, and visiting leaders, and all the people. Grace takes many forms, including graciousness — "thank you," "please," "that was beautiful," "can I do something to help?" "let me get it for you."

8. *"Keep the primary purpose continually before singers and congregation."* The work of the choir is not to entertain, to impress, to be "nice," any more than the church exists to lift the moral standards of the community, or to save money in the bank, or to keep kids off the streets, or to give old people something to do with their time. The mission of the church is to glorify and praise God, to nurture God's people for the ministry, and to live out the Good News in the world. All groups need constant reminders of this purpose. Such a clear mission, a sense of unique and supreme purpose, will *attract* people, even as it will leave some people behind who want less demanding reasons for being, for singing, for working, for dying.

The prelude

There are some churches where most of the congregation comes in eagerly anticipating the organ prelude. These are usually churches with fine organists, fine organs, and the preludes are showpieces of one kind or another. There are many other churches in which the congregation talks through the prelude. So who said there had to be a prelude? Perhaps it all started when we got paid accompanists and realized that they were getting enough money to do more than accompany three hymns. So somebody said, we'll have them play something in the beginning and the end and when the offering is being taken up.

As musicians, we are constantly re-examining why there is music in the service. Worship is not a concert, as we all know and often forget. Worship does include fellowship, the gathering of this specific group of the people of God, many of whom do not get the opportunity to relate with each other during the week. As people enter, they are glad to see each other, glad to share events and feelings and concerns. Marvelous! Perhaps the order of service is too structured for this to happen

44

later. So the prelude is often an interruption of the fellowship, a signal to stop relating to each other and to settle down and listen to the piece of music offered by a soloist.

Complicating the situation is our experience of Muzac, the musical device of the Devil, which teaches us subliminally that music is something-to-do-something-else-to. Fun things like washing the dishes are even more fun if there is music in the background. Waiting for the plane to take off is less nervous-making when there is music. Slaves work faster to music, in offices as well as in chain gangs. So there are very few times when the average person sits down and really listens to music. The church in its structure tries to force the congregation to listen a number of times whether it wants to or not. And herein lies the problem. Why? Or, to quote, "To what purpose is this waste?"

There are a number of things we are trying, mostly to preserve the prelude (though we have questions as to whether or not we should, really) that may be helpful or of interest. We offer them to you in this context.

1. If it's a prelude on a hymn tune, invite the congregation to turn in the hymnals to that hymn and read everything they see on the page: the name, the composer, the lyric writers, the dates, the metrical numbers, the words, the notes, the fly specks, whatever, as the music begins.

2. Have a sign or poster or banner with the title of the prelude held up by some person where the congregation can see it.

3. Choreograph a dance or a pantomime or set up a human frieze that relates to the music. We are planning a series of choreographed preludes in which the dancers will start in the choir loft near the organ and, just like jazz musicians, will trade dance phrases in which the dancers move with music phrases in which the dancers point to the organ and organist.

4. Lower the lights as the prelude starts and light the organist and the instrument, if possible.

5. Include other instrumentalists, preferably from the congregation and preferably good ones.

6. Invite a few members of the congregation to go up and sit or stand where they can see the organist playing.

Obviously all of these should be done only with the appropriate music and on the appropriate day. They should not be done purely to draw attention to themselves but only to educate and to increase the sense of worship for that specific worship experience. The same suggestions can apply to the offertory as well as to the postlude. It all gets so difficult when we start asking questions. It would be so much simpler if we just followed the customs of the past, however meaningless they may be, simpler for us leaders and more agonizing for the congregations. "Nobody said it was going to be easy...."

Music on a budget

Of course the disadvantage of music is that it is expensive. And with many music budgets being quite small to sumptuous, choir directors have to plan carefully. Here are four ways to answer the problem.

1. Use anthems in a variety of ways. Many of our suggestions to stage anthems, to "space" them, to put them up on their feet, to use props, and so forth are simply ways to put a known or semi-known composition into a new context where different things are heard in the specific performance. (We do not mean wrong notes, or right notes for a change.) Most congregations have sung "O sacred head now wounded" often enough that it is very familiar and because of its familiarity we may overlook things, ideas, words. If the choir sings it while slides of Durer etchings of the Passion are projected on a wall or screen, the strength of the words comes through again. Take a hymn like "Fairest Lord Jesus" and do an anthem arrangement in each season of the church year. During Advent with pictures of the baby or a family with a living baby the words may sound like a projection of the grown man. In Lent they may become very strong as Jesus strides through his three-year ministry. On Good Friday they may become loaded with horror and terror. On Easter they become transcendent. Just think: That would be six performances of the anthem to bring out different meanings. Think of the money saved! And think of the challenge of doing it differently each time, a different tempo, different emphases, different dynamics. It's exciting!

2. Get a collection that has a lot of good songs, anthems. No one hymnal can possibly have all the good and great and needed songs and hymns of the church it in. So we suggest a standard hymnal and then one like our "Avery and Marsh Songbook" or start, with permissions, your own looseleaf hymnal. That is for the congregation and choir. For the choir alone judge your choir's ability and find a collection.

3. Borrow from a friendly neighbor choir director. Borrow but do not steal. By that we mean *do not make copies of the borrowed music*. We have borrowed on occasion from our friendly United Methodist Church across the square. If it is something that we have then done a lot, we decide to get copies of our own.

4. Memorial music! Have someone give an anthem or larger work as a memorial gift instead of flowers or a plaque or a piano. We recently got thirty copies of Bernstein's "Chichester Psalms" with money from three groups of people who wanted to give something large but were not able to pay the whole bill themselves. Try it ... they'll like it!

Energy and tempo

"When nothing else in the service moves me, at least the music can get to me." We have heard this statement countless times. We are now hearing, more than ever, another equally sad statement about the state of worship: "The music in our church is so slow, it's so proper and so dull!" A combination of those two complaints would be enough to keep lots of people from the church — and probably is doing just that.

If the readers and preacher and ushers are lackluster in tone and quality, at least the music can be energetic. Unfortunately, that statement is a myth. There are still lots of organists and choir directors who believe "holy" means anything from slow in tempo to dull in texture and lacking in energy.

Part of energy is excitement. Somehow, as conductors, we must rediscover the excitement in the Christian message, and then excite our choirs to committed singing. One of the things that Don does is to rehearse a given piece at a number of different tempos, insisting to the choir that each tempo be considered legitimate. Because, of course, any tempo is legitimate depending upon its relation to the context in which the work is sung. We know of nothing quite so agonizing as hearing a child practice a piece we know, unbelievably slowly, in order to get it perfect, note for note. It is much more exciting to the listener to hear an energetic, moving performance of that same piece, even if a few notes are lost on the way.

Having said all of that, every once in a while, when we hear a performance of some of our songs by other people and groups, we are keenly reminded of a discipline essential to good church music. Many of these performances please us very much, but some seem insensitive both to what the songs are about and to the possibilities of the rhythm. It's not that they always go too slow, it's that they often are done much too fast, so that the words are lost to the congregation or lose their meaning and so that the rhythmic interest is gone. No bounce, or oomph, or force, or syncopation. A rule for us all: Try hymns and songs at several speeds before determining which is best, with the possibility of varying the tempo for the stanzas — as *the words* indicate. The key is sensitivity, thoughtfulness, understanding.

The hymn-sing

What a rich heritage of Christian faith and understanding comes to us through the hymns and carols of the church! How casually and thoughtlessly we usually treat these songs in weekly worship! And what a helpful step the consideration and experiencing of these songs can be for the renewal of worship!

As you plan events of the summer, include a "Service of Hymns" on the Sunday morning schedule. It can brighten the calendar immensely, breaking the summer routine with a fresh experience. (It's especially interesting as a union service for two or more congregations.) But make it more significant than an "old-fashioned hymn sing." You can preserve the pleasures of that old-time Sunday night event but also provide a mind-expanding and educational experience with a carefully planned program that sets forth the story and meaning of diverse and representative songs and includes songs that are both very old and very new.

Here are some ideas for your planning. A couple of sample service outlines are given later:

1. Organize the service with groups of hymns relating to particular themes or topics. Let there be three or four groups of songs, with a variety of styles and periods represented in each group. The sample service in this issue has three sections: Songs of Celebration, Songs of Communion, and Songs of Challenge. Other possible thematic structures include: songs of the life of Jesus (the Church Year Cycle), songs relating to common human experiences (joy, loneliness, anger, protest, commitment), songs about God (the God of nature, the God of history, the God of my salvation).

2. Mix the songs chronologically. Don't sing songs in the order of their composition, or people will make immediate distinctions between old and new rather than let each song express the theme in its own terms. Mix them up. For example, present a medieval chant about Christ, then "The Rebel" or "Put Your Hand in the Hand," then "What a Friend We Have in Jesus." (Other examples are in the sample services.)

3. Have a narrator or the pastor tell the story of each hymn's origin — by whom and why it was written. Many old favorites were composed in response to interesting historical events or personal experiences, and many were rather controversial when first presented. These stories can give the hymns lasting meaning for the congregation. Moreover, when old songs are understood in their native context and their meaning appraised, the use of new music is seen as reasonable and necessary in the church.

4. Commission the composition of a song for the occasion. Have one of your local poets or singers write a song with the service's themes in mind. If possible, encourage the writing of both new words and a new tune, but it's possible to ask for new words for an old tune if that tune is in public domain (written before 1925).

5. Employ a variety of presentations in the service, but let the congregation sing most of the hymns.
  • Have soloists sing particular stanzas
  • Have the choirs or ensembles do more elaborate arrangements of certain songs
  • Use instruments
  • Have organ preludes on hymn tunes, and
  • Read occasional stanzas responsively or in unison.
In other words, try to explore the meaning and emotional content of each song. Don't just sing the first stanzas of a long list of hymns and do them all alike.

6. Advertise the event in the public media. Some people will come to a service of hymns who will not ordinarily attend a regular service.

Sources for a service of hymns are not hard to find. Check the local public library and other church leaders' libraries in town for books on hymns. Many denominations also publish some sort of "companion to the hymnal" that tell the stories of their songbook's hymns.

Probably the narration should begin with the authors' and composers' names, where they were writing, the dates of composition, and the tune titles, then the location in the pages of the hymnal you are using. This immediately makes worship a bit more interesting and creative, as people realize that the old hymnal did not just fall out of the sky with the Ten Commandments.

And don't forget to use spirituals, folk songs, and other songbooks or bulk reprints of new songs that are available from many publishers. Everything God has inspired is not in the denominational hymnals!

A sample service of hymns - 1
Here is the outline of a service held in our church, with a few words to indicate possibilities for the narration and a few ideas for the presentation of the songs. A bulletin printed for the day need not contain more than general information about the songs' origins — names, centuries, etc.

At the top of the bulletin or program: "Songs of the People of God" and, beneath this title somewhere, "from all kinds of people from all times and places."

Call to Worship: Verses from Psalm 95

Introit: "O For a Thousand Tongues" (Sung by several soloists standing one by one among the congregation without announcement, joining on succeeding lines of the song.) Narration (in this case after the singing): We have begun with a song from the pen of Charles Wesley, the eighteenth century writer of the words for 6,500 hymns. The hymns of Wesley, who helped his brother John found what is now the United Methodist Church, have shaped our understanding of the faith ...

Invocation

Songs Of Celebration

"All People That on Earth Do Dwell" (Old Hundredth)
Narration: We go back to the sixteenth century and to Geneva, Switzerland. Louis Bourgeois wrote music for the emerging Reformation church there. William Kethe, a Scotch refugee, wrote this adaptation of the One Hundredth Psalm for singing. This is the oldest hymn preserved from those early days of Protestantism.

"The Lord of the Dance"
Narration: This song combines three elements: a poetic picture from the Middle Ages of a dancing Jesus, a "Shaker" tune from early America, and the composing talent of a contemporary English song writer and performer named Sidney Carter. (The song might best be done by a soloist on the stanzas and the people joining on the refrain after a quick rehearsal. Use light percussion.)

"My Hope Is Built on Nothing Less"
Narration: A cabinetmaker and reporter named Edward Mote became a Baptist minister at the age of 55 and wrote many songs to express his faith. This happy and bouncy gospel song is one of them ...

Songs Of Communion

"Savior, Like a Shepherd Lead Us"
Narration: These anonymous words inspired by Psalm 23 are sung to a tune by William Bradbury, a New York City music teacher and conductor ...

"To Thee Before the Close Of Day" (in the *Episcopal Hymnal* 1940)
Narration: This is one of the very oldest hymns still sung, with words from the seventh century and a tune from the sixth! The whole song consists of just four notes, typical of the simplicity and starkness of the music of the ancient church.

"When I'm Feeling Lonely" (in *Hymns Hot and Carols Cool*) (with solo stanzas sung from around the room)
Narration: We leap across 1,300 years for another hymn of personal communion with God, one from our own time and from the United States. Richard Avery and Donald Marsh wrote this song in response to the loneliness and the probing questions shared by members of their congregation in Port Jervis, New York.

"Be Still, My Soul"
Narration: These words are by the German poet, Katharine von Schlegel; she wrote them in the eighteenth century. The tune is from the majestic orchestral work "Finlandia" by the composer Jan Sibelius of Finland.

Songs Of Challenge

"Once to Every Man and Nation"
Narration: This is a century-old protest song. These words are from a poem of 1845 by Harvard professor James Russell Lowell, written to protest the war with Mexico. This tune was in Welsh legend said to have been washed ashore in a bottle; thus it is called "Ton-y-botel," "Tune in a Bottle" ...

"Turn, Turn, Turn" (By a soloist, accompanied by guitar, with congregation invited to join on the repeated words, "Turn, turn, turn")
Narration: This is a song by contemporary balladeer Pete Seeger based on words from the Bible's book of "Ecclesiastes." It was one of the most popular song hits of the 1960s — a call to repentance and wisdom.

"God of Our Fathers"
Narration: Daniel C. Roberts, an Episcopal rector in Vermont, wrote the words of this hymn for our nation's centennial in 1876. A prayer for our nation's future, it is still relevant in the decades after the second centennial in 1976. The tune is by George Warren of St. Thomas' Church in New York City ...

A sample service of hymns - 2
Theme: The Life of Jesus Christ — musical responses in the history of the church to the story of our salvation, songs reviewing the church's year. (Here we offer brief examples of what narration can contain. Add personal and local bits of relevance.)

Introit (possibly sung by a choir from the back of the church without announcement): "Wake, Awake, for Night Is Flying" (Wachet Auf). Narration (following the song): We have been called to worship by a song that claims our attention for the imminent coming of the Savior. Both words and music were written in 1597 by Pastor Phillip Nicolai in Germany and was harmonized a century later by the great Johann Sebastian Bach. Nicolai wrote the song as a message of comfort and hope during an epidemic that killed 1,300 of his parishioners.

Opening Hymn: "All Hail the Power of Jesus' Name"
Narration: Let us sing a hymn of honor for Jesus, who is himself the theme of this musical service. The words were written in 1779, about 225 years ago, by a London pastor, Edward Perronet; the tune "Coronation" appeared thirteen years later, composed by Oliver Holden and published in the city of Boston ... (Announce the number, wait for attention, then the narration.)

The Birth Of Jesus

"Angels We Have Heard on High"
Narration: Popular hymns and carols of Christmas come from many nations. This carol is from France and from the eighteenth century. It was also discovered in the French province of Quebec, Canada. It's distinguished by the chorus with its echo of the angels' song ...

"Mary, Too" (*Avery & Marsh Songbook*, possibly as a solo or as an anthem published by Agape).
Narration: This song was written by Richard Avery and Donald Marsh in the late twentieth century to emphasize the humanity and humility and reality of the Holy Family. It also suggests that a loving Savior probably emerged from a loving marriage ...

"Go Tell It On The Mountain" (Write your own final stanza about your own town — as we did: "Go tell it in Port Jervis/through West End and Matamoras ...")
Narration: From the great heritage of American black spirituals comes a rousing and popular Christmas proclamation.

The Life And Ministry Of Jesus

"Fairest Lord Jesus"
Narration: The words of this popular hymn are anonymous, coming to us from Germany and from as long ago as 1677. The tune dates back almost as far. The hymn affirms the supremacy of Jesus in the Christian's life over all experiences of nature or human nobility. Hear first the original German first stanza sung by the choir (or a soloist)....

> *Schonster Herr Jesu, Herrscher aller Erden,*
> *Gottes und Maria Sohn!*
> *Dich will ich lieben, Dich will ich ehren,*
> *Meiner Seelen Freud' und Kron'!*

"See and Come Running" (*Avery & Marsh, Book No. 7*)
Narration: This joyful hymn was written in America in 1975 to witness to the excitement and exultation appropriate to the sharing of the gospel and to protest the drabness and casualness of much Christian worship of the twentieth century. In the same way as "Fairest Lord Jesus," it speaks of the surpassing worth of Christ as he appeared to the multitudes of his own time.

"I Heard the Voice of Jesus"
Narration: The words of our next song come from Scotland, from the pen of Pastor Horatio Bonar, who wrote them in 1846. This Edinburgh pastor wrote several hymns which have endured to this day. The music is that of another man whose hymn tunes are part of the experience of millions of Christians — the Englishman John Dykes. In contrast to the last two songs, this hymn is a uniquely personal and almost mystical statement of the meaning of the ministry of Christ.

The Suffering And Death Of Jesus

"The Royal Banners Forward Go, The Cross Shines Forth in Mystic Glow" (found in the *Episcopal Hymnal* 1940)

Narration: This is one of the very oldest Christian hymns, with words by Venantius Fortunatus, written 1,400 years ago. The tune is a plainsong melody of the same ancient period. Listen to the choir sing the mystical poetry, and note the symbols which are mentioned in the stanzas, uniquely strong metaphors....

"When I Survey the Wondrous Cross"

Narration: Here is another song that takes us in our imaginations to face the death of Jesus. The words are by one of the three or four key figures in the history of hymns, the Reverend Isaac Watts, of the eighteenth century. He wrote some 600 hymns, many of which are still found in Protestant hymnals. This tune is by an American church musician, Lowel Mason ...

The Victory Of Jesus And His Eternal Presence

"The Strife Is O'er, The Battle Done"

Narration: The music of this hymn is by another great figure in the history of music, the sixteenth century Italian composer Palestrina. The joyful words are from a Jesuit songbook of 1695 ...

"Every Morning Is Easter Morning"

Narrator: Most Christians worship on Sunday — instead of Saturday as the Jews did and do — because it's the day of the Resurrection. Every Sunday is Easter. Moreover, each day of the week is given new possibilities by the fact of Easter. That is why Avery & Marsh wrote our next song which is in a style suggesting Latin American Calypso music ...

"In Christ There Is No East or West"

Narration: The British novelist John Oxenham wrote these hopeful words early in our own century. Here they represent the growing sense of Christian unity across denominational and national and racial boundaries ...

"Rejoice! The Lord Is King"

Narration: No service of hymns would be complete without the words of Charles Wesley, co-founder of Methodism and writer of literally thousands of hymns. This poem appeared in 1746. It's a poem inspired by the words of Paul's Letter to the Philippians, chapter 4, verse 4: "Rejoice in the Lord always; again I say, rejoice." The metric pattern of this tune by John Darwall was called the "Hallelujah Meter" in early American hymnals because of its vigor and joyfulness. It provides an appropriate conclusion to the musical consideration of the life of Jesus, our Lord. Stand up, hold the hymnals up, lift your voices boldly.

Other ideas

1. Sing to your church windows

As simple as that. Look at the stained glass windows in your sanctuary or chapel and devise a worship service or program that relates to what is pictured in them. To give some ideas and suggestions as to types of music we will describe the windows in our church in Port Jervis, New York.

Each window is like Tiffany glass with lots of curlicues and abstract design that encircles the focal point in the center. The theme of the window will lead to suggested hymns and songs.

Window: Wheat tied together with "I am the Bread of Life"
Hymns: "Break Thou the Bread of Life," "Shared Bread" Summerlin (*Songbook for Saints and Sinners*, Agape)
Anthems: "Bread of the World" by Palestrina (Fischer), "Take, Believe" by Wexler (Asmi)

Window: A bunch of grapes
Hymns: "Sons of God" (*Hymnal for Young Christians*)
Anthems: "Taste the New Wine" by Avery and Marsh (Agape), "O Sacrum Convivium" by Messiaen Durand, Schirmer

We would divide the choir in two sections or use two quarters. Each group would stand before a window and the window should be lit from behind with God's natural light or a spotlight from outside. The group before the "wheat" window would sing the first verse of "Let Us Break Bread Together." The second group would sing the second verse as they stand before the "grapes" window. On the third verse, "Let Us Praise God Together," the two forces would sing together (1) where they are or (2) gathered together down front or (3) the first group would sing the first phrase, the second group would sing the second (repeated phrase) then join together from "When I fall on my knees ..." to the conclusion of the song. Or the congregation would be invited to join in the third stanza. There are many variations you will come up with. Any of these methods could be used with any of the suggested music above. A communion service could really be highlighted with a number of these pieces of music sung by various groups as the elements are being served.

Another of our windows features a harp. When the window was cleaned or releaded it was put in upside down which could be pointed out as a reminder that we are all human. A group could sing the spiritual "Li'l David, Play on Your Harp." A group of women and a harpist could be placed before it (or near it) to sing all or parts of Britten's gorgeous "Ceremony of Carols." Someone could play an autoharp before it as accompaniment to the hymn (by group or soloist) "Let me sow love" by David Yantis (*The Contemporary Hymn Book*, Word) which is a setting of St. Francis' Prayer: "Make me an instrument of your peace...." Yantis' collection is very good and we recommend that your church have as many copies as possible.

Another window has the tablets of the Ten Commandments as the focal point. Tallis' "If you love me, keep my commandments" (Schirmer) would be an appropriate anthem to be sung before it. The congregation could enjoy singing "Just a closer walk with thee" with the focus on this window.

The idea is pretty clear by now. New songs can be found and learned for services or programs that focus on the windows. Or familiar songs, twice-heard anthems, even popular songs, and folk songs will be heard differently in the context of the windows. And the windows will never be the same for the congregation that has experienced this sort of contextualizing.

You may ask, "What do we do about the windows in our church? They are clear glass, or colored glass." The answer is obvious. *Sing about what you see through the windows.* If it's open country, various settings of Psalm 23 would work. If it is a city or a ghetto scene, sing "Where cross the crowded ways of life." If the glass is colored, find music that either mentions the color or has some relationship to it. A green window reminds us of pastoral music; a deep red window of the Crucifixion. And so forth. Remember that someone has said that architecture is frozen music. Well, perhaps stained glass is like music in the form of glaciers. Glaciers are still moving, still liquid and so is stained glass, being thicker at the bottom as the years go by.

2. Encourage participation

One of the major changes that is happening in all Christian denominations is that congregations want to do more than sing three hymns as their part of the music in the worship service. Many hymn-anthems invite the congregation to sing in the last verse, for instance, but those of us in charge of the music should consider inviting the congregation to sing even in anthems in which a part for them is not written, including having just the women in the congregation sing the melody on, say, a third verse which is harmonized more complexly in the lower parts. Aside from a new kind of participation, this may turn out to be an occasion where some people discover they can join the choir and enlarge the soprano section.

We once sang the big arrangement of "The Battle Hymn of the Republic" by Peter Wilhousky (CM 4743, Carl Fischer). In the short section for men only, which is very "barbershop" in feeling, we invited all the men in the congregation to sing the melody while those in the choir sang the parts as written. It had a tremendous effect and if we had been using our heads we would have followed it with the women singing melody on a verse, all of it reaching its climax with the congregation and choir uniting in the splendid last verse.

3. Choose hymns theologically

One of the advantages of music is that the average churchgoer learns more of his or her theology from the hymns and songs and carols they sing than they do from the sermon. The sermon they hear only once, the music they sing over and over and over again. This is a reminder to be very cautious about the theology of the hymns that you choose to sing over and over and over again.

4. Explain your musical decisions

We have heard of pastors and choir directors and organists who control the musical taste of the congregation from their biases rather than from the needs of the congregation. We can only assume that they do not give the people a chance to state some preferences. If those in charge could explain why they do not allow certain things, the spirit of sharing and the spirit of love would be much more noticeable. We all have some prejudices, but for the church to be run on some leaders' prejudices, unchallenged, seems to us to be against the spirit of Jesus. Isn't that what the Pharisees did? It is so easy to become pharisaical and pontifical when we reach a certain stature. Jesus preached against that temptation all the time. We need to look in the mirror of what we say and write.

When we say we don't like somebody's music/words we explain why: Wagner — too longwinded, too static, too simple and simplistic; Beethoven's "Missa Solemnis" — unsingable, conception is inhuman yet written for human beings to sing, tessitura is too unmanageable; Gaither's music/ words — too simplistic, lack of depth, and out of touch with daily reality. "We use absolutely all kinds of religious music in our church worship because our congregation is a multi-tasted one. We have never refused to present any kind of music in worship including some of the above when it is requested because it obviously speaks to someone."

5. Don't print all the words of a simple song

We are appalled when visiting churches around the country to find sometimes the compulsive printing in bulletins of words that don't need printing. We're thinking of black spirituals like "He's got the whole world" or "Let us break bread together." In many cases people know the songs very well anyway, and in all cases they can learn them and sing them better by following a leader than by looking at the words on the bulletin. It seems silly for a line of lyrics to be printed three times when it is simply repeated word for word with a simple tune. And, let's face it, most of us will bury our heads in the bulletin and read those lines diligently even though we don't need to, instead of standing tall and looking around at our brothers and sisters and singing out. Let the leader just say the words ahead of each stanza, or sing the first line and let the folks join in. Those spirituals seem to have caught on quite well back in slavery days without the slaves having to read off printed bulletins!

How we write music

It may seem presumptuous of us to use this space to explain how we write our songs and anthems and larger works, but we feel that if you know our standards (which we don't always meet, unfortunately) the works themselves will mean more to you. And if you accept our standards, then you can apply them to music by others. (Or refine your own standards.)

1. We made an agreement to each other that as far as the **content** goes, we will try to write songs and hymns that could *not* have been written in another time and, in our experience, have not been written before. For this reason, we rarely set words directly from scripture without paraphrasing them in language of today, unless there seems to be no musical setting of some strong passage we want to sing. It's very hard to write for tomorrow or the future; let it suffice for us to write for today. We no longer do settings of the Psalms or just repeated Hallelujahs! And probably no more songs are needed that simply tell the Christmas story; we need songs now that explain what difference the story makes! Each of our songs for the Christmas season has taken a new and different approach from the one before. We have been moving in a specific direction of "humanizing" the event and the people so the story can relate to our real lives.

2. As far as the **music** goes, we need to break it down into four categories: melody, harmony, rhythm and texture.

Melody in hymn writing for us is the part that most especially needs to be almost immediately accessible to the congregation. As we write a tune, we work hard to make it seem natural, inevitable, without being entirely commonplace; simple without being dull; interesting without being complex. Someone said recently of Oscar Hammerstein that he *worked very hard to make things simple*. We do not have time nor can we create occasions for the congregation to learn new or old hymns and carols outside of the worship experience itself, so we feel the melodies must be readily singable and the lyrics must make the people want to sing them.

Harmony is our way of coloring the text. Quite often we take a melody and deliberately put a wrong set of chords behind it to bring tension, if that is appropriate to the text. Sometimes in this process the tune itself has been changed to find some meeting places for tune and harmony that give anchors to the singer. A suspended chord or an unresolved chord or a tense chord immediately gives a different feeling to a phrase, putting the text in the context we are searching for. In some instances, other musicians have changed a ninth chord in our music to a regular consonant chord,

55

thereby destroying the very tension we intended. Major seventh chords sound entirely different from regular chords or dominant sevenths and we choose carefully. (Have your organist or local pop music piano player show you the difference.) Many of our pieces of music for the church have much richer and more diversified harmonies than much if not most of the classic literature. Some of the favorite pieces of classic music for worship are on the harmonic scale of the simplest 1-4-5-1 pop songs that are looked on as being too simplistic to be taken seriously by cultivated church musicians. A simplistic classic is no better than a simplistic pop song.

Rhythm is the lifeblood of music and was one of the first things removed from church music when the church began to feel guilty about joy (among other things). We are living in a world and time of rhythm, and so we feel it a very important and serious part of the music we write. With almost each composition, we try to create a rhythmic pattern that expresses the emotional content of the text, one that can be repeated and then broken for contrast. The importance of the accompaniment editions that we produce lies in the rhythmic patterns we suggest as well as the chordal ones. Although tempo is not really a part of rhythm, tempo is an essential part of our work. Patterns that are too difficult at a very fast tempo are wrong for our music. Not everything should be taken fast, fast, fast. On the other hand, we all now know that "Holy" is not just "Slow!"

Texture is the most difficult aspect of our music to put into print without writing out full and complicated scores. (We have been asked to do this with some of our songs and we plan to in the future, but at present we can only show it on cassette tapes.) Too much of the music done in churches sounds alike because leaders work for a certain rich "Choral Tone" that is then used indiscriminately. Texture depends upon the spelling of the chords: wide open or close harmony, four parts or sixteen; it also depends upon the instruments that accompany: organ for sustained and piano for brittle rhythmic effects; and it depends upon the range: the accompaniment can be in the same register where we are singing or one or more octaves above. The sound of both accompaniment and vocal part can be sustained or staccato, lush or spare, covered and dark or open and white, sharp and accented, or smooth, etc. All of these choices are put into performance when the works are done in the service of worship, but they need to be practiced a variety of ways at choir rehearsals so the choir can truly lead the congregation in the singing of the new hymn.

3. The **words**, the lyrics, are the most challenging aspect of our writing. We set very high standards for ourselves formally, both in scansion, meter, rhyme, understandability, and in theological content. We try not to use words or phrases that are passing fads (tell it like it is) but sometimes we risk them. Rhyme is used as anchor, for rests, for breathing spaces in long complicated thoughts, for fun and pleasure, for impact and shock. Outer rhymes, inner rhymes, hidden rhymes, and assonances, are set up and stuck to in all stanzas as long as they help the meaning of what we are saying but are discarded if they get in the way. You would probably be surprised how many times we write and rewrite a lyric to simplify, to make more direct, to make clearer. And we check the Bible constantly for the accuracy of the paraphrase, both historically and textually. We talk a great deal as we write about the theological viewpoint of the words and can answer questions asked about it. Sometimes we have deliberately phrased a point in such a way that it arouses questions. In an introit we used the words: "Mary's baby, Joseph's baby" knowing full well that some people will assume the parenthood of Joseph is being implied. We say to this that it might bring about a very interesting theological discussion and if so, it should be encouraged. Some leaders of worship, instead, just don't allow the song to be sung. They might be surprised to find out how many of their parishioners are already talking about or discussing such things among themselves. Our words must always be

looked at in the context of the whole song and not pulled out of context to be twisted to mean something else.

We struggle to use correct grammar. We struggle even harder to avoid inversions that are endlessly used in former hymns in order to achieve a rhyme. At one time inversions were the custom, now they are only confusing, and often throw the wrong syllable or word on the wrong accent. This is the kind of thing we mean: "When *to* a *grasshopper* I *was* knee *high*...." The inversion created the faulty accent and cut down the seriousness of the line.

We could go on endlessly about words because they are so difficult and because they are so loaded, by themselves and in phrases. Enough to stop at this point and suggest you look hard and long at the words you put into the mouths of your congregation and choir. No wonder some people would prefer lovely Latin that sings so beautifully and means naught, or want just another setting of the same old words so the music can be time out from worship instead of the challenge and joy it should be.

We try to keep our standards high. We know we have made some mistakes. And we are still trying to correct some of them, meanwhile believing that the song as a whole is working and is important to get out at that time. With all the musical and lyrical and theological choices available to writers for the church, this is an exciting and challenging and difficult time to be trying to communicate with God's people.

As we've mentioned elsewhere, our music is available from:

Hope Publishing
380 S. Main Place
Carol Stream, IL 60187
800-323-1049
www.hopepublishing.com

Worshiping During Advent

"Advent" comes from the Latin, *advenit,* meaning "he comes, he is coming." So this, the first season in the Christian year, has a sense of excitement about it, like adventure! Four Sundays with four services of worship, four times when the whole congregation gets together and shares. Shares what? Shares what it knows about Jesus, his family, his forerunners. Shares the fact that it, as a whole congregation and as individuals, needs to prepare for his coming. Shares confessions, hopes, anxieties, desires. This can be a most exciting adventure. And it can be done only when the whole church will meet at worship, not just in Sunday school classes, not just at home with one family, but as this specific group of God's people who are your church.

Each Sunday can have a different prevailing mood or theme:
- One Sunday: *wonder*! Amazement that God would act in such a way as to deliver salvation in the man Jesus, who, like everybody else, was born a baby. Wonder at the history leading up to this event. Wonder at how salvation works, has worked, is working, and will work.
- One Sunday: *listening*! To John the Baptist. A lot of them didn't listen. Have we listened? Are we listening to the Prophets of today?
- One Sunday: *preparing*! Rehearsing new songs. Making things to decorate, to give away, to show we have been saved and want to help others.
- One Sunday: *excitement*! He is almost here! Let's shout and cheer and let all within earshot know that we know whom it is who's coming!

The color is purple, the color of royalty and the color of penitence. (In some churches the color is blue, a color of hope.)

The mood is expectant. There are things to do while waiting but "I can hardly wait!"

Planning

For creative worship to happen in Advent, we must begin planning early in the fall. This means not only that the rehearsal of Advent and Christmas music must begin soon, but that pastors and worship committee members must begin determining *strategy* for the season. What do we want to happen in Advent? How do we provide for the possibility of new experiences of the meaning of Christ? What new or traditional forms will provide access to timeless truths related to the coming of the Messiah? What new bonds can be forged, what new connections can be made, what new directions can be illuminated with the congregation?

Our basic suggestion is that you *turn Advent planning over to the people*. If you have a capable and imaginative Worship Committee, give the four Sundays to them, or ask them to appoint a rather large sub-committee for Advent. If you don't have a Worship Committee, recruit or have your church board appoint a Planning Task Force for Advent. Include all ages in the group, all kinds of people. Give them books on symbols, books about liturgical and seasonal traditions, books on early American holiday customs, and the Lectionary of readings for the season. Get them started early, first brainstorming about the meaning of the season, then about what the themes of Advent mean to them personally. (Don't let clergy dominate the discussions!) Then let them spout off ideas for art, music, sermons, staging, drama, family events, etc., etc. In November, let them shape the ideas into the four services and related events they may have in mind.

Advertising AD-VENT

Well, let's face it: the Bible is not subtle or hesitant in its announcing to the world that the Savior was coming. John the Baptist shouted it out in the wilderness and in the valleys, and we can imagine the news bouncing off walls of rock and sandstone and echoing through the valleys until others picked it up. Everyone who checked out their prophets, such as Isaiah (who started the advertising years before), found the information correct and started talking to others about the approaching day with excitement. So, let us take our directive from the Bible and the world we live in today with its tremendous focus on advertising and let's ADvertise (Adventise!?) that not only are shopping days before Christmas piling up on us, but also that Advent is here.

VENT, according to the dictionary, is an opening for the passage of liquids, gasses, etc.; an outlet; means of escape; a slit in a garment. As in such phrases as give *vent* to it means to utter or express; to give vent to one's anger; to give expression to. And all these definitions apply beautifully to what Isaiah says, speaking for God, and to what John the Baptist says in arousing the people to action before the one comes who carries his winnowing shovel with him to thresh out all the grain, gathering the wheat into the barn and burning the chaff in an eternal fire! Wow! Strong words, those. No mincing words, no sentimental analogies. Powerful statements from and for the All-Powerful One!

And the good side of the announcements is sheer beauty: the peaceable kingdom, swords into plowshares, the desert rejoicing and blooming. Wonderful words, wondrous words! Powerful statements once again. We need to retell the promises of Isaiah: "Be strong and don't be afraid! God is coming to your rescue, coming to punish your enemies." We need to get this message heard by the strangers on the streets, that *with* Jesus all these things are more possible than *without* him. It isn't just a cute little baby who's coming; it's a baby who will grow like us, live through the same things we live through, and show how to survive and surmount the things that we are falling prey to without knowing where to look for help. We need to remind them that Jesus is Help! And we need to ventilate their lives with this bright, clear, fresh wind.

So, let's get busy to start Advent with a resounding trumpet blast, a Gabrielic announcement that he who is coming to dinner and longer is someone worth listening to and shouting about! Here are some ideas.

1. Tell people personally

Of course, there will be people who object, people of other faiths, and people with none. But they are the very people we are trying to reach with the message they have avoided or discarded or perhaps not heard before. How can we do this? We have resented being approached by people on street corners and at breakfast tables in restaurants asking us if we are saved. How can we avoid that, since other people are put off also? Let's improvise a possible scene:

> "Have you heard the good news? ... It's Advent again ... Do you know what that means? ... It means that it's time again to remember Jesus and what he stands for ... Have you been unhappy or disturbed or frustrated lately? ... If you have, and most people have, perhaps you need something or someone to hold on to ... I know I do. Well, I have *him* to help me ... He's not really here in person, in his own flesh, but he is a living presence in my life and my life is easier than it used to be ...

I know you've probably heard this before, about Jesus, I mean, but he particularly helps me at this time of year, when he's about to be born again for all of us ... He helps me with my Christmas shopping and the terrible rush we all get into ... he helps me select what gifts I give to people in the name of the Prince of Peace, for instance, I don't give guns, real ones or toy ones, or Star Wars toys. The kids get enough of that ... And I don't give too many gifts to one person. Most of us don't need fifty presents to know we are loved; we need to be told we are loved and given fewer material things that break so quickly ...

Anyway, since there is so much pandemonium at this season I thought you would like to hear the Good News, and so I invite you to think about it for yourself ... I hope I didn't bother you ... I didn't ask you if you were saved ... But I will remind you that you are saved and now it's up to you to accept that amazing gift at Christmas ...

I'd like to talk to you some more if you would like to talk ... My name is _____ and my phone number is (fill in the blank) ... Good-bye ... Did you know that means 'God be with you'? We'll talk about that some time, too ..."

2. Use billboards

Some organizations take billboards; how about the church doing it? "Jesus is here again! Visit him at First Presbyterian Church at Sussex and Broome streets, particularly Sunday mornings when there is nothing in the world *better* to do at 9:30 and 11. Meet you at the stable!"

3. Use radio and television

Radio time is available is some areas for free and in other areas at minimal cost. You need to check with your local radio and television stations to find out what kinds of opportunities they offer in Public Service Announcements, package deals (two commercials for the price of one) or similar things. Try some commercials to combat the "Ho ho ho's" of Santa Claus. Try something like these:

- "Wow! Guess who's coming to town — again? That's right; Jesus! In four weeks he'll be back again to everybody's minds in everybody's hearts. Take time to visit him at the First Presbyterian Church ..." We suggest something like this.
- "Done your Spring cleaning? How about your Fall cleaning? Now it's time to clean out everything and make room for Jesus. As John, you remember, the Baptist said: 'Straighten up the highways and your lives for he is coming.' Take time to remember with other people, at the First Presbyterian Church ..." Always include times and addresses, phone numbers and e-mail addresses.
- "For many people Christmas is the loneliest season of the year. Invite the single and the lonely to share Jesus with you at the First Presbyterian Church ..."

4. Try street banners and signs

Check on the legality of a street banner announcing the same information as above. Of course, you can put as many signs as you want to on the outside of your church building or even place a manger on the porch or ground in front of it, a manger which you add to daily with further announcements of who will fill it and how and what the average person can benefit from a new or renewed relationship with Jesus, lover of us all and solver of many of our problems.

5. Use flyers and posters

Flyers sent out announcing the news and programs and services for the season may not draw a large response, but you know they will be seen. Posters placed on bulletin boards in supermarkets can be effective. We know. A stranger showed up at a Bible study after seeing one such poster. Flyers or posters put up in local motels and hotels can remind visitors to your area what is available to them during the season. Many people are *not* home at Christmas. Share in newsprint, on posterboard, with every manner of advertising, the startling fact that *God still cares and is still sending the Son to prove it!*

The Advent wreath

Since the Advent wreath is widely used in churches this time of year, here are two ideas to make it more memorable:

1. A special wreath and ceremony of lighting

On the First Sunday of Advent start the service with the presentation and ceremony of the wreath. Since the wreath goes back to the pagan cartwheels decorated with greenery, find (beg, borrow, or buy) a large wagon wheel. Anchor it on a table or stand large enough to support it without taking the focus away from the wheel itself. Anchor it with picture wire tied to the legs of the table or stand. Put some kind of clear plastic covering under the circumference of the wheel *on the floor* so the dripping wax will not hurt the carpet. Put *four* purple candles on the rim of the wheel, an equal distance apart. Put *six* white candles between each set of two purple ones. That's *28* candles in all: four weeks of Advent with each white weekday being holy and each purple Sunday being something extra special.

Then add greenery in the spokes of the wheel. Since Advent is a season of preparing, it might be appropriate to put the candles on and the greenery while the congregation watches. Prepare the other things beforehand since they will take quite a bit of time. (If a church has two Sunday services, there should be two Advent wreaths.)

Get a family of seven or seven individuals (it should not be restricted only to married people) to put the wreath together in this fashion. When all is ready let the father light an extra candle and with it light the first purple one. He then passes the other candle to the mother who lights the white one next to the lit purple one. She then passes the candle to the oldest child who lights the next white one. This continues until seven candles are lit representing the first week of this season.

We wrote a special song for this occasion in our church,"Advent Proclamation, Four more weeks till he arrives" (Proclamation Productions, Inc.). While the candles are being lighted the organist or pianist (or combo orchestra of some kind) plays the music very slowly and softly and mysteriously. When all the candles are lit, the music picks up in speed and excitement and the choir starts singing the song. It is written in such a way that the congregation can sing each line back after the choir has sung it.

The Second Sunday of Advent another family or group of people comes forward at the beginning of the service. The first person lights *all the candles for the previous week* and then lights the second purple one and passes the lighted candle to the next person in the line. When the second week of candles are brightly burning, the choir and congregation sing the above song again changing the words to *"THREE more weeks till he arrives."*

The Third Sunday and the Fourth Sunday see the natural continuation of this brief but moving ceremony. On the final Sunday, it could be quite beautiful if all the people who had participated the three previous weeks could join in and make a glorious "lineup" as all 28 people relight or light for the first time a candle that becomes a special thing for them and for that church family. We suggest that if you use twelve-inch candles they will last through four services of normal length.

2. Name the candles

Many churches have Advent wreath ceremonies, with different church families or groups of members, lighting a new candle each Sunday. Some churches name the four candles, identifying themes of the season — usually for Love, Peace, Hope, and Joy, or other great themes. If you use the lectionary as the basis for sermons of the seasons, we suggest you name the candles and build parts of the service around the following themes that are a bit more loaded and provocative and less "commercial" now:

- First Sunday: PEACE, especially from Isaiah 2, with its message about disarmament.
- Second Sunday: JUSTICE, from Isaiah 11 and the preaching of John.
- Third Sunday: HEALING, including the healing of nations, as set forth in Isaiah 35 and Matthew 11.
- Fourth Sunday: FULFILLMENT, including the idea of the fulfillment of history, especially from Isaiah 7.

Each Sunday, let prayers focus on these themes — and don't just pray for yourselves! Pray that these meanings of the Advent of the Messiah may unfold for all the peoples of the world! *Explore* what that unfolding would mean in those times of prayer.

Using music in Advent

In choosing music, prayers, media — relate to the tastes of all the people in the church and community. Claim the rich and fascinating heritage of diverse cultures as they celebrate the coming of the Savior of the whole world. Mix the styles flamboyantly and gratefully in regular services. Several ideas follow:

1. Present old songs in new ways

"O Come, O Come, Immanuel" (*The Oxford Choral Songs*, x194 SATB, arr. John Rutter, Oxford University Press) is familiar enough to present as an anthem in which the congregation can also participate.

- Space it: have a small group of singers in an area to one side and near the front; a baritone soloist at the rear (in the balcony); keep the rest of the choir in the choir loft; any way so the sound will be coming from three different directions. The congregation should feel as if they are surrounded with the sound of longing and are thereby a part of the hope.
- Sing it: The small group sings the first verse, unaccompanied and with an Old Testament feeling. The soloist sings the second verse. The rest of the choir sings the third verse. All the men, *wherever they are*, sing the fourth verse. Everyone, including the congregation, sings the fifth verse, with a few people singing the descant.

Why? The congregation will listen more intently to the music when it is *staged or has a focal point* (such as props) or is done in an *unexpected place.* The music becomes a more important part of the service, a more integral one.

2. Teach the congregation a new song

"O Jesus is coming so sing this song" (Advent carol in *"More, More, More!"* Proclamation Productions, Inc.), is one of our songs that has been done in a number of ways with the congregation joining in. Take time to teach the song, quickly, with the help of the choir. Then invite the congregation to make other "holy" sounds like *clapping* (see Psalm 47)*, snapping, stamping, slapping thighs, oom pah pahs, whistles, rattling keys, etc.*

After this rehearsal start the song with everyone joining in. At some point, after the third verse, for example, invite everyone to make excited parade-type sounds while the accompaniment continues. It may last a number of choruses. Encourage them to use the sounds they had rehearsed previously. Then pick up the song with the fourth verse and continue to the end. Why? If we have parades for the astronauts and rock singers and VIPs, shouldn't we get at least that excited for Jesus? And shouldn't we be allowed to show our excitement in ways that everyone knows and understands?

There are lots of people in the congregation who cannot carry a tune in a bucket, but they can thump the bucket! It's time they were allowed to participate in the musical parts of worship. Another suggestion: Pass out instruments to people in the congregation: wood blocks, finger cymbals, small drums, bongos, etc. Invite them to play along whenever they want to. Children should not have ALL the fun.

The advantage of music is that all ages can get involved; we learn much of our theology from the songs, hymns, and carols that we sing repeatedly; music mirrors the seemingly endless variety of our moods and gives us the chance to express them; music is for lovers and we, the church, are lovers.

3. Use the songs of Luke

Advent is the season when you can stress the Magnificat, the Benedictus, the Gloria, and the Nunc Dimittis, the four "songs" in Luke 1 and 2. You could plan to devote time each of the four Sundays of Advent on different settings of one of the canticles from Luke. For example, there are organ pieces titled "Magnificat" and you could have the organist choose one to play as the prelude. Soon after this, as the order of service allows, have the scripture reading from Luke 1, either read straight or have the situation told or acted out with a Mary and an Angel improvising in contemporary language the events that lead up to Mary's gorgeous canticle. At that point an arrangement could be sung by the choir. One we recommend is a setting by Vaughan Williams (G Schirmer 8813). There are many others.

With some words of explanation such as noting that this is such a fantastic poem for women, we would recommend turning to the back of the hymnal (almost all hymnals have settings of the canticles, usually in the back of the book with other responses) and have all the women in the choir and congregation singing this setting. Perhaps the organist, finding a number of beautiful settings for organ, would then play another setting for the offertory. We have publishing settings in a Neo-Byzantine style of all four canticles for soprano and tenor (both with very wide ranges and quite difficult) that Don wrote and have been performed successfully at a number of occasions. The Magnificat is marvelous text for a sermon of course, and finally another setting from a different period can be played as postlude.

Zechariah's fantastic words, also from Luke 1, the Benedictus, has been set by Healey Wilan (Oxford University Press, No. 529 SATB). It is set in such a way that the pastor or soloist can sing the cantor's lines with the choir, in unison and in parts, sings alternate lines. If your church is not noticeably a "liturgical church" it would be a great experience to do such a setting and get the choir to sound as much like monks as is possible.

The Angels' words, the Gloria, found in Luke 2, have been set hundreds of ways. One of the most exciting versions is the Poulenc setting for Soprano soloist and choir. It is really beautiful music and since it is extended writing it would be a major part of the service of worship, taking some 25 minutes or so.

Simeon's words, the Nunc Dimittis, also in Luke 2, are some of the most beautiful in the Bible. Vaughan Williams has a setting that is included in the G. Schirmer octavo mentioned above. And Calrton Young has a marvelous blues setting that is swinging and builds in excitement, published in Fourteen Canticles and Responses" (Agape, AG 7129). This arrangement can be done with piano or organ and rhythm instruments.

We feel the important thing is to put the words in context by reminding the people of the situations in which the words were said. All of them are tremendously dramatic situations. Acting them out will get even the youngest and squirmiest people in the congregation to listen and under-stand them. It seems well worth the risk. And don't have just the choir sing the settings; use the ones in the hymnal that the congregation can join in.

4. Rewrite "Santa Claus Is Coming To Town"

If yours is the kind of church and congregation that can use popular songs in worship to make a point, we suggest that you do a rewrite on "Santa Claus Is Coming To Town." Set it up as if John the Baptist is a contemporary person wandering around saying the sort of thing he is quoted as having said and then let words be sung:

> You better watch out, you better not cry,
> You better not pout, I'm telling you why,
> Jesus Christ is coming to town.

That old pop song has been used through the years by some parents to bribe the children to be good or scare them into being good or else no *presents*. That seems a cruel pop song. But John the Baptist sang an even harsher song and for strong reasons: shape up or you will be zapped out. If you sing the new version often enough it will become a commercial for Jesus' arrival as well as or along with Santa.

5. Use "Follow the Star"

Our songbook, *Songs For All Seasons*, includes a simple song from the Christmas musical "David's Town" called "Follow the Star." This would be a good theme song for Advent. It starts obviously talking about the baby Jesus in the manger but then implies a continuation of following him until there is the personal realization of what it means to be one's self, a follower *and* believer.

> Follow the Star, follow the Star,
> And someday in its presence you'll find out who you are.
> Learn how to see
> Learn what to do.
> Then you'll learn the things that God has planned for you, so

Follow the Star, follow the Star,
And someday in its presence you'll find out who you are.

6. Sing carols of the nations

We suggest that you take time each Sunday of Advent to sing two or three carols appropriate to the season, each of them coming from different countries of the world — adding up to eight or twelve songs through the season. Let the songs be sung by different choirs, soloists, and small ensembles, families, organizations of the church, and by the whole congregation. In each case tell as much about the writing and/or the origin of the song as possible. As you study about these songs you may find that they also represent many denominations; mention that fact, too.

Finally, at your Christmas Eve service or on the Sunday after Christmas, sing a stanza from each of the songs as a "Christmas Around the World" medley.

7. Use music from *Godspell*

The word used to be Godspell and became Gospel. The people who wrote and produced that great show reminded us of or taught us this piece of information. Yes, this musical has been around for a number of years, but it remains timely, so use music from it during this season.

- "Prepare ye the way" could be used as a call to worship or as a liturgical response somewhere else in the service.
- "Day By Day" is a great song for the theme of illumination, particularly as we hear and/or sing the line "To see thee more clearly." The song can get further use as the pastor or somebody asks questions while the choir or congregation keeps singing the song, questions like: How do you see Jesus more clearly each day? Is it by reading the Bible? By having conversations with others about him? By reading devotional and theological books and articles? By looking more carefully at other people around you? And so forth.
- "Turn Back, Oh Man" from the show can be very interestingly coupled with the great traditional hymn setting in most of our hymnals. If you do both in the same service, be sure to point out that the words are so great that both musical settings are valid with personal preferences set aside.

You should be able to order the recording and the music from any store than handles recordings, books and music, or you may find it on the Web. We have heard recently that a number of music dealers are saying some music is not in print any longer, when what they are really saying is I don't want to bother with dealing with the publishers. If you run into this experience, ask for the publisher's name from your dealer so you can check on it yourself. So many of us choir directors and organists have to deal with clerks and dealers who are in the dark and we need to bring them to the light of our needs, beliefs, and demands. If they know how serious we are about demanding a certain piece of music, perhaps they will work a little bit harder and be better prepared to satisfy us.

Special offerings

Now don't get nervous; read on. Special offerings can be made memorable too. It is important to get the congregation actually participating, *moving down the aisles,* as they *offer* things from the variety of their lives rather than having someone else *collect* it from them or drop it in a box at the back of the church.

1. Tie offerings to Sunday themes

On a Sunday with *preparing* as the prevailing mood, have a time when the people come forward and put on the altar or Communion table things they have brought to put the church in order: cloths, soaps, glass cleaner, mops, brushes, hammer, nails, silver polish, etc. Make a regular procession of this. Make sure that sometime during the season all these offerings are used!

On *listening* Sunday have the people write on a furnished card something special they will do for the local church or the church at large or the community: baby sit for free to free some mother for a special meeting, use the glass cleaner, address envelopes, wash dishes, do some typing, call house-to-house, talk to someone they don't like, etc. This makes for a stronger commitment than just telling yourself you ought to do something. People can sign their names if they so choose or leave them unsigned. Have the people bring their commitments forward and put them on the altar or communion table.

On *excitement* Sunday have each person bring an ornament of some kind and actually put it on the Christmas tree himself. This ritual or liturgy could be a highlight on that specific day. We have seen people actually crying with joy as they place their ornament and watch others doing likewise.

On *wonder* Sunday have the people bring forward to the table something to make a child's life happier: a rattle, a doll, a toy, etc. Make it clear that these things will be used in the nursery program of the church, given to underprivileged in the town, sent to hospitals or homes for retarded children, or used in some similar fashion.

2. Bring mystery for nursing homes

A bad pun but a good idea: have people bring mysteries (or other books) to be taken to old folks' homes.

3. Use the youth group to energize the offering

We will never forget the occasion in our church when a traveling group of young people led us in a very moving creative worship service. As a young guitarist started playing a guitar selection, the rest of the teens in the group walked up the aisles, some carrying the offering plates, and all shaking hands with the people, smiling and talking with them and inviting them to make their offerings. The outgoing energy from the young people was contagious.

4. Dance your offering

If you have some dancers in your church, on a specifically joyful Sunday, let them choreograph some simple movements with which they could go up the aisles and smile and dance the offering. The important thing is to make the worshipers aware that they are offering their pledge and not being accosted for it. We won't forget a young person's description of the ushers in their large suburban church: "You could hear them marching down the aisle behind you like storm troopers, but you knew they were good guys because they were wearing plastic carnations."

Scripture and sermon

Let's go deeper and let's go broader.

Going deeper means getting beneath the religious clichés which come so very easily to our lips, the glib platitudes which we have lifted out of biblical contexts and mean so little to modern women and men, boys and girls. They may offer a certain easy security and even foster a rosy glow of good will but will not get us through the hard decision-making required in the trenches. It is especially easy for preachers to sound like preachers, to fall back on religious language without working at clarity and persuasive and educational communication.

In Advent, as we take up the traditional themes of the season, let there be a commitment to talk like human beings instead of institutional figureheads, to communicate with everyone as if they were completely new to the whole experience (not dumb, not unsophisticated, just undomesticated as far as household jargon is concerned). It's the difference between assuming that everyone knows what the Bible means by *sin,* for example, and knowing that sin must be clearly redefined according to biblical standards for our own time. In Advent it's also the difference between assuming that people understand what the "Second Coming" means for life now and knowing that this doctrine needs profound, thoughtful discussion. Thus we can go deeper.

To discover the meaning of the gospel in *breadth* we challenge you all to give the scripture texts for this year a "second reading" (for this terminology we are indebted to our friend Dieter Hessel and others who are leading us to a better understanding of the Bible's messages). The "first reading" is our habitual approach to the scripture in which we find messages for individuals and perhaps for families — for our personal moral decisions in relation to ourselves and our immediate environment. The "second reading" involves listening to the Bible as if it were addressed to groups and nations about our life together on this planet, which is precisely how much of the book was written! This does not mean that individual responsibility is set aside but that we are each identified as figures in the ongoing history of God's actions in the big wide world.

One thing this means for us as planners of worship is that we take the Old Testament more seriously both as the channel of God's Word to us and as essential background for the New Testament. In this light Jesus is heard as a son of the *prophets* who spoke to the nations just as he is heard as the savior of individuals. And New Testament teachings, such as the Second Coming, taken up in the Advent season, is interpreted as it impinges on political strategies and national goals.

A book edited by Dieter Hessel and published by Geneva Press sets forth patterns for this "second reading" approach: *Social Themes of the Christian Year.* Our own chapter in that book was on this season of Advent, as "social themes" may be interpreted in Sunday services and educational programs. Some suggestions in this issue will duplicate what we wrote in that chapter at greater length. But we heartily recommend that book, which offers many authors' dissertations on possibilities in the Christian year and the lectionary to help planners of worship go both deeper and broader.

In Advent and Christmastide, perhaps it should be our goal to plan and lead services that go beyond what the congregation will describe as "nice" or "lovely" to what they can describe as "full of surprises" and "stimulating," and even "historic" and "earth-shaking." Join us in discipline.

1. Talk about prophecy

The so-called "Messianic prophecies" of the Old Testament are very much a part of Advent and Christmas traditions. And the last of the Old Testament prophets (who appears in the New Testament), John the Baptist, is a major Advent figure. (And, of course, the prophets of Israel and their prophecies are very big parts of our year-round Christian heritage.)

But most people have very fuzzy notions about all these things. The words "prophet" and "prophecy" are — we must face it — identified primarily for the average person-in-the-pew with television weather predictions, with Jeanne Dixon and her ilk, with Jehovah's Witnesses and other bizarre "Adventist" groups, and with radio preachers who offer "inspired" interpretations of Ezekiel and Revelation relating, they claim, to the end of the world.

Distorted concepts of biblical prophecy are always around with naive "Jesus movement"-style groups boosting "Late Great Planet Earth" — and "Left Behind"-type tracts to staggering popularity. Upon hearing of prophets and prophecy, few people in our churches would think of Amos or Jeremiah's calls to justice for the poor, of second Isaiah's images of vicarious suffering, of Elijah's denunciations of idolatry. And most people, as they hear the familiar prophetic words we read in Advent and Christmas (like Isaiah 7, 9, 11, 35, and 40) think of them as visions rather magically inspired, words written in trance-like states by ancients with pictures of Jesus in their spinning heads.

So, let's consider prophecy this advent. Some ideas:

- Don't just read or sing those "Messianic" words from the Old Testament as predictions, but as expressions of longing and hope by real people. Take a moment to introduce the readings, to anchor them in their troubled times, to relate them to our own feelings and to world issues now.

- Give real attention to John the Baptist as a prophetic figure.

- Stress the social implications of the four poems in Luke 1 and 2 attributed to Zechariah, Mary, the angels, and old Simeon. They do contain rather revolutionary ideas, and we've made them sound so — well, religious.

- Stress the ethical dimensions of the prophets' teachings and of John's preaching. (His demands for "preparing the way" are quite relevant to present patterns of corruption and greed.) Prophets of the Bible had visions of a new social order, of a new Israel that sets standards of obedience, of a Messianic kingdom quite different from our society. The purpose of Advent is not to make everybody feel good about themselves and their patterns of living.

- Preachers, explain carefully what "prophet" means, what "prophecy" is, what it means for a church to be "prophetic." Challenge magical and superstitious ideas of Jesus' coming with a serious effort to explain what difference it makes to us and the whole society that he was born. Help people get ready for a Christmas that is more than pretty, and nostalgic, individualistic in effect, and simply confirmative of things as they are in white, materialistic America.

One thing we are urging is that Advent be Advent, not just an early, long Christmas season. The old, traditional themes of the four weeks provide opportunities for in-depth biblical preaching and study and provide an authentic background, a context for the celebration of Jesus' coming which we think is essential.

2. Bring the messianic passages alive

As you use readings through this season of the traditional Messianic passages in the Old Testament prophets, tell briefly but pointedly: Who wrote the words, when, why he was longing and hoping, how his words deepen our understanding of God's work. Use the words as dramatic readings by a solo reader, responsive readings, spoken or sung choral selections — a variety of presentations.

3. Freeze a sermon

Improvise a scene of John the Baptist crying in the wilderness. Have a person with some acting or improvising or role-playing experience walking up and down the aisles bawling out the congregation and reminding them that they are sinners and need to confess and be baptized. Have the actor read the gospel stories on John the Baptist so he can adapt the language into contemporary English.

Costume him historically or in contemporary counterpart (like clothes many counter-culture people wear) or let him wear whatever he usually wears to church.

Let the preacher call it to "ACTION!" to get it started and "CUT!" to stop it. If the preacher wants to preach about certain points or verses a suggestion would be to have the actor freeze at the call of the preacher and remain in that statue-like pose until the cue "ACTION!" Then the actor continues until told to "FREEZE!" again. The sermon, because of the stopped and frozen action, would be listened to by all ages with much more concentration and commitment.

4. Dramatize "prophecy"

Illustrate the different ideas of the concept with four people doing short monologues before the congregation: No. 1 comes up and starts doing a TV News weather report, pantomiming pointing to a map, predicting tomorrow's temperature and humidity. No. 2 does a Jeanne Dixon kind of clairvoyant act, predicting some dramatic event for the coming year, as in a kind of psychic state, holding temples, and describing slowly. No. 3, speaking fast and threateningly with King James Bible in hand, calls for repentance and uses some images from Revelation and announces a specific date for Jesus' return — suggesting a wild-eyed street corner preacher (maybe standing on a box). No. 4 reads Amos' denunciations of injustice, as an angry and sad preacher. Then let the pastor explain what biblical prophecy is.

5. Converse with the congregation

"Who are the voices in the wilderness today?" Following the definition of a prophet as "a spokesperson for God" who challenges the world, ask: Who may turn out to be today's prophets? (It took a long time for people to honor Amos, Hosea, Jeremiah and the others; can we do better today, or do we still "persecute the prophets"?) Let the members share some of their ideas of who and how, assuming tolerantly that there will be wild variety in the congregation, variety which may be thought-provoking for all.

6. Sound the ethical demands of Advent loudly

Inspired by the lectionary readings suggested for the season this year and by the condition of the society right now, we suggest you let the ethical demands of Advent sound loudly in preaching and all parts of worship. The Gospel Readings for Advent all contain strong moral challenges, and those from the lips of John the Baptist in Luke 3 are quite specific. The world is in great confusion about many moral issues, or where there is not confusion on these subjects, it is largely because people have completely given up any concern for biblical or traditional Christian teachings.

In our city, there is no longer a question about the normalcy of unmarried men and women living together, about bribes in various trades and businesses, about many forms of gambling, about cheating on school examinations, about teenage drinking, and most other matters of "personal morality." This is not to mention the larger and troubling issues of defense spending, attitudes toward the poor, and patterns of consumption. Advent offers a chance for strong and clear coping with such issues — and, probably, with more people gathered in worship than in some other seasons of the year.

7. Hang from the family tree

A series of four sermons for the four Sundays in Advent on four (or more) giant figures from the Old Testament who were in the line from Abraham to Jesus. The list is in the "Begats" and if you do the litany on the first Sunday, it would be worth repeating each Sunday in some manner, taking it up to the name of the person who is the subject of that day's sermon. In this new context, familiar figures like Abraham and David take on a different meaning. It is also the occasion to preach on some lesser people like Boaz, Jesse, Solomon, Joseph himself — lesser only in the sense that we don't hear about them as much.

8. Let Isaiah speak

Many of the Old Testament readings for Advent and Christmas are drawn from the writings of the "Second Isaiah." These include some of the most beautiful and thrilling lines of scripture. As we have suggested in other years, such a sequence of readings deserves special treatment. Assign them all to one or two of your church's actors for preparation and let these persons read the Old Testament lesson each Sunday. You may want to have the reading come from a special place other than the lectern or pulpit. You may wish to have musical accompaniment to that reading. You may be able to think of a "prop," a symbol for each reading or one for the whole series that could be held up or worn each Sunday during the reading. You don't have any actors in your church? Sure you do. You have someone who would respond to such a challenge maybe with great delight and creativity. Plan ahead.

9. Let the prophets' words live

If the Word of God in the Old Testament is to be heard freshly, providing a strong context for Advent thoughts about the coming of Jesus, we must prepare creatively. The lectionary's readings from Isaiah are very strong, but, let's face it, most people won't listen to them very much because most Old Testament readings in most churches are "throwaways," ho-hum moments in the service. Three suggestions for these great readings:

- Assign them to different groups in the church for choral reading — perhaps four different groups, one for each of the readings. Give them general ideas about how choral readings can work (dividing lines, solo voices, occasional repetition, etc.) and tell them to be as dramatic as the words require.
- Prepare them as responsive readings for the whole congregation, but explain them in brief introductions so that the reading won't be dull and plodding. Whoever leads the responsive readings needs to prepare carefully to lead excitement and proper tempo.
- Assign them to your best lay readers for preparation; don't let the clergy read them! In our experience over several years of worship workshops, we have found that lay people almost invariably read scripture better than ministers, who make everything sound "holy" instead of real. Have lay readers read the prophets' words from *behind* the congregation each Sunday, as if coming from the past, with great force and urgency. Let the words live!

10. Let John walk among you

Turn John the Baptist loose in some way during Advent. He is the principal figure of the season until we come to the birth of Jesus himself. Do you have in your church a few people with interest and experience in drama, in theater? Turn the stories of John over to them; ask these folks to bring John alive for a few moments on the second and third Sundays. Not only can the second Sunday's reading from Matthew 3 become a compelling dialogue between John and those who came to him (people coming forward from the congregation?), but the situation in Matthew 11 can be quite moving also. Picture poor John rotting in prison, awaiting possible torture and death in that ancient dungeon, wondering, "What if I made a horrible mistake? What if he's not coming? What if this Jesus is not the One? And here I am, throwing my life away for nothing." Can such a poignant scene be dramatized, even related to situations of persecution and oppression in today's world?

11. Preach on Advent phrases

Some phrases that recur from John the Baptist's wild speeches to the listening crowds are another way for us to focus in Advent on things to do. "Prepare ... take stock ... inventory ... confess ... make room." All these can be the *subjects of sermons* and the entire *worship service.* An example: Consider how "Make room!" applies to the church family as a whole and as individual families and as individual people. Make room in the continuing life of the church for Jesus. Is the church so busy doing things like putting on plays and dinners, studying theology and reading books about the great reformers, and so forth, that it is not ready to accept a baby, a living baby named Jesus, the Son of God? As individual families, are we so busy with Little League, football, cheerleading, Tupperware parties, meetings, and rehearsals, and so forth that there is not time to hear the baby's cry that is the trumpet blast announcing the coming of the kingdom? As individuals, are we working too hard at keeping our houses beautiful and so forth that we have no time for thoughts on what difference a baby will make in the home, not just the new baby in our family but the baby Jesus, too? Can we make room for Jesus at the office, at the table, in the election booth, in the supermarket, at the movies, etc.?

12. Discuss the Second Advent

Since the second coming of Jesus is a major theme of Advent through the centuries, and since most mainline churches have dealt with this major New Testament theme rather vaguely and nervously through the years, plan to share the search for understanding. One way to do this is to have an Advent discussion group in which you lay out some of the real meanings for present-day Christians of the biblical descriptions of the return of Christ. Then share these with the congregation during a sermon in the season.

Another way to do the same thing is to have the discussion — more briefly, of course — during the sermon period itself, opening up the theme to the congregation. For example: "Some of us may believe that Jesus will actually return on clouds of glory with trumpets and angels, while others may understand these stories more symbolically; but what difference does it make that Jesus will return at the end of history? So what? How do you feel about these teachings?" Or this: "What would you do today if you knew he was returning soon?" Such a topic may need preparing for in your congregation, but other churches may be more readily conversant with such heavy themes.

A third approach might be a dialogue sermon with two ministers or a capable layperson and the pastor, with one playing devil's advocate — "You can't think that we should really expect Jesus in physical form to come down from the sky!" Consider the possibilities, but don't forget this major theme. And don't forget that can have major implications for our attitudes in the world of nations.

Other ideas

1. A display of Advent words

On a wall before the congregation, on organ pipes, on a big display board, on a large cloth, on windows around the room — somewhere, have different groups or classes (out of a study of prophecy, perhaps?) or families or a single committee post key words from assigned Advent readings. On posters, decorated and in different styles of print, tastefully done and mounted, put words like "repent," "light," "Messiah," "wonderful counselor," "the zeal of the Lord," "prepare the way."

2. Build a totem pole of prophets

Get the large size Quaker Oats boxes (round boxes of any kind will do if they are large enough) and cut a hole in the bottom and top. Study the prophets for personal attributes. Design a face and draw it with magic markers on some construction paper and paste it on the box. Make a beard of rolled construction paper in an appropriate or surprising color, cutting it to look like tresses. Do the same with the hair, the eyebrows, sideburns. Have fun with it; be imaginative. Paste all of these on the face on the box. Then on the Sunday in which Isaiah's prophecy is read, have someone ceremoniously walk up to a large dowel on a stand and slowly put the head on the pole as the prophet is being announced by name. The following Sunday add that week's prophets' likeness to the pole. By the fourth week the totem pole is built. If you want to use more than one prophet a Sunday it might be more profitable (ha-ha) and of course the totem pole will be larger and a thing of beauty as well as education. If you are afraid to do this in the sanctuary, use it in your Christian Education program.

3. Road signs

Relate certain prophets or other Advent themes to road signs, and use pictures of road signs, borrow real ones (with permission), make them out of cardboard or wood or whatever. Use the roadside designs that people recognize as they drive along so that after seeing them used in the worship of the church the signs will take on religious significance as well. For instance, the sign saying "Children" can be used for Isaiah; the sign "Curve" ("make straight") for John the Baptist. Check the available road signs and then check the passages appropriate for Advent and relate them. The signs can be used as props in the front of the sanctuary, as calls to prayer or drawn on the bulletins, or placed on the walls, whatever way makes them work best in your situation.

4. An Advent scrapbook

There is so much to remember about Jesus that a scrapbook is very helpful. It's very much like the reminders of our marvelous Holy Land trip that Don put in a scrapbook: photographs with moving or funny remarks beneath them, postcards of places we could not get close enough to, some wildflowers dried and put into plastic, a bit of palm branch that had dried by the Sea of Galilee. You know the sort of thing you probably do around your house. Well, we have a great series of scrapbooks in the back of the church for guests to look at and for members to enjoy that Don has kept up for about fifteen years. So we are suggesting that you consider the scrapbook concept and use it in a variety of ways:

- Turn it into a Sunday school program that is used in the regular service of worship, contemporary or traditional, small or large. If you have small worship services for different classes let the scrapbook as it is being built be passed around. Eventually let this happen in the major worship service of the week.
- If you have exhibit space in the rear of the sanctuary for the season of Advent put up pictures or objects that are appropriate. This can be done *historically* or from a *contemporary* standpoint. Historically, use pictures of artwork or drawings or paintings (use a variety of forms and techniques) showing Joseph and Mary going to Jerusalem, a pregnant Mary (if you can find any such work of art), that sort of thing. From the contemporary standpoint use pictures from magazines and newspapers that relate to the Advent story: a mother and child

refugee, a birth certificate, a book on natural childbirth, the things that all parents get ready for the arrival of their expected baby. If you turn this over to a committee or a family that is expecting some time soon, it can take on an even more personal meaning for them and the church family as a whole.

5. Advent drama

Put on a staged version or even a reading version of the "Annunciation" and the "Salutation of Elizabeth" scenes from the Wakefield Mystery Plays (Anchor Books). The language can be adapted if it would be difficult for your congregation to understand, but it is a beautiful work. Another book that has a variety of medieval mystery and morality plays is Religious Drama, Number 2 (A Living Age Book, Meridian Books).

6. Family Advent banners

Invite all families of the church to make a banner, large or small, for Advent. Give them lists of Advent symbols, key phrases, hymns to look at. Get a consignment of felt and other materials from a local store for them to buy cheaply. Plan a workshop to get folks started. Encourage use of different kinds of sewing and construction. Have them bring them for display — in the church, not out back! — on the second or third Sunday of the season.

7. Wear purple

For Advent's first Sunday, or each Sunday of the season, invite everybody to wear something purple. (But don't insist so hard they'll go out and spend lots of money to do it.) Then have them exhibit the color joyfully in the service, in honor of the Royal Son who comes.

8. Sense the sanctuary

Yes, that's right, explore the place of worship with *all* the senses. Or the first Sunday of the new church year or on any other appropriate Sunday, invite the whole congregation or perhaps a part of the congregation — representing all — to take five minutes and explore the room with touch, smell, sight, hearing, and taste. Ask them to move *all through* the room. Beyond the five senses ask them to test the spaces to jump, turn, reach, crawl, and climb, to discover the feelings of aisles, chancel, and other open spaces.

Afterward, ask them, while they are scattered about, the following questions: What surprised you? What is especially beautiful? What is amusing or curious or bizarre? How does God speak through the various sensory perceptions? After discussion, "line out" a few lines of Psalm 84, as people still stand all around the room. Or if you can't line out Psalms, have three or four different people read the Psalm antiphonally from different parts of the room.

This experience has been found very meaningful as a way to increase our appreciation of the rooms in which we worship. Each time we have done this in different places, people discover things that they would not otherwise have noticed in the room. Thus, worship becomes much more interesting, and the traditions of the church as contained in its architecture come alive and speak to us.

9. Skip the bulletin

Here's an idea that continues to be a startling one and an appealing one in many of our workshops around the land. Stop printing the order of worship every Sunday, we advise fervently. The season of Advent with all its symbols and drama and color — all its visual excitement — is a good time to start. There are reasons why not having a printed order can be most beneficial to worship. These include the simple encouragement of attention to what's going on instead of to the "agenda" on the piece of paper. People notice things and see each other with much more awareness without the bulletin. (Yes, you can still have a list of announcements for the week printed for everyone and accomplish this same increase of participation.) Tell the people on Advent Sunday that you simply want them to enjoy the sights and sounds more and be free of the words on the page. Do it for the season and see what happens. (Think of all the secretarial time you will save.)

10. "O, Come, O, Come, Emmanuel" with newspaper headlines

On a Sunday early in the season, in between the stanzas of the Old Testament hymn, have people stand in the congregation and loudly read the opening paragraphs of newspaper articles about the problems and troubles of the world. Have them hold the newspaper up visibly as they read. The organist might hold a low suspenseful peddle note during the reading or very softly improvise on the musical theme. End with the last stanza of the song and its refrain of hope, singing boldly and confidently.

11. Prime the pump

Most sports figures, most actors, most singers, all dancers, in other words, most professionals, aside from warming up whatever equipment they use, also prime the pump (as the saying goes) by breathing deeply, jumping around, whatever, just to get the adrenalin going. Leading an hour of worship, whether you are the preacher, the reader, or any one of the musicians takes a lot of energy and stamina. Figure out what you need and how much, and prime the pump before going into the service. To most of the people listed above, this would be an obvious and natural thing. But to church people who are used to being interrupted, threatened, argued with, etc. as they are going into the service, this might be a startling idea. Don has said that because of the noise made by the lined-up choirs, it takes him about fifteen minutes into the service before he is able to worship. Because of the seriousness of dealing with God's Word, sung or spoken, you should be at your best, so though it may seem silly at first, try it. If you are like the actress our secretary heard interviewed, who said she needed to do at least one primordial scream before she went into performance, find a suitable place. Remember, it is Good News we are sharing and such a scream might indicate just the opposite if the congregation were to hear it!

12. Bring greens

Lots of churches do a Hanging of the Greens (this always made our friends Sid and Anita Greene nervous!). Our question is: What greens? Many churches get these from the local florist. Here we are suggesting that you invite the congregation, perhaps by families, to bring the greens and formally present them as a special offering in the service. Invite the congregation to bring them forward and to put them on the Communion table or altar. Have a prayer of gratitude for the miracle of the evergreen plant and, after the prayer, let the families place the evergreens in the appropriate place. The phrase, "the appropriate place," implies there has been somebody in charge of decorating the sanctuary in Advent. There should be one person in charge, or it seems to us bedlam might take over.

13. Vocal exercises or mike practice

If you know of certain people who will be reading parts of the service in forthcoming services of worship, gather them together in the sanctuary and let them practice. If you always use microphones, have them practice reading a passage very close to the microphone, a short distance away, and farther away. The microphone will always supply some energy for the reader, but knowing how to speak intimately, for instance, close up to the microphone, is an exciting technique for the reader to learn. It is also important for them to know when to move back and when to move in closer. Since John's crying in the wilderness is used for at least one of the Sundays in Advent this would be a great passage to practice with. If you are not in the practice of using microphones, have the readers stand at lectern or pulpit and shout, and then practice projecting their voices to the back row without shouting. The reason for the rehearsal is so they can get over the self-consciousness when their time comes to read. There is nothing wrong with having some technique.

14. Promote the beginning

Start ahead of time to build interest in the start of the new Christian year on the First Sunday of Advent. Tell the people "Happy New Christian Year!" in bulletins, newsletters, and announcement periods. Remind them that on the same weekend as Thanksgiving celebrations, we start the new "Season of Expectation" — to build more reasons for thanksgiving. If you have Advent traditions, such as the wreath ceremony, remind them of such moments and encourage them to get back from any Thanksgiving Day trips to be in worship on Sunday.

15. For when Christmas comes on Sunday

If this is one of the years when Christmas Day falls on the Lord's Day, here are a few suggestions:
- Come on strong, announcing and planning, with the *assumption* that everyone will come to worship to celebrate the Lord's birth.
- Skip Sunday school and have a festive and participatory fellowship service late in the morning, with all ages sharing in leadership, and with a special effort to involve the children.
- Invite everybody to bring one gift to show and tell about in the service. Invite some of different ages to come up front to the microphone and do this, and let others just communicate with their neighbors in a two-minute period in the service. Invite them to share also one event, *idea* or experience connected with Christmas that they consider a "gift from God." Now some folks may speak just of these spiritual gifts instead of presents they found under the tree; others may do both. As you lead this time of sharing, speak of gifts as signs of love and care — which they are.
- Communicate to the congregation your own love for the people of the church on this joyful occasion. Give the gift of *yourself* to the people whom God has given to you as partners in the gospel.
- Pray earnestly for those people who know nothing of the birth of Jesus, or those for whom it has no meaning.
- Let there be some *silence* in the midst of the merriment, so people, even the excited children, can consider the deeper meanings of the celebration on this day.

16. Let the children's choir introduce themselves

Use a song available from us at Proclamation Productions called "Step, Step, Step." The words are:

Step, step, step, step up and be counted.

Step, step, step, stop and shout your name.

When we do it, and we do it every two years with the choir from kindergarten through third grade, we have a set of stairs (the kind you buy to get into mobile homes before they are permanently grounded) placed with the back facing the congregation. Each child sings the short refrain, climbs the steps, shouts his/her given name, and comes down. Honestly, most of the comings down are inspired leaps off the deep end. The congregation loves it, of course, and we feel whether or not Presbyterians would love it, Jesus would. (Tsk! Tsk!) There is a further part of the song that you need the music for but the above can be done without music. Just have each child chant the lines and do his/her own thing. Very soon the congregation will recognize the young singers with their individual personalities. And soon they will get to know their last names and who the adorable kids' parents are. And so the family grows and gets to know each other.

17. Emphasize the "Christian" in Christian names

The long-held theory that children show their respect for their elders by calling them by their last names has fortunately been disproved. For 25 years children in our church have been calling Dick and Don by their first names and there is no lack of respect. If anything, the reverse has happened, plus the added fringe benefit that the young suddenly feel they have a new and treasured friend. Our suggestion is to set aside one Sunday to trade Christian names. After all, it is not by accident that we have the phrase "Christian" names. Make a ritual or a litany inviting the people to come forward to the front of the church and use a microphone, if possible. Have one member of the family introduce the family by the last name. Then have each member of the family move to the microphone and say clearly: "I am _____." Of course, this will take time. If it takes too much time on one Sunday, divide it up over two or three Sundays; or do it alphabetically on separate occasions, alerting the whole congregation to that fact. Get to know the family.

18. Make symbols for the season

Choose symbols for each season of the church year and turn them over to a committee or to the whole church. When we did this, one Epiphany ended up with more indoor stars in our sanctuary than have ever been seen before, except in our galaxy. We had batik stars with enough of the wax left in them so they shone like stained glass, glass stars, paper stars, tin and other metal stars, whatever, and we suggested that the whole church school design stars. When they had all been made, the committee figured out where to hang them, so that that season, particularly, was a season of great light and joy. Consider what could be done with symbols of Advent.

19. Clean for Advent

Emphasize cleaning as preparation for the coming of the Savior in such a way that everything is brighter and thereby illumined and find appropriate props. For instance, silver polish and a rag and a silver chalice on the Communion table, Lemon Pledge and a rag on the piano, a basin with soap and water or even ammonia or Mr. and Ms. Clean for the stained glass windows, etc. These props can just be in place and explained or used as part of the service. Have somebody use them to remind us all that some of the Lectionary readings for Advent are about making ourselves ready and clean and shining so we will be prepared for a surprise appearance of the Savior.

20. Act out Isaiah 35:1-6

Have the congregation cover their eyes and pull them back for the lines about the deaf hearing, and have them leap in place on the lines about the lame leaping and dancing. It will be simple enough to figure out other such activities for other lines in the reading. Incidentally, all of these are other examples of illumination: the blind seeing, the deaf hearing, etc.

21. Illuminated the coming of the Child

Buy a clear, plastic model of a woman in which you can see the interior. If somebody in your congregation has recently given birth or will soon, making use of this figure as being light, particularly to the children, could be very effective as you remind them that the large stomach was an indication that inside was/is the baby that has been born or is about to be, a baby coming from darkness into light.

A final word

Let us look at Advent in the context of energy, all sorts of energy.

Consider the energy of the star! The energy of the pregnant mother! The energy of the baby growing within her! The energy it took to make the trip to Bethlehem, of the riding mother and the walking father, and the bearing beast! The energy of the kings riding their camels and nearing the place where the baby is born but we move now through Christmas to Epiphany!

So, let's go back to Advent, and the energy we know it will take to get the work done in preparation. The energy it will take to clean and decorate, for the season to become alive and redolent with its specific symbols of growing things. The energy it will take the organist to prepare exciting and appropriately moving music that the congregation will want to hear (this is sometimes called the energy of Hope). The energy it will take the choir director and the singers and instrumentalists to rehearse and re-rehearse (after having hearsed once) the music that should be the musical highpoint of the church year. The energy it will take the congregation to organize and appropriately allot their combined and individual times to include coming to worship with expectations that great things will happen. The energy it will take for all of us to think and hear and cry and laugh and wonder and be grateful and be proud as we acknowledge the awesome size of God's energetic love for us. And most importantly, the energy it will take the preacher to gather together and absorb and then share with us this most tremendous event for which we prepare.

What does energy need? Strength, risk, sleep, commitment, faith, knowledge — that's all! As the adult Jesus will say later in his life to each of us: "I want from you everything, only everything, that's all!" Let's take a sentence or two to reconsider each of the above:

- Strength — most of us are rundown, if not entirely fatigued, by the end of Advent. This should not be so. Our tiredness probably comes from too much focusing on gift-giving and the appropriateness of the things we have bought for people, instead of our concentrating on this special gift that we will receive. We say this special gift because we're so focused on present giving that we forget the obvious gifts God has already showered on us: space, place, time, the senses to receive all these gifts, our minds, our bodies, each other. These things can sound so platitudinous until we take the time and energy to re-examine how these things are gifts for us.
- Risk — having a child is always a risk. Having Jesus was a risk for Mary, for Joseph, for God, and for us. There are sermon topics there. Specifically in worship, the risk aspect of

energy is very important. The story that we tell and sing and show must be splendid, awesome, shattering and not sweet, precious, or bland. And to achieve this means risking on the part of all the leaders in worship. Consider how to make the job of the usher, receiving the offering, a risk.

- Sleep — energy requires replenishing. We need sleep. God knew what he was doing when he offered one third of our daily gift of time to be spent in sleeping. Without sleep the singer's voice wobbles, the dancer's knees are unsteady, the pastor's enthusiasm wavers, the worshiper gets drowsy — what an offering to present at worship! Surely we must allocate time for rest in order to be the energetic receivers of God's gift.

- Commitment — if you have doubts about what you are saying, your energy may be low, or you may come on too strong. The energy of some preachers condemning some of us to hell very often looks and sounds like doubts (with the parallel hope) about the prospect. Would that they spoke as energetically about grace and needs and joys! As a one-time professional actor, Don tells actors he is directing, that sincerity is easy to simulate and also not enough to get by with. Commitment to the role, to the belief, is paramount and results in energy.

- Faith — blind faith stumbles into all the pitfalls; aware faith moves ahead quickly, looking at and working at the problems as they arise. Blind faith sits back and thanks God for doing something or not doing anything; aware faith asks: "What do you want me to do now?" and, discovering it, moves ahead.

- Knowledge — we started a song with a question, "Why die wide-eyed and innocent when you've got the opportunity to learn?" A muscle that is not used atrophies, a brain that is not used atrophies. Part of energy is using that brain to test information and ideas in every way possible, and then using the resultant knowledge. The solo setting of "I Know That My Redeemer Liveth" has the highest, strongest note on the word "know" rather than on the word "my" or the word "liveth." The singer singing it needs to give that word the highest degree of energy. Likewise, the pastor reading Scripture needs to energize the known truth, the known facts, in the reading and in the preaching.

Four weeks, 448 waking hours to examine, prepare for, understand and try to assimilate the tremendous event of Christmas. Lets do it all with excitement, with increasing interest, with energy. Let there not be said about your church, "There is an energy crisis." The supply is endless, and it is only worth anything when it is spent. 'Tis the season to be spending!

Worshiping During Christmas

Christmas is the shortest season in the church year calendar. Why? It is almost everyone's favorite season and yet it is given such short shrift! Why? A season that includes the exchanging of presents, enjoying looking at the baby Jesus and all other babies and little children, the gift of God's Son to us, New Year's Day with its growing possibilities, and New Year's Eve with its glowing (the rosy glow) possibilities would surely be allotted more time. God knows there are more carols and songs about Christmas than about any other season.

In fact, we are not given enough time to sing as many as we would like to sing. There are more Christmas Oratorios and Cantatas and Musicals than any other. We have to do a different one each year and all composers keep on writing more of the big works as well as the small works. There is no way to catch up. It's a season that demands that the choir director and organist make choices: What style of music will be most appropriate this year? Should I mix it up? Each choir could sing each week or should we offer some variety there, too? Should I pull in other instruments along with the organ since there is so much literature? Help!

The preacher also has to make choices. Of course, the lectionary helps us with the choosing of texts but what is the best way to preach what to the people who will be there on Christmas Eve/Christmas Day and may not show again until Easter (what we might call the "Ground Hog" Christian)?

We have a sneaking suspicion that whoever decided on the lengths and names of the church seasons very specifically wanted us to touch on the wonder of it all, the Nativity, and then get moving into following a grown man with only a three-year ministry. It was their way to get us to move beyond the sentimentality that always appears with babies, to learn to speak to Jesus in some other manner than "baby talk," and go with the excitement of a growing faith. Pentecost, when we the people of the church take over, is probably the least popular season (Day, yes, Season, no) since it lasts for many denominations until the next Advent begins. That is as long as a marriage and takes as much hard work, in contrast to the short season of "courtship" called Christmas.

The exciting coming of Christmastide provides challenging opportunities for worship-in-depth and worship-in-breadth. Give to all the scriptural texts around which our services revolve this year a "second reading." Let all the lections and themes of the unfolding seasons be interpreted not only as they relate to individual lives but also to the life of the nations and social groups of which we are a part. In this issue we urge approaching the celebration of Christ's nativity. And when better?

People are uniquely open to global concerns and to caring about others and the dynamics of social problems at this time: The experience of Christmas each year opens our hearts to the plights of others as does no other experience of the year. Call it "Christmas Spirit" — with a capital S for God the *Holy* Spirit, alive and working among us. People will be moved by concern for peace on earth; by demands for justice for those who suffer oppression even as most of us celebrate merrily and lavishly; by regard for families without food and shelter, while we feast with *our* families in beautifully decorated homes; and even by news of violations of human rights, as we move about the communities in our season of joy with freedom and laughter. People are especially vulnerable to calls to compassion as the lights of Christmas candles and the music of carols surround them. So let us not fail to celebrate the *whole* gospel for *all* God's children.

It's all there in the sacred story, of course, the story of the Word become human flesh during a time of political turbulence in which many were victims of political oppression. It's the story of the Word becoming flesh and quickly becoming a refugee from tyrannical and paranoid political power. It's the story of the Word becoming flesh in a working-class family. It's a story of the Word becoming flesh and growing up to be "the light of the nations" who soon upsets vested political and religious interests while finding friendship among the outcasts of society.

Christmas themes

1. Illumination

Consider using the theme of *illumination* for this year's services. Christmas is the season of light-in-the-darkness, and the metaphors and symbols of light may be very helpful to you and your congregation as a key to understanding. The symbol emerges strongly from at least three basic pericopes of the season:

- Isaiah 9 — "The people who walked in darkness have seen a great light."
- Ephesians 1 — "I ask that your minds may be opened to see his light, so that you will know what is the hope to which he has called you."
- John 1 — "In him was life, and the life was the light of humanity; the light shines in the darkness."

Consider the *light of hope*. Many hurting and confused people need to see the light at the end of the tunnel in their lives, at least in our community. Alcoholism, severe economic problems, divorces and separations, the inevitable disappointments of popular patterns of self-indulgence — these are harsh realities for many people. What hope is there? What real, sound, lasting hope? (We see some disenchantment with the self-centered "personal renewal" movements. What *real* hope can we find as we press through to the meaning of the carols' lyrics, to the personal meaning of the old familiar words of Luke 2, to the light?)

Consider the *challenge to the children of light*. In this time when the campus mood is dominated by a "What's in it for me?" philosophy, and the news is bogged down with speculations about broken international agreements, the financial wheeling and dealing of some powerful people, and perpetual demands by private interest groups, is there a unique and special way of life for the Children of Light? Let Christmas be a time for preaching and praying and singing about Christian ethics. Jesus was born, we accept him, so what do we do different from everyone else? The emergence of the theme of conflict right after the birth narratives — as with the lectionary's scheduling of Matthew 2:13ff for the First Sunday after Christmas (in year A) — suggests that the Christian way is a hard and narrow way. If we are to bear the light in the darkness, we must know what that means, how to be different. And Christmas, with its crowds and heightened attention to the church's words and music, is a good time to learn of this difference.

The place to start may be with a consideration through Advent of *Christmas giving*. More and more Christians are becoming frustrated with the pattern of giving that's popular in society. Alternatives are being proposed widely. Take up this matter with your congregation in advance of Christmas: What causes can we support instead of giving more knick-knacks and candy to each other? What people in the world need special concern? What forms of outreach and visitation and help can we offer with the hours we have usually spent shopping before Christmas? (Do you realize how much time is spent shopping, as well as money? How many lonely people could be visited with that time, how many people outside the faith could be contacted, talked to?) No, this is not specifically a liturgical matter, but on a profound level it is a liturgical matter — for our worship is hollow if our behavior is unworthy.

2. Peace on earth

Beyond the pandemonium, beyond the "pretty," beyond the pious nostalgia, beyond the panic, and even beyond the poignancy: Let there be Christmas, with heady meaning and lasting effect. (Plan ahead!) And let there be *peace on earth* as a theme to think about and sing about and pray about and act out. We offer the words from the angels' song, "peace on earth," for the Twelve Days of Christmas.

Wars continue with haunting persistence. Ours continues to be an age of violence and terror, all over the world. For some, it is also the Age of the Tranquilizer. (Where is peace?) And of course, there's the economy.

More specifically for some of us, this is also a time when squabbles within the church and the churches continue to be hot and heavy and occasionally ugly and scandalous. It is also a time when many professional church leaders are anxious, worried, uncertain about the shape of their careers and searching (often creatively, to be sure) for new answers, styles, and forms. (Where is peace?)

Is it possible, as we look ahead to Christmas, to look first at ourselves? Have you found a "peace that passes understanding"? Is it possible that Christmastide can be a time for us to be open to receive what God can give us of his peace? (Think: Are there peaceful times and places and people for you?) And can we provide moments, hours within the twelve days for people to find the peace of God, to consider its meaning, as the world goes its hectic, inebriated way through the season?

Consider the possibilities: Silence, long times of silence (without muzak) within the services of Advent's Fourth Sunday and Christmas Eve and Day and on the the two Sundays surrounding the start of the New Year ... Special prayers for peace within the wide world and *within us* in all these services ... A sermon-conversation with the congregation, perhaps most easily on the first Sunday after Christmas, on the question "What are the deep-down threats to our peace?" and then on the question "How does God actually give us peace? What are its channels?" ... List the specific answers to these questions in a big display for all to see as they begin the new year ... Let church leaders and staff members share together their own sources of peace, in a meeting or with the whole congregation ... Emphasis in sermons and prayers on the opportunities Christmastide offers for reconciliation with other people, for the settling of old problems among friends, for the asking of forgiveness, for the granting of forgiveness in the form of gift, letter, touch, or smile. (Could there even be — miracle of miracles! — a time in or after a service for people estranged from one another in the church family to seek reconciliation and offer an embrace of peace?) ... A "Twelfth Night Party" with special times of prayer for troubled and warring peoples around the world — in honor of the Magi who came from far away to the Prince of Peace ... A one or two-day retreat during the Twelve Days, for anyone in the congregation, with some of the above times and opportunities and much silence for prayer, meditation, and reading ... Emphasis in the church on giving for those in need at Christmas rather than for ourselves, and on cutting back in how much we spend in favor of other forms of showing love ... Consider the possibilities. Peace to you.

Using music during Christmas

1. Focus on lyrics

The *disadvantage* of much church music is that it is so pretty that we forget the words, the depth of the words. One of the major differences between lyrics and poetry is that since lyrics are to be sung they cannot be too loaded since the singer will most often sing them in such a way that their strength and meaning are lost. Poetry needs a different sort of time, a time that allows the listener to savor the words and phrases. Lyrics very often need to say a thing simply or to repeat an idea in order for the listener to get the true depth of meaning. This is even difficult to explain simply. So, let's take an example: "Faith of Our Fathers." We sing the tune more and more sentimentally all the time, slurping and sliding as if it were some sort of drinking song. We overlook the fact that the words are about the martyrs who suffered and died for their strong, unsentimental faith. And we promise in verse three to "love both friend and foe in all our strife ... by kindly words and virtuous life" in such a lovely way that the words better be garbled or the lie becomes patent.

So the season of Christmas is the one that suffers most with pretty and cute music. Lovely, beautiful, and moving are not the same as pretty. Ironic, clever, even arch are not the same as cute. The baby Jesus is *not* the same kind of cute and sweet baby as any other. He is a baby with a profound destiny. He is to be sung about with awe, particularly by those who are no longer just in theological kindergarten. Simple is not simplistic, simple is simple-minded. A simple melody like many of the folksongs and tunes from *Southern Harmony,* for instance, have been honed down. It is far easier to write a complex melody than a simple one. Martin Luther, after saying that it was time that there was church music to be sung in the vernacular, elongated complex phrases of poetry into understandable lyrics and honed down complex melodies into tunes that the common people could, not only *could* but *would,* sing.

So ... examine the words of the carols everyone wants to sing and study them in worship with the whole congregation or in other groups so that this year's singing will be different from last year's. "Joy to the World" includes "No more let sins and sorrows grow, Nor thorns infest the ground; He comes to make his blessings flow Far as the curse is found." What on earth does all that mean? What sins? What thorns? What blessings? For whom? What curse? What do those words mean today? After studying and discussing them, sing the song again in a renewed way, in a changed context because we are who we are and now is where we are.

2. Use music to challenge the "year of the gun"

This season more than any other we are aware of the advantage of music. But if we are using the theme of Peace on Earth, we must admit that most years end up being the Year of the Gun. It would be food for those who think the church is irrelevant if we were to ignore that fact and fail to look at it in the light of the birth of the Prince of Peace. Therefore, the music we suggest for this Christmas idea is aimed at Christian statements about this problem that will never make any headway in Washington until Christians *recognize* they are daughters and sons of the Prince of Peace and must be radical about gun control. To the literalists we say: Jesus never had a gun. To those interested in history: Jesus never carried a weapon except his tongue and God's truth. To the liberal: How can we say, "Peace," on one hand and ignore the increase in use of guns on the other? From *The Genesis Songbook* (Agape Pub.) we recommend three songs: "Let There Be Peace on Earth," "When All [Folk] Shall Walk Together," and "Down by the Riverside." And we suggest staging all three:

- "Let There Be Peace on Earth" ... have two children come up front and have a tug-of-war with a present. As they struggle, they pull the wrapping off the gift and pull out something like a truck or a doll and they continue with the struggle with the toy. They freeze on a given cue and a solo voice sings the opening line through "and let it begin with me." Two women then come up front and fight over a sweater on sale, all of this in pantomime, until they freeze and another soloist sings the same first line. Then two men come forward with an earth globe and go through the same struggle and freeze. On this one let one soloist stand in the choir loft and sing the first line and hold the note on the word "me." A second soloist down front in the congregation (in civilian clothes, not robe) stands and starts the same line as the first singer hits the word "me." A third singer farther back in the congregation stands and does the same thing the second singer has done. Then start the song again with people in the choir loft and congregation rising whenever they want to as they sing the whole song through. Have the three groups of people remain as frozen statues throughout the song. As the singers hold the final "me" have the two children face front and while still holding on to the toy put a finger to the mouth or to the forehead as they ponder the words of the song. (Let the other two statues repeat this sequence.) Then as the pastor speaks, let each duo go back to their places and sit together still holding the prop. The pastor can say things to the effect that we need to recognize the problem first and then think about it and hear what the Bible has to say about it in the birth of Jesus, Prince of Peace.
- "When All Men Shall Walk Together" ... first of all change the word "men" to "folk" so that everybody in the congregation will be included. Get a trumpet player and have her play the tune good and slowly and heavily from the balcony or somewhere behind the congregation. Have a drummer start a march rhythm. Then let the combined choirs march from the rear in a procession. Have them march up to the front and turn and face the congregation looking as angry and martial as possible (this is easy as it is the normal look in many Christian churches). No music as they are marching forward. When they are in place, have a trumpet blast that moves from the germ of the melody into a free jazz-like, soul-like, spiritual-like melody that leads obviously into the song. As the singers start the first verse which deals with "guns no more" have them drop the martial look and stance and relax and reach out and touch the other singers, or link arms, or do anything that is meant by the word "brother-hood" (or a non-sexist substitute, such as "kinship" or "fellowship"). On the second verse, which deals with "sharing," have the singers pair off and move toward the aisles. On the third verse which deals with "the beauty of the earth about us" have the singers look obviously around the sanctuary and through the windows if they can be seen through. On the fourth verse which deals with "understanding" have them move up the aisles and greet people in the congregation, young taking the hands of older people and older singers taking the hands of the young.
- "Down by the Riverside" ... do this song on the Sunday before New Year's Day and have the pastor talk about the tired old thing called New Year's resolutions (or even "revolutions"). Perhaps have someone carrying a picket sign saying: "Change! Make resolutions!" Have a soloist move forward singing her or his resolution to stop warring in the new year. Have another join in the second verse and chorus, moving down front. After a while, let the jauntiness of the spiritual take over and bounce along as other singers in groups of two or three come forward singing. Plan, if possible, to have a display of guns from different periods of American history somewhere in the back of the sanctuary. During the singing of

the song have some people coming up carrying the various guns and have them put them down. Let the pastor rise and say things to the effect that laying down guns means putting them to rest in trophy racks, or historical societies or museums, reminders of what we have done in the past but hope never to do again.

3. Stage a giving song

Jane Marshall's setting of our song "Give a Little Something Special" can hit harder if it is staged. There are three verses in this Agape anthem. The first one deals with giving a gun for Christmas. As it is sung, have a young boy pantomime opening a present, discovering it's a gun, trying it on for size, then very deliberately turning toward the congregation, and pointing it at them. During the second verse have a woman trying on (in pantomime) a new, expensive fur coat while another women on the floor pleads (silently) for food. On the third have a couple (preferably an older couple because they know what it's all about) walk slowly toward each other, touch hands, smile, then go into an embrace, and perhaps a kiss. All three should remain frozen while the chorus is being sung by the choir. Recently we did this, and the high point of the whole two-hour evening was the embrace by the older couple. At the end Don likes to get up and say: "We know the importance of guns and how necessary they are for certain occasions. But doesn't it seem weird to give a gun in the name of the Prince of Peace. If you must give a gun, give it on a more appropriate day, like Memorial Day!"

4. Dramatize a hymn

The hymn "Watchman Tell Us of the Night" lends itself to some interesting staging and singing. Start it with someone in costume walking through the congregation calling out: "Eleven o'clock and all is well." Cut to a watchman up in the balcony repeating the phrase as a watchman in the towers of Jerusalem. Have the pastor point these out. Have a person dressed as one who watches crossing the street for school children. Radar, sonar, satellites, helicopters, etc., are other contemporary "watchmen." Have these live, in models or slides and then sing the hymn back and forth between the congregation and the watchmen placed around the room.

5. Mix message songs with carols

Especially if you are having a carol sing on Christmas Eve or some other evening in the season, mix some songs (such as mentioned in 2 and 3 above) in with the old familiar ones. When you go caroling around town mix them in. This is such a fantastic opportunity for the Christian to make her or his voice heard in the real world in a real way when they least expect it. Don't be Christians espousing cheap grace; grace is expensive. Be biblical! Stand up and be counted! Stand up for what Jesus stood up for! In fact, stand up, stand up for Jesus, Prince of Peace!

6. Use singing families

Since Christmas is the time in which we are most aware of the beauties and joys of family life, we suggest this would be a good time to start a musical program in which you would invite various families in your church to present special music in services of worship. We are fortunate in our church because we have a number of sizeable families who are all very musical. Our song "Sometimes" in the *Avery and Marsh Songbook* was written for the Ross Decker family who eventually sang it in a memorable service. Lines of the songs obviously relate to specific members of the family. At this point in our non-sexist climate, some lines are admittedly close to clichés, but then let's face it, a cliché cannot become a cliché unless it fits the majority of people or situations. The father sings the line, "Sometimes after TV viewing," the mother sings, "Sometimes after chicken stewing," the daughter sings, "Sometimes after hair shampooing," and the oldest son sings, "Sometimes after airplane gluing." Obviously these lines can be reversed according to the family situation! (When the Decker's sang this song their second boy stood in front of the piano waiting to sing an "Amen" while the surprise third son, still a baby, sat on the top of the piano staring at accompanist Don, and rocking in an appropriate rhythm.) This song is listed in our songbook as "A Song for a Happy Occasion." What happier occasion can there be than Christmas? Look through the list of families in your congregation to find out what riches you have that you have either forgotten or overlooked.

7. Have people sing carols from their ethnic background

Encourage individuals, groups, or families to each choose a carol to sing in a Christmas service, one representing their ethnic or national origin. Or have different groups sing "Silent Night" on different Sundays in different languages with the appropriate accompaniments.

8. Sing about peace — in Latin

If you want to do a major work with punch, drive, and great music and lyrics, do Vaughan Williams' "Dona Nobis Pacem." It is a really great musical work with the reiterated phrase "Dona nobis pacem" (give us peace) sung in Latin while the rest of the words are by Walt Whitman and selections from scripture. It's hard, very hard. But when the choir gets to know it, they won't forget it.

Other ideas

1. Celebrate the season, not just a day

Each year we remind you and ourselves that there are twelve days of Christmas. Plant this idea early in your congregation's mind, and use the season for a variety of liturgical experiences — some loud and joyful, some quiet and meditative, some disturbing, some pointed outward in service and mission.

2. Come on strong with the Word

There are strong and eloquent texts for this season. Plan how to present them and interpret them boldly and forcefully: Let the words of Zechariah, Isaiah, and Job ring out; let the words of Paul be personal and provocative. Let the Gospel readings grab the imagination. For those lections: Use different readers; let them sound from different places (like the prophets speak from behind the people); use musical backgrounds; use drama to present the Word. And take time for those sermons. In short, focus the church on the Bible. Anchor Christmas in the Book, more than the tree, the candles, or even the songs. We need the Book now, in a confusing time. (And not in a superstitious, simple-minded, idolatrous form.) Get the people to read the stories of Christmas in the pews and at home. Get them to study the lections with you in the classes for adults. Explain the biblical origins of carols, anthems, organ music. Emphasize the singular role of the Book in transforming Christmas from a sentimental, nostalgia trip to a time of renewal.

3. Suggest alternatives to commercialism

Don't just knock commercialism and greed this Christmas, offer alternatives. Offer alternatives to Christmas spending and getting as the season comes near: Mission projects, ways to combat hunger, times of visiting the lonely and suffering, forms of outreach to the unwanted and unattractive. Interpreting at least two of the assigned lectionary texts, leaders of worship in Christmastide might explore the meaning of joy, in contrast to "pleasure" or "comfort" or "escape."

4. Display baby pictures

Have your Sunday school classes make a scrapbook of drawings and paintings of the baby Jesus. Christmas cards will be a great help here. Also add pictures of contemporary babies from foreign lands as well as from the U.S.A. (Remember, to the majority of the world the United States *is* a foreign land!) And pass the scrapbook around in worship services that happen in church school as well as the regular service.

If in Advent you put up pictures and objects relating to preparations for birth on exhibit space in the rear of the church, now add appropriate words for the birth itself. A series of pictures about birth could remind us of the miraculous process that has been photographed so stunningly in a variety of magazine and books. A birth announcement, further write-ins in the Baby Book, can be shown. This would be a lovely time to exhibit pictures of babies born into the church family during Christmastide (if there are any). An exhibit of baby pictures of those born in the past year could be fun. What would be the most fun of all would be for everyone to bring in a baby picture and then have people guess who it is. Even your oldest members may have a baby picture somewhere that would baffle even other elderly members. Celebrate life in honor of Jesus!

5. Explain the Christian names of members

There are many books on how to name the baby (our local library can't keep copies, borrowers always keep them!), that explain this and for children particularly it is an exciting thing to find out that John means "gift of God."

6. Highlight the names and phrases that describe Jesus

There are so many people who still think Christ is Jesus' last name. This would be a good season to go through the list of phrases that are used in the Bible and in hymns to describe Jesus. "Emmanuel" means God with us, for example. Many hymnals have a topical index with a heading "Christ." Under it we find such phrases as Advocate, Our Captain, the Conqueror, the Friend, our Guide, Judge, King, Lamb of God, our Leader, our Life, our Light, Master, our Savior, Shepherd, Son of God, Son of Man, our Teacher, the Way, Prince of Peace, Wonderful Counselor, etc. Just the names themselves can be exhibited or used as thematic material for sermons, as well as for banners, and posters containing a litany of names.

7. Make family Christmas banners

Continuing the Advent idea, suggest that families make a Christmas banner and bring them to church to display. Also suggest they put it in a window at home during the season. For a number of years we have put our Christmas cards up in the windows of our sun porch. Everyone who passes by looks at them and we make sure to put the most obviously religious ones facing the street. It is really a beautiful sight. Of course, the plants die but something has to be sacrificed.

8. Wear white

White? After all the gorgeous colors people are now wearing (they're not just for the birds any more!)? Yes. White is the color for Christmas and Easter and the year that Don showed up in a white shirt and a white tie, it really was electrifying. Or if you normally wear a robe, switch to a white one.

9. Do caroling with a difference

Mix *new* songs of Christmas in with the familiar old carols everyone hears over and over during the season. And do some simple staging of some of the songs. And put the birth of Christ in its biblical context by singing a Good Friday song and an Easter carol along with the songs of Christmas!

10. Use light symbolically

Symbols are important in the church. The fish, for example, is one of the oldest symbols in the church. The Greek word for fish is ICHTHUS. Early Christians who were being persecuted at the time used the fish as a secret sign for recognizing each other and for recognizing Christian homes. They would wear ornaments in the shape of a fish or they would put fish signs over the doors to their homes or as symbols inside the home. One reason for this was probably that several original disciples were fishermen. Moreover, the Greek letters of the word ICHTHUS can be the first letters of words in the Greek phrase "Jesus Christ, God's Son, Savior." So we used the fish, the *Ichthus,* as our symbol for Advent since the focus is on the birth of Jesus.

A key Christmas symbol is *light*. Here are a number of suggestions of how to create forms of this symbol:

- The Christ candle. Many denominational stores sell a variety of Christ candles. Some ornate, some simple. Perhaps somebody in your church who is into candlemaking can make a special candle and somehow use symbols of Christ on the candle itself in some sort of design.
- A spotlight. We have been in some churches that are equipped to have a dramatic spotlight focus down on the altar or Communion table. Once this spotlight has been used and explained, the color can be changed to red for Pentecost as a symbol of the Holy Spirit. If your church can be darkened, it would also be possible to change the color to purple for Lent and green for Epiphany. There is also such a thing as a "blacklight," which really means a bulb that looks purple but brings out white objects and others that have been painted in fluorescent paint. Such a blacklight shining on a prepared cross or chalice might work very well for Holy Week or Good Friday alone.
- A construction with a bulb inside. This is hard to describe but if you have a crafts person or an artist in your congregation let him use his imagination as he creates some abstract or realistic form out of papier-mâché, plastic (preferably translucent), alabaster, or Lucite. Use either a bulb with a battery or plug it in to the electricity in the room, so that there will be an eye-catching symbol of light that will be explained to the congregation.
- Ancient lamps. While Don was in Greece and Italy he obtained two lamps made in the style of the time of New Testament Christians. They both have wicks in them. Vessel lamps like these are surely available in large department stores or specialty shops. You can look these up under "Lamps" in most books on symbols of the church. Lamp oil is needed and you can get it scented or unscented in most drugstores. The light made from burning such a lamp is quite different, we discovered. It also makes smoke, but if it's put on a nonburnable, it's perfectly safe. Several such lamps cannot only make charming decorations in the church;

they can create a bridge to biblical-history and make certain biblical parables come alive. "Keep your lamps burning...." (Fire codes in some communities may prohibit using this idea indoors, but you may find a way to use these lamps outside, near the entrance to the church.)

11. Build a whole service on these little lights of ours

"This Little Light of Mine" has been sung so often in so many churches that many people belittle it. "Brighten the Corner Where You Are" is another song that has had a similar fate. Gather together all the things that you can think of that provide light and create a litany relating the light to Jesus' parables of the seeds and how people listen to the Good News. For instance, get a match, a candle, a sparkler, a flashlight, a tensor light. (What else?) The match lasts maybe five seconds; the candle lasts several hours; the sparkler burns brightly and quickly fades out; the flashlight either needs new batteries or bulbs or is designed to be thrown away when it's worn out; the tensor light gives brighter illumination for a longer period of time but then almost explodes as it goes out. And notice that many lights must be "plugged in," as we must be plugged in to the Word and Spirit. Using quotations from both Old Testament and New Testament that deal with light, a litany can be written in which we confess that some lights (some people's faith and commitment) don't last very long, and also rejoice in the fact that other lights last a long, long time. Either of the songs mentioned above can climax the litany. This program can be done in the daylight but is obviously more exciting and more fun if it's done in a darkened room or sanctuary. This may be a useful presentation for one of those services of Christmastide with the big crowds!

12. Remember prisoners at Christmas

When you go caroling, include stops at the city and county jails. When you pray, pray about prisoners in your own area, youth and adults of your own town who are "in trouble" — not by name, probably, but at least with thoughtful mention of specific reasons for being in jail — stealing, prostitution, drunk driving, non-payment of child support, etc. Also when you pray, pray for those people in the world (thousands, hundreds of thousands?) who are imprisoned and persecuted because of political or religious beliefs.

13. Share hope, identify conflicts

We repeat from a Christmas issue a few years ago the suggestion that you invite your congregation to tell what they hope for. Invite them on Christmas Eve, or Christmas Day, or on January 1 to stand and tell — in a few words — what they hope the future holds, for themselves, for families, for your own church, for the town, the nation, the world. Intersperse these offerings of hope with stanzas of "Joy to the World" or "God Rest Ye Merry Gentlemen."

Another time, invite the congregation to identify forms of conflict, within people and within society, which results from the coming of Christ. Do this in response to the story of Herod and the Flight into Egypt. This may be hard for your people at first, so give them an example and give them time to think.

14. Give new meaning to the candlelight

If you have a ceremony in your Christmas Eve service in which candlelight is spread throughout the congregation, with each person holding a candle, consider how that ceremony may have greater significance. You may wish to suggest that each person light his or her candle as a sign of commitment to make the meaning of Christmas come true by *working* for peace and justice in the world. Or ask the people to think of one specific way they can each make the world brighter for those who suffer around the world — as they light their candles. In Advent, you may have already identified the meaning of the symbol of darkness. Now the candlelight can represent hope for *change,* and not just a pretty and heart-warming sight to us well-fed, free, and comfortable Americans.

15. Pray for those who are afraid

Some analysts of the current world scene believe that much of the trouble around us is caused by the *fear* in people's hearts. (Visitors to Russia, for example, are amazed at the continuing memories Russian people have of the horrors they suffered in World War II, and the fear that war may come to them again.) Many people are afraid of economic problems, others are afraid of personal rejection by a harsh society. Invite two or three people to respond to the Christmas angel's message, "Do not be afraid!" with prayers for those who are. (Let them name what fears they see and know about, without the minister's prompting.) Include these people with their prayers in the service on the Sunday after Christmas.

16. Give some time to Herod

Since Herod figures prominently in the Christmastide readings, give him his due. Have a sermon about him, relating him to movements and moods in the world today: What fears does he represent in us? How are leaders of our world like him? What corrupts civilized governments so they do horrible things, "slaughtering the innocents"? Also in the service, *pray* for leaders of the U.S. government and foreign governments, that they may be free of the insecurity and blindness that motivated Herod, that they may recognize God's action in the world in distinction from human schemes. Pray also about "national security" — that we may know what it is and how to find it, so we won't be resistant to changes in the world God may be initiating. W. H. Auden's long poetic work *Christmas Oratorio: For the Time Being* has a funny and pathetic speech by Herod that may stimulate your thinking about this tragic, misguided figure.

Look for Christmas carols and hymns that mention Herod and those that clearly seem to take seriously the prominence of evil in the world. The issue here, you see, is that the power of evil is dramatized from the beginning of the story of Jesus, and that power is manifest even among sophisticated, well-organized structures like that of the Roman Empire. President Reagan once identified the Soviet Union as an "evil empire"; can the U.S.A. also become an evil empire? Is there such a thing? How does it happen?

"A Day for Herod" may be very appropriate for January 1, as we desire to start a new year with eyes open to the evils around us, among us, and in us. Are Herod and Orwell's "big brother" related in their desire to control their world and their capacity to destroy?

17. Remember the refugees

When they aren't making daily headlines, it is easy to forget that there are millions of homeless, exiled people in the world, and that many of them are knocking at the doors of our own country, and others are waiting in this country for some kind of settlement. Because of Herod, Jesus and his family quickly became refugees, identifying with all those displaced persons of history. So let's pray right after Christmas for the refugees. Is there someone in your congregation or town who has been one and could lead such a prayer with particular authenticity?

91

It may be interesting to dramatize the plight of the Holy Family in their "flight into Egypt" in contemporary terms: Have a mother, father, and baby of your congregation come forward and be introduced as refugees from a current country in turmoil. Then have someone get up and tell all the reasons they should not be admitted to our country — sound reasons about how "we must take care of our own," how jobs are hard to get, etc. Then ask the refugee family to tell their names, and have them say: "My name is Joseph." "My name is Mary, and this is our new baby, whom we have named Jesus." *Then* have prayer for refugees of the world, victims of Herod-like tyrannies.

18. For when Christmas comes on Saturday

When Christmas comes on Saturday, that means three special days in a row: Christmas Eve on Friday, Christmas Day on Saturday, and the first Sunday of Christmastide is on December 26. Plan with your congregation and choirs for a special kind of service on that Sunday, not just something humdrum for "the Sunday after Christmas" with its anticipated letdown. Do something extraordinary and highly participatory, but don't just try to sustain the volume and vigor of Christmas one more Sunday. (Times of sharing by family groups? Long silences? A mission-emphasis day?) And also plan carefully for the first Sunday of the New Year, on the ninth day of Christmas, January 2. It can be a great day, with New Year's Eve behind us and with the restfulness of New Year's Day also behind us. What can happen on January 2? Think about it.

19. For when Christmas comes on Sunday

Some of your churches may be used to Christmas Day services, but for many of us that's a special concern when Christmas comes on Sunday. What shall we do? You could try making the Christmas Eve service shorter and a bit more simply focused, a candlelight Communion service with not so much pageantry as usual. Then make the Christmas Day — Sunday — service a "family event" with much participation and joy and physical action. And promote and talk about these services in advance more than usual, so people can plan their gift-openings and family trips accordingly.

Worshiping During Epiphany

Epiphany is most readily thought of as the season of illumination. As traditionally observed, these Sundays which follow the twelve days of Christmas set forth the message of Christ as "the light of the world," the revelation of God amid human darkness, the appearance (epiphany) of God's love and power in the human scene. Whether or not you observe all the seasons of the church year consistently, whether or not you regularly deal very much with the whole idea of Epiphany as a season, we recommend strongly the themes and theme passages this season holds for us.

Depending on when Easter falls each year, the number of Sundays following the day of Epiphany until the beginning of Lent varies between five and nine.

As we think about Jesus as the light of the world, our thoughts naturally move to the question of how this happens, that is, to *evangelism* and to *mission*. These Sundays are a good time to stress the outreach of the church, the world ministry of the church, as we try to relate the Christmas gospel to the challenge of the new year. Let your prayers, your announcements, your music, and your sermons respond to or contain this concern.

And so we move on to Epiphany. MOVE ON! to Epiphany. Get going! The hottest season, which has so much ground to cover in such a short time. And it's a season of variable length. So we have to cover the ground in a period of nine Sundays at most. And what is it we have to cover? Well, first of all we start with the Wise Men, the Magi, the kings. Call them what you will, they are the visitors from foreign lands who upon finding the baby Jesus, worship him for what he is going to be, not what they see before them at the moment, a baby. Their gifts are gifts to be used in the future when he has grown up to being what has been destined for him by God. They waste no time with his cuteness, his mildness. They recognize the future leader and savior. And having worshiped him, they don't dawdle around with King Herod, but hightail it back to where they came from. And so they have become symbols of the mission of the Church, the moving out to tell others what they have seen and heard.

That story takes one Sunday and in a few short weeks we have to deal with Jesus' Transfiguration, the moment when Peter, James, and John see what and who Jesus is — and he is a fully grown man with twelve busy helpers, the disciples. The Baptism, John's shouting in the desert, Jesus doing miracles, getting into trouble by preaching at home, gathering his close friends and followers, and so forth: That's a lot of material to dig into so we can't linger too long on anything. Perhaps this is why for many church people Epiphany is the forgotten season. We call it the Season of the Star, Season of the Kings, Season of the Manifestation, Season of ... ?

We like to imagine singing the carol "We Three Kings" in the usual slow tempo as we celebrate the coming of the Magi. We then imagine doing an extra verse about their *leaving* in a different, a faster tempo. And explain to the congregation the need to get back and tell the world. If you do this, add percussion in a double meter underneath to emphasize the sense of urgency. In fact, it might be very interesting to talk to the percussion man/group in your church (come, come, if you don't have one, it's time to get one) about working out some drumbeats that could become the background sounds for Epiphany in your church. Each service would start with the soft drumbeats in the distance (sometimes called the balcony), even before the organ prelude. This would encourage the organist to look for different sorts of musical material for all three expected places in the service. Each service should probably end with the drumbeats, after the postlude, hurrying the worshipers on to their planning meetings, their dinners, and linking nicely with the football games on television. If they noticed the excitement of the crowds and the bands on television were an extension of what they just heard at church, they might think: "Hey, the church has something to do with this outer world. Now then, what was it we were all excited about?" If that happens, we're a step ahead.

As we think about it, it wouldn't be a bad idea to start the drumbeat in Advent, building to a shouted series of responses: "He's on his way!" and "He's getting nearer!" and "He's only a shout away!" and "He's just about here!" to "He's here!" Each of these would lead into a service that dealt with the tempo of necessity, of hope about to be realized, the culmination of dreams both personal and public. If you have not only a good percussionist but a set of tympani, you're on your way! Move it, and God be with you!

Epiphany themes

The season of Epiphany can be a very *stimulating* season, as we focus on the emergence of the revolutionary figure of Jesus himself, without the pious and mystical and otherworldly accretions of later thought and belief. The texts of the season may ask more questions and raise more challenges rather than give answers, comforts, or resting places. So be it.

Here are themes commonly raised by the lectionary readings during Epiphany:

1. Unity and reconciliation, the gathering of God's scattered people

This theme moves us to plan for a series of prayers for the unity of our own church, the whole church with its many denominations, and the world — perhaps a different prayer for unity each week of the season. We are also moved to think hard about the unity of our own congregation. According to a recent exposition of the early chapters of 1 Corinthians, God does not expect an elimination of our differences but enables us to love each other *with* our differences within the body of Christ. Does this happen in our church? In yours?

2. Justice and liberation

Whatever we think of the so-called "liberation theology" (which some people have dismissed without knowing anything about), the passages assigned for these weeks demand our concern for the freedom of the oppressed and imprisoned. What is our church doing specifically to accomplish what the Bible demands? What is yours doing?

3. God's coming to us and our quest for meaning

Certain of the assigned Gospel readings and many other texts having to do with the start of Jesus' ministry show how he appeared to eager people, longing people, suffering people. This moves us to ask about the appearance (epiphany) of our particular congregation of the body of Christ to our community. When people of the town see us, do they see him revealed? How about your congregation? The scriptures move us to appraise the forms that longing for God may take among people of our community: What are the signs of the quest for God among people outside the churches — intellectual struggle? Involvement in cults and lodges?

Using art in Epiphany

Art, which for centuries has been supported primarily by the church, is at last back and thriving after years of absence. This will not be news to many of you, but we want to look at this fact from a slightly different angle. Epiphany, which invites us to focus on Jesus' life and ministry, is a good time to bring great works of art to your members' attention, for much of it, particularly the works of the old masters, portrays scenes from Jesus' life.

For a long time we all have been using the various forms of art as an essential part of our church school programs. In the earliest grades the emphasis has been on art, since the children are more accomplished with pictures than they are with words. But there has been a tendency to drop art from class procedure when the child becomes more word conscious; then it is often picked up as an extracurricular program for adults. Too often these programs are merely for the adults to have fun and not primarily as a method for significant self-expression or for exploring ideas. Serious artists — by which we mean professional artists and even many Sunday artists — don't think of art just as fun or something to pass the time. They are using whatever techniques they already know and can learn to communicate a perception of the complexity of reality. We cannot always stay in the artistic nursery.

Pick art carefully. Much Christian art of our time is, in a single word, atrocious. It is sweet, sentimental, precious, shallow, and often unbiblical as it prettifies the strong concepts of Jesus. It is also often garish and unreal, abstracting faith from reality. This is probably due in part to the fact that many book, music, and art stores want to have some inexpensively made things to sell, like gaudy pictures or statues of Jesus, Mary, Moses, et al, made of plaster-of-paris and with little imagination or insight. Those of you who have traveled to Italy know very well what we mean when you remember the hideous, cheap imitations, expensively priced, outside cathedrals and museums that house some of the great Christian artwork of our time.

Because for the most part the church is not serious about art, we are giving children of all ages terribly low standards, as they will generally accept any "religious" picture or statuette that we present to them. Museums around the world are crowded daily with people who are looking at paintings and sculptures that are very complex and they are paying extra money to have these explained to them. Depth is not come by easily, but it's worth the digging. So many of us spend quite a bit of money buying lots and lots of little pieces of art, like dozens of cute, little porcelain kitty cats. Much more can be learned and enjoyed if that same amount of money is spent on just one more complex, challenging, or original piece. (It also saves an awful lot of dusting.)

Many churches not only have a variety of art courses available to members of the congregation and of the community outside, but also have annual art shows to which lots and lots of people come. Artists outside the church are suddenly being encouraged by the church both by word and by money. We have seen some church art shows that have very demanding standards, and only very good work is exhibited. Excellence is no longer a snobbish or a bad word. Not every piece of childish play-dough is put on a pedestal and revered as a religious statement. If you think we are being unkind, remember that Jesus picked up a whip and started knocking over tables in the Temple courtyard bellowing to those people who were trying to make money by exploiting religious impulses of the people of the community. If Jesus did not accept every so-called religious practice, why should his church?

At one time there was no subject that was not available to artists in the church. All of the seven deadly sins were open subject matter to artists of all kinds, as well as the seven joys. We have gone

95

through a number of periods in which the ugliness of the world has been kept from the churchgoer as if the time spent outside the church was a time in which they wore religious blinders. We are living in a time now where most Christian people are forced to look at the world as it is, in light of their faith. And we are taking humanity itself more seriously and joyfully. This is one of the reasons serious artists are interested in doing work for the church now.

For example, in our Christmas dance performance of Lloyd Pfautsch's *A Day For Dancing,* the early carol "Adam lay ybouden" dealt lyrically and physically with God's gift of sex as the way for the human family to recreate itself. Our church is a small one in a small town and there were a few, but only a very few, comments such as: "Wasn't that a little bit too sexy for the sanctuary?" Our answer was: "In the sanctuary we deal with everything in the context of the Christ experience in God's world. It seems ungrateful to God to dismiss his good gifts as 'naughty.' And we can't imagine anything more frustrating or debilitating than always having to sugarcoat any real experiences." The arts, all of them, can and should be used as methods whereby our lives are illuminated, or as Isaiah said it: "The eyes of the blind shall be opened, the ears of the deaf unstopped."

Using music in Epiphany

We have had so many cards and letters about the problems of *getting music* we have recommended, that we are going to take time right now to deal with the problem.

It has come to our attention that many dealers (music stores) do not keep enough music in stock because of limitations of space, and that they are also tired of or annoyed at ordering small quantities from publishers. The publishers themselves do not mind getting small orders; they literally thrive on it. So we suggest writing directly to the publishers themselves. Find the address on the music. If the publishers tell you themselves that the piece you are interested in is out of print, ask them for permission to make copies of that out-of-print selection including the following statement: "Copied by permission of the publishers." Or check with other churches for copies.

1. Put up a display about music
As part of our theme of illumination we suggest this is a good season to put up a display about music. Here is a possible list of headings and categories:
- **From these comes music** ... and have some instruments including some organ pipes in a display.
- **From this comes music** ... and exhibit copies of music written from ancient times to some anthems that have electronic sounds indicated in them.
- **From them comes music** ... pictures of living and deceased composers with a copy of a hymn or anthem by each that your church has done. Writing to living composers for pictures for such an exhibit can be fun. One catalog of Contemporary Music put out by C. F. Peters, New York (718-416-7800. www.edition-peters.com/home.html) has facsimiles of statements in the composers' handwriting. A marvelous and moving sight to see!
- **From here comes music** ... and have a Bible open to, a Psalm or to a scriptural passage that has been set to music with a copy of the setting beside it.
- **From those comes music** ... and have pictures of the choirs and ringers and instrumentalists of your church with their names.
- **But the music is in the *hearing and the singing*!** ... and have pictures of the congregation listening to the choir and singing themselves.

Have different members of the music program of your church work on the display. It can be an exciting and stimulating project for the group as a whole. Their history and the history of how music is a part of the illumination of God's Word in God's world can be a treat for the whole church fellowship. Enjoy it!

2. Greet the composer

There is a national music organization called Meet the Composer, so we choose to title this idea as we did. We have a moment each Sunday in our worship service where we meet and greet each other in the congregation, usually with a specific sentence Dick as preacher has suggested. Here, in this idea, we are suggesting that we take time to greet the composer whether the composer is there in body or only in spirit. Perhaps it would be even better to *thank* the composer (and lyricist, or perhaps this should be done at a different time). We, the congregation, so quickly forget the composers of our favorite hymns as well as those we join in on but do not consider our favorites.

Who wrote "Beneath the Cross of Jesus" and "How Great Thou Art" and "Fairest Lord Jesus" and "Be Thou My Vision"? Does it matter? Yes. And we don't say this because we are composers. Our church has a tendency to thank everyone for something well done (or even done, period). But the composer is given short shrift because we do not remember that some member of a congregation in the past wrote for their church a special song that was taken up by other congregations until it became a popular hymn and it was published in a hymnal. Since we do spend a lot of time and money on music in and for the church, let's be a little nicer about giving thanks to those who created it. Many people say that it was a gift from God, but it did come *through* some person.

Don often told his father that he was leaving not children but songs behind him, children that did not cause many problems in the world nor take up too much food and space. Composer Gilbert Martin, who led one of our "At Home with Avery and Marsh" Musical Workshops, was very proud in showing off his growing photograph collection of his children, his songs and anthems. He told us how they were conceived, how they grew and how they developed through agony and love into the creations we saw before us. When you hear a composer say: "And then I wrote ..." don't groan unless you groan when a parent or grandparent pulls out the raft of baby pictures they want you to see. Take time to be nice, and it may turn out to be a holy time.

3. Perform music from Gil Martin

One of Gilbert Martin's beautiful selections is called "The Jesus Gift" and is very, very right for this season of the church year. Look at the words of the beginning for a moment and relate it to your own child as the possibility of spoiling your child rotten creeps into your unconscious (ha ha; sure, unconscious) mind:

> Shall I gather em'ralds, shall I bring him gold?
> Shall I shower diamonds, white-hard, bright-cold?
> Shall I spangle jewels like stars above?
> (And the choir answers the soloist's queries with)
> Give him laughter, bring peace-filled laughter,
> Offer him warm laughter and love.

"Of course," you might say. But you say that only because it's so real and so natural you assumed it was *always there.* Lovely, expensive words set to a glowing, contagious melody and you will be singing it, every now and then, for the rest of your life.

Gil told us that he has lots of "oo's" in his choral arrangements. He's been told that some choirs sing "ah" or "oh" instead and he says that's all right. But he means "oo." And we know why, though he may not. The simple reason is that so much of his composed music as well as arranged melodies by others, known and unknown, are so *gorgeous* that "oo" is the only response. Think about that and tell your choir or congregation and we bet you that they sing it differently.

His Christmas and Epiphany anthems include "The Love Carol," "The Mystery, Miracle Moment" which includes a reader's part, "This Perfect Stranger," and "When Christ Was Born of Mary Free." Have a Martin Christmas; it will be memorable.

"I'm But A Stranger Here" has an opening solo that fits right in to the Temptations of Jesus which are considered in Epiphany:

> I'm but a stranger, here, (he sings in the desert)
> Heaven is my home.
> Earth is a desert drear, heaven is my home.
> Danger and sorrow stand round me on ev'ry hand (hunger, power, Satan)
> Heaven is my father-land (a whole new meaning in context), heav'n is my home,
> Oh, heaven, heav'n is my home.

All of these splendid anthems of Gil's are published by Hinshaw Music (www.hinshawmusic.com).

4. Use star songs

"Without a Star to Follow" is a short, responsive song that admits that we are lost without a light to lead us. It mentions some of the things that can divert us and seduce us from following the star and reminds us that we have the real Star, Jesus, to follow all life long.

"Follow the Star" is another short song, which asserts that we find our true identity as we follow Jesus. Both of these songs can unite the congregation in thoughtful expectation, we have found.

Both songs are from our collection, *Songs for All Seasons*, which is offered as a supplement to your regular hymnal. In other words, we wrote the songs and hymns in the collection to be sung by the congregation, by all ages together. Obviously they can be sung as solos, duets, small group presentations, but they are basically for the whole congregation, the "larger choir."

Sermon and scripture

1. Talk about how Christ answers needs

In many churches, Epiphany has long been the season of greatest emphasis on the world mission of the church, a mission first represented by the Three Magi from the East. A profound examination of this story and others of the Sundays after Epiphany can get at the question of how Christ answers the needs and problems of the present world. What were the Wise Men seeking? Did they find it? What does it mean to call Jesus *Messiah* today? Can he really be the "Light of the World" today?

In this world-context we prepare for Christmas and think about Epiphany and their symbols of light and their messages of hope. And even more than biblical writers could imagine, the destinies of nations and parts of the globe are bound up with other nations and parts; inextricably, for good or ill, we cannot be separate.

No, the meanings and concerns of these sacred seasons are not *just* global, political, social. Nor should these dimensions make for services heavy with gloom or guilt or hour-long seriousness; as if they could. Christmas should still be merry and full of laughter, and it will be. And Epiphany should still be a season of exuberance, and it will be. But don't forget the world, the real world.

God didn't.

2. Identify the situations of injustice

In a way similar to No. 1 above, or in a sermon, invite the members of the congregation to pinpoint as many kinds of injustice in your own community or within their larger environment as they can. Acknowledge for the folks that there will be differences of opinion about what is injustice and what is "just deserts" or self-inflicted trouble. The important thing is to get people thinking and have them do the identifying, and not the preacher or other leader of worship. Do this in relation to the readings of Isaiah 58 or Isaiah 42 or similar readings.

Other ideas

1. Name your differences

This will be a bold gesture but a biblical one. Invite the congregation, as a preparation for prayer, to list specifically all the differences among them: political differences — "some of us are Republicans, some Democrats, some real Liberals, some real Conservatives, some pretty Radical" — differences of theological opinions ... differences of personal style ... all they can possibly think of. Then pray for ability to love and respect each other, and for your corporate life to be enriched by these differences rather than held back.

2. Make stars for the sanctuary

The main symbol for Epiphany is the star, and we are having the whole church school make stars. We have discovered a new thing to do with the tops and bottoms of tin cans, all sizes. Ask the congregation to collect them. Then cut star shapes from them with heavy cutting scissors: five-pointed, six-pointed, off-shaped — use your imagination. Hang them in the sanctuary and as they turn in response to gravity or candle flames and smoke they will pick up light.

3. Create a teaching space in the sanctuary

Our choir loft has an arch about twenty feet above the floor. There is about a fifteen-inch deep space from the top of the arch to the ceiling behind it that hides the lights from the congregation. It suddenly occurred to us that putting a pole as wide as the choir loft up in that hidden space would give us a way to hang all sorts of arts and crafts and even screens for projecting slides. So we gathered a group of teenagers (two) who love to work with tools and lights and ropes and wood and they figured out a pulley system so we could put up that long pole and take it down easily to change the exhibits.

Our first use of it was on the First Sunday after the Epiphany. The entire church school had made stars out of tops of tin cans, had colored them with magic markers, and in some cases applied glitter. At the end of the church school time on that given morning, everybody gathered in the sanctuary not to do "the hanging of the greens" but the "hanging of the stars." There was one large star, looking a great deal like an explosion, that was vaguely five-pointed, and then there were about seventy stars in a variety of shapes that dangled and jiggled and turned and glittered as Dick preached about the baby in the manger who was going to light up the world. He used the decoration somehow in each of the services of Epiphany and now our congregation knows the symbol of the star.

And, what's more, the children do, too. And they also felt a great pride in ownership: "That's my star, the green one that looks like a fish," said a proud creator. These were removed and nothing was hung until Pentecost, at which time the church school hung their multi-colored Tongues of Fire, which hovered mysteriously over the heads of the choir. Examine your sanctuary to see if there is a place that you might use more fruitfully in communicating the Bible, the Word, the gospel — with symbols made by the members of the church school and the congregation.

4. Try blinking stars

On a large sheet of poster board, draw a series of stars over each other — black ... red ... blue. One star should be in red, another in blue, another in green, one in black. Then set up floodlights of each of the colors you have included in your large drawing and put blinker discs in the sockets. (We don't know what they are called, but they are things that make whatever light you have them attached to blink at regular intervals. Check with your local electric appliance store.) When the red light is on, the red star will vanish; when the blue the blue, etc., etc. The large star will look like it's blinking as it changes shape and form before you. (Pastors may want to turn them off during the sermon, but only with the risk of losing the children!)

5. Affirm and encourage male participation

One of the major historic realities of the past 150 years of the church is the disproportionate abandoning of the church by men. In many, many, many places there are almost twice as many women as men in the church. The reasons for this go back at least to the nineteenth century, to patterns of society and church life of which we are the inheritors and victims. Now, in an age where the role of women is being asserted, we must not fail to include and encourage all kinds of men to participate at all levels of church life.

As you plan worship, consider: Men and their unique roles and current concerns and problems should be prayed about and taken up in preaching, and ordinary men — including "blue collar" types — should be "up front" in positions of liturgical leadership. Regarding style, while the church is in error if it reinforces the *macho* image of masculinity, it is also in error to make Christianity a soft, irrelevant, sentimental, and effete way of doing things. Let's have more on this subject in later issues.

6. Hold a "Festival of Baptism"

Or call it "A Water Festival." On the First Sunday after Epiphany, celebrate the Baptism of Jesus, with due festivity and seriousness. In the history of worship, Jesus' baptism rather than the Magi was the focal point of the season after Christmas. And, God knows, we need all the help we can claim for ourselves in understanding and acting upon the meaning of baptism.

First, schedule baptisms that day.

Second, turn loose your creative people in the church with the theme of *water,* especially its cleansing and renewing power, and the symbolic meaning of crossings of water — seas, rivers — as experiences in our lives.

Third, let that group and other groups in your church study the Bible's water crossings and other "types" or metaphorical antecedents aid explanations of meaning for baptism. That curriculum for study should obviously include the Red Sea crossing, the Jordan crossing, Psalms that refer to parting of waters, Isaiah 43, and other passages in the Old Testament and Paul's teachings as found in Romans 6 and elsewhere. Then there are John's references to "water and the Spirit."

Fourth, let groups studying about water and baptism prepare litanies, prayers, or some other form of reports — banners? posters? pantomimes? — which present their findings, and plan to include these in the "Festival of Water" service. For example, we have done a large and joyful and interesting pantomime, involving a large group of people, of the Crossing of the Red Sea, using the aisle of the church and having a lead actor as Moses responding to Exodus 14 as it is read.

Fifth, have children cut out all the pictures of water they can find in magazines and other sources and put them all over your church building for that Sunday (and maybe the Sunday before as promotion of interest leading up to "Water Sunday"). Big pictures, small pictures: Water all around!

Sixth, plan a Reaffirmation of Baptism, or a "Remember Your Baptism" ceremony. In the service ask people who were not baptized in your church building to tell where they were baptized, at least any persons who were baptized in unusual places or situations. Ask them to remember *who* baptized them, and have a moment of silence for all to thank God for the minister who did it. Then, when you have the Sacrament of Baptism in the service, reclaim the medieval custom and let everybody be splashed! Have the minister take a bowl of water and go up and down the aisles throwing handfuls of water over the people's heads, calling out "Remember your baptism!" (Do announce that it is an old, old tradition, so they won't think it's just a new, crazy idea.)

But that splashing ritual should probably follow a time of solemn and serious commitment to the meaning of baptism as a source and sign of identity. Perhaps this can happen in silent prayer; perhaps with a show of hands as the congregation is invited to rededicate their lives to live out their baptism; perhaps — in smaller churches — with all the congregation gathering around the baptismal font. Or — what other way can you think of?

Then follow the splashing with all rising to declare, with hands on their heads, "I am baptized! I am chosen! I belong to Jesus Christ," then have them mark their neighbors' foreheads with the sign of the cross.

Finally, we still will have no great number of songs to recommend about baptism, because there are very few old ones which serve us well as we celebrate this Sacrament, and few new songs have been written, apparently, about its meaning. So we must still suggest our own "Passed Through the Waters" (in the first *Avery and Marsh Songbook*) ... and what others? Yes, there are several hymns about the baptism of children, and many hymns about personal dedication, but few about the biblical meanings of the sacrament. Check all the hymnals you can find.

Such a "Water Service" would be quite appropriate, of course, for an ecumenical gathering, as we remember Ephesians 4: "There is one baptism." And it may be a strong beginning for any season of emphasis on the mission of the congregation.

7. Respond to what's happening in the marketplace

We recently had a long strike among supermarket workers in our area. It was a tough time for the workers, their families, the customers, and the managers of the stores. So we had a person in our congregation who was not directly involved but was sensitive to the issues pray about that strike. In the same way, it is important to respond in prayer to food prices, to the failures of businesses and industries in our area, to new economic developments that raise the morale and well-being of people and to other kinds of critical changes in your community. And let the responses be prepared and led by lay people who know about them and are somehow affected by them.

8. Pray often for those who don't believe

Especially on the Sundays after Epiphany, when we think about the church's mission, have prayers for people in your city and in the world who just haven't responded to the Gospel of Jesus Christ. Have the prayers led by a variety of people and ages.

9. Celebrate baptism as an initiation to ministry

Early in the season of Epiphany we are called by the story of Jesus' baptism, a traditional focal point for the start of the season, to consider the meaning of our own baptism. In keeping with the emphases of Epiphany, let's identify our baptisms as *baptism to ministry in the world*. If you have baptisms on the day you read the lection about Jesus at the Jordan, take the opportunity to explain the sacrament as a commissioning to make a difference in the world. Some people we meet still seem to think of baptism as something you have done to be marked for heaven instead of hell after death, or as a "nice" thing, like having good family connections or a pretty home. Instead, relate baptism to issues of social justice and community ministry in prayers of concern in the same service. ("As your baptized people, dear God, may we stand alongside the poor and rejected; may we vote according to your will for our governments and not according to human judgment ..." etc.)

10. Invite a couple to share their "encounter"

Marriage Encounter is a growing movement and a source of rich blessing for many couples. Let other couples, old and young, share the blessings: Invite a husband and wife who have been on a Marriage Encounter weekend recently to report for five minutes in a service on their experience, as a way of pointing beyond the contemporary chaos and tension of many marriages to other possibilities. Marriage is a place we need to encounter the living Lord of Epiphany.

11. Present meditations on the Lord's Prayer

In a time of prayer let the pastor say a phrase of the Lord's Prayer and a lay person read a personal interpretation of that phrase, a short paragraph of his or her own composition, also in the form of prayer. Go phrase by phrase in this way through the prayer, perhaps alternating between a man and a woman doing the interpreting. Then, at the end, let all unite in praying the prayer slowly and thoughtfully.

Worshiping During Lent

In Christmastide we sang:

> Fill full your hearts and minds, your hearts and minds
> Fill full of joy!
> Past promises and present possibilities meet in this crying baby boy
> He cries for love, he cries for care, he cries for tenderness;
>   As he *will* cry *throughout his life* in city and in wilderness.

And now we come to Lent, the season in which we remember how he cried, *against* whom he cried, and *for* whom he cried. Perhaps this year, as we look deeply into the scriptures for the season and plan worship, we need to stop and consider our own crying. Consider how we cry — or don't cry — about our own sins and our involvement in evil ways of the world; consider our crying for pain that is being inflicted on the world — the many by the few; and consider our crying out to those inflictors, whether they be our own people or those labeled as the enemy — our crying out "Stop!" We have cried for ourselves in the past, the cries of self-pity, the cries of pain for our own injuries, and we shall continue to do so, since we are human beings. But one of the differences between Christians and non-Christians is that followers of the Master do not just cry for themselves.

Let one major concern of this season be *true repentance*, our sincere crying out in remorse for our real sins against others, including the sins of our nations and our groups. And then consider: Have we been crying as Jesus did over Jerusalem because of what has happened to the city of humanity? Have we cried out for what is happening to the wilderness? Have our cries, private as well as covenantal cries, been heard by the people who should hear them? As Christian congregations we need to exercise our prophetic lungs as well as our priestly hands.

In the musical *Fantasticks* the cries of the people being burned and tortured are covered by pretty music, waltzes, and personal pleasures. Is that a true, rather than fantastic, picture of us, of our churches? Particularly of us Americans?

Lent is often a time to think back, to evaluate our lives, to examine ourselves. And that is most appropriate. Lent is also often a time to look back at the old story of Jesus' suffering and death. And that is also most appropriate. But Lent should be loaded with thinking about the future. We know historically that the crucifixion was inevitable. But must there always be crucifixions in the future? Must history repeat itself? Is the Christian making a difference in the world? Are we among the complainers or the shapers, the watchers or the workers?

As we relate the old stories of Jesus and as we consider our own sins and the evils of the past, let another theme of Lent this year be the issue of *power*. Many of the scriptures for the season, pose the problem of the corruption brought by power, e.g. as Jesus confronts the leaders of his time. In our time there is also suspicion that national leaders are often prone to play power games while the common people want only to go on with their lives and be friends with peoples of other nations. Are there similar issues in the "world of religion" — among church leaders, hierarchies, and in centers of scholarship? Does wealth corrupt the churches of America? Does the economic power in which we Christians are inextricably bound in the U.S.A. bar us from covenantal relationships with the rest of humanity? If the Gospel is the story of salvation through the "weakness of God" in the "suffering Servant" — where does that leave us who are among the powerful, the confident, the strong, the assertive, the comfortable?

A third theme for possible focus in Lent is *the encounter of newness* with old patterns of sin and death. In the biblical stories of the healing of the blind man, the dialogue of Jesus with the Samaritan woman, the raising of Lazarus, and Triumphal Entry, we behold the breakthrough of new realities into human experience — often to the shock and dismay of the powerful and even the victims themselves. The Easter hymn which announces "'Tis the Spring of Souls Today" summarize this Lenten theme nicely, for these Lenten stories are "Previews of Coming Attractions" in relation to the Easter Gospel of an open future.

In a book we highly recommend, *Social Themes of the Christian Year* (edited by Dieter T. Hessel, published by Geneva Press), Walter Brueggeman expounds of this *old situation/breakpoint/ new situation* sequence in his chapter on Lent. In this holy season let us think hard about the "breakpoint" and the emergence of the "new situation" in our worship, our preaching, and all our church experience.

As we read through these assigned passages for the season, we find ourselves wondering once again about our own expectations for the worship experience. Not that we should have "goals for worship" — that's the business of the Holy Spirit; worship is an end in itself. But do we expect things to happen on a particular Sunday? Do we expect people to be *changed?* Do we have faith in the Spirit to move and transform and renew us? The thoughtful Hollywood preacher Lloyd Ogilvie said it in our hearing recently: What happens to people on Sunday morning may correspond rather directly to what the preacher expects to happen! Do we hope for change in ourselves and others as we encounter the living God? Lent, as a time of personal introspection and evaluation, is a time for worship leaders to face such questions.

A general suggestion for the season is that you give the congregation the opportunity to come to know the whole story of the life of Jesus and of the content of the whole Bible. Lent, with its emphasis on discipline, is a natural time to encourage systematic Bible reading and to relate the Sunday service to the reading of scripture done at home. Urge your people to read one of the Gospels exclusively through the season, then use it in your services. Continue to outline for your people the sequence of events in the life of Jesus during the whole three years of his ministry. Sing hymns about him, meditate on his experiences, study about what he did for people and to people, assuming that many people really don't know the story.

The theme of sacrifice

Since sacrifice is so often considered the main theme of Lent, it deserves special attention here.

First, let's focus clearly in our worship on the sacrificial life and death of Jesus himself. Not just grimly, not with morbid interest, but not sentimentally either, as if it's all sweet and tear-jerking. And let's move beyond the often-empty clichés of "he died for me" and "saved by his atoning death" to clarity. What do these words really mean? *How* did his dying save us, and what does it represent in the (political, social, personal) history of the world? Not only must the centrality of the cross be a basic issue in the church, but we must also strive for clear understanding of what happened and why and what it does for us. In sermons, prayers, explanations of hymns, testimonies, anthems, let there be clarity about the death of Christ and the meaning of salvation.

Furthermore, what can we learn from his sacrificial lifestyle about our own lives? What sacrifices does he ask of us? What is gained when we relate the simple life, the poverty and humility of

Christ to our own lifestyles, and to the decision-making of the church? What differences in our values are made when we start taking the demands of Christ with complete seriousness? What sacrifices must we make when we try to follow him who "has nowhere to lay his head"?

What this theme of sacrifice means for Lenten worship we aren't sure, except for a few tentative ideas:

- Our *forms* of worship must always be seen as temporary, not of the substance, not a "lasting city to dwell in." We must travel light.
- The harsh demands of the Gospel must never be soft-pedaled in our services; the distinctions between the kingdom and the world never watered-down.
- The cross — in words, music, architecture, and drama — must be our central reality.
- We must seek out materials for preaching, prayers, music, and all parts of worship from Christians of other countries, other cultures.
- Joy and beauty are to be seen as essential but *not all there is* to worship. Just as joy may be unbridled, there may properly be very intense struggle and honestly traumatic penitence in a Christian service. "We're here to be happy" but we're also "here to be *moved*" — says one of our songs.
- Worship should rarely, if ever, be luxurious, posh, steeped in human glory. Leave the high-priced vestments to the lodges, leave the deep carpets to the country club, leave the regular paying of singers to the television producers, leave the high-priced printing of glossy, throw-away bulletins to the government.

More personally, the theme of sacrifice speaks to us about our own egos. We are called as leaders of worship, choirs, and organists and all, not to exalt ourselves, but God; not to win approval, but to win people to the cause of Christ; not to advance our own salaries or status or popularity but to advance the church's mission of compassion and justice.

Always, as we enter with vigor the way of sacrifice, we shall find that we gain instead of lose, live more fully as we die. This is ultimately an affirmative theme.

What follows are some specific ideas for the sacrifice theme:

1. Let the lectionary set the mood

Let us keep in mind that the way of *sacrifice* is still the Christian way, the hard way leading to eventual victory, a pattern hardly more popular in the church than outside it. So let prayers and hymns of the Lenten services take their thrust and direction from the strong Gospel lections. Let anthems be chosen carefully to illuminate these texts, or to "bounce off" them. Plan. (Don't have the choir singing "Soft Were Thy Hands, Dear Jesus" just before the story of Jesus cleansing the temple!)

2. Add "taking on" to "giving up"

Since Lent is traditionally a time for "giving up" something for a season, take the opportunity to consider both *"giving up"* and *"taking on."* We are thinking in particular of the misuse of alcohol, a problem that is increasing among the people of the world in an alarming rate. We are also thinking that more and more Christians seem to be willing to "take on" the responsibility for particular neighbors in the world, their economic plight, and their need for friendship. Both of these themes of Lent can enrich the Sunday morning service.

3. Sacrifice for others

Lent is probably known most widely to millions of people as the time to give up smoking or drinking. Let us consider this a moment and see what some of the other, less self-centered possibilities might be. We may get to be known by what we give up, by something that makes relatively little difference to anyone except the person who is making the sacrifice. Smoking, for instance, is often given up by the person who knows she shouldn't smoke because it's bad for her health and God knows she's tried but she has to have something to do with her hands and besides cigarettes are relaxing and if she stopped can you imagine the weight she would put on and you know where. Very seldom is it given up because it's not good for the people *around* the smoker. The real man doesn't smoke; he doesn't need to because he's secure. The woman for others doesn't smoke, because she also is for others and for herself.

If this larger reason for giving up smoking is tried perhaps there will be fewer returns to it with a passion after Jesus' Passion is over, and we can get back to the normal (!) Easter world. And one way all of us can share with this person is by giving her the chance to stand up and share her decision in a *Litany of Trial and Denial* in one of the Lenten services of worship.

4. Try good-mouthing

Another marvelous thing to give up during Lent is gossip, or as our secretary says, "Bad-mouthing people." We know of a church where there is a lot of behind-the-scenes aggravation happening because of a number of people who spend so much active time gossiping because "others really ought to know what's going on with so-and-so and I'd tell it to her face if I ever got the chance and I know this'll never get back to her but something should be done about her and the trouble she's causing doing such awful things to people who are only minding their own business and care a lot more for things than some people we could mention and...." There's another person who is going around deliberately tearing down somebody in the church family, at every opportunity, including worship.

We all fall into these patterns and habits so easily; we need the chance to practice the New Life, the life for others, in which we admit in a *Litany of Confession* that we are trying during Lent to not only *not* gossip but to not start it, by consciously reversing the thing we are about to say.

5. Strengthen the body-temple

We have been told that our bodies are our temple in which and through which the Holy Spirit lives and moves. And look at what we've done to them! Try a *Litany of Expectancy,* a shared time when the worshiping congregation can make decisions and try to stick to them with the help of other members of the church family. Discipline alone is hard; with others it's easier and sometimes even fun. Here are a few suggestions of ways to strengthen the temple:

- The Body — find a friend or two with a mutual sport, like tennis, racquetball, walking, swimming and set *aside time* to do it at least once a week. Don't overdo it. We don't want the temple to be lopsided.
- The Mind — Read a book about something, not escape fiction. The Time-Life series of books on almost every subject in the world is a great place to start looking. Share the reading time with a friend; share the book with him.
- The Heart — read a devotional book (hate that word!). There are lots of them available now, check the church library to read Robert Raines, Frederick Buechner, Lloyd Ogilvie, Gary Demarest, etc.

- The Social Part of You — visit, with a friend, somebody from the church who is shut-in, sick, not coming much, never heard of you. Share part of the conversation at the appropriate time given to such things in your service of worship.
- The Private Part of You — set up a time for you to be alone to think deep thoughts, to pray, to look anew at the world or things that you are taking for granted, to listen hard, a variety of possibilities.
- The Whole You — read the Bible. That sounds so commonplace, so pat. But the Bible can strengthen every part of you. Particularly reading a part that you don't often read, the Prophets, the Song of Songs, Proverbs, Ecclesiastes, Numbers.

Church renewal during Lent (Or, What's the matter with your church?)

"I don't know what's the matter with our people. The attendance had been awful recently, and I'm getting discouraged. The morale is low, and well, frankly, I'm thinking of moving." Have you heard that kind of feeling expressed by neighboring pastors? Being honest, most ministers would admit to having said or at least thought such thoughts at some time themselves. So what *is* the matter with your people, or with that neighboring congregation that is so unresponsive?

Let's look at the issue positively: Where does the renewal of the church begin? What has to happen to "turn a church around" — greater interest, more active involvement, people inviting others, more concern for mission, etc.? Yes, there have been almost as many answers through the years as there have been askers of the questions. Small groups obviously revitalize many churches, so do retreats, and various kinds of lay training events, not to mention the grace-filled crises that can renew people's faith in surprising ways.

As we think about worship, the weekly Sunday worship of the congregation, the question of renewal may come into focus a bit more clearly, but the first answer remains the same. Robert Hudnut, Presbyterian pastor and writer on the renewal of the church, speaks powerfully on a *Thesis* theological cassette, stating that *the renewal of the church begins with the renewal of the pastor.* We presume to believe that the renewal of worship begins also with the renewal of the principal worship leader and preacher. Even more obnoxiously we believe that "What's wrong with our people" or with attendance at worship may be primarily a question of "What's wrong with the pastor?"

At any rate, in Lent, all of us church leaders need to *look at ourselves* with a gracious, but self-critical view, to stop complaining about others and to see where we need to change and grow.

The pastor-member of the team preparing this material knows for sure that the quality of his leadership on Sunday is often directly proportionate to the amount of real praying he has done during the week. And it is also clearly related to the nature of his *personal* struggle with the scripture texts on which the sermon is based. Moreover, the quality of his leadership is also related to his preparation for his own participation as a worshiping person in the Sunday service. This preparation must include time for awareness of personal need and for a "gathering of gratitude" for one's own blessings.

One other less obvious issue in assessing one's leadership is the evaluation of personal strategy. What worked before may not be working here and now. We sometimes meet pastors who are frustrated in their work because things in their present churches are not going like they did in the last position. The problem may be that they are trying to do things in the same way — without listening to the new congregation to find what is really needed and desired. Listening is a large part of the renewal of the church, beginning with the pastor's ability to listen to the people; the customer may be right: desires and opinions of the people may be the voice of God to the leader.

"Business as usual" is a questionable policy for the pastor whose church seems unresponsive. "Full steam ahead and damn the torpedoes!" may indicate a hardheaded, conceited person rather than faithfulness to the true gospel. For example, we often hear people complain around the country that worship is DULL, but that the pastor just goes on doing the same things (though maybe louder and more angrily). Maybe worship is dull because the pastor is no longer excited about God's love! Maybe the pastor's life has lost its zest and interest! Maybe the pastor needs to spend more time with his/her spouse or children or alone with God or playing. On the other hand, maybe the pastor has to work harder at preparation of the service, and more creatively.

Lent is a good time for the hard questions about one's own life, and for changing patterns. At least we may be aware of our own complaints — and turn them back on ourselves. Would *you* want to come to your church every Sunday? Would you want to sit out there and hear your sermons week after week? What feelings would you get out there in the pew if you were watching and listening to yourself lead worship? What kind of person would come across to you if you heard your own prayers or announcements or watched yourself relating to people in the congregation — the old, the young, the new, the grouchy, the hurting? Would you see someone who is close to God and in love with God and delighted about the gospel if you watched yourself?

Using music in Lent

There are so many great chorales and hymns in our various hymnals for Lent that we are so tempted to turn the music for the season into a heavy emotional putdown or "guilt trip." So as you pick your hymns and other music, make sure there is a variety of styles and a variety of content. One song reminding us that we are guilty sinners is enough. Two is barely understandable. Three sets us against the idea and we revolt into indifference. The Good News needs to be sung as well as heard and preached about in Lent. So take time to balance the service and send the people home ready for the week ahead and eager to come back for more next Sunday.

1. Use "Cross-Cry," but sparingly

We recommend one of the great Lenten anthems, Gil Martin's "Cross-Cry." It is tremendously dramatic. It is so dramatic that you should probably not do it except once every five years or so. On the other hand, here is a suggestion of how to do it a bit more often.

First, just do the anthem as written, with a lot of work on the diction so that the powerful words can be understood easily (don't give the solo part to your bass with a wobble!). Make sure the presentation in the worship service has time *after* it for the congregation to absorb it, to say wow! and pray. Preacher, liturgist, don't jump into the announcements! Be sensitive, both to the congregation and to the composer.

Some time later, possibly the next year, *stage* it. There are two ways to stage it. One is to set up friezes of Jesus and people in frozen attitudes, like statues, that either get a light on them for each episode, or have the people move into position before each episode is sung. The other, more complex way, is to have it choreographed and danced by soloist or group. This will take much more work. Both can be equally effective. When we say effective, we mean that those who don't understand words, little children and foreigners, will be able to understand the friezes or the dance. The choreography, we feel, should be very specifically related to the episode. You ask: "What episodes?" The answer:

> I think I heard him say, when he was *strugglin' up the hill.*
> Take my mother home
> ... when they were rafflin' off his clothes ...
> ... when they were liftin' up the cross ...
> ... when they were nailin' in the nails ...
> ... when he was givin' up the ghost ...

All of Gil's splendid anthems are published by Hinshaw Music (www.hinshawmusic.com).

2. Give up "beautiful" music

Since we are talking about Lent and sacrifice, perhaps one of the things the "serious" church should do as fasting is to give up serious music that is merely gorgeous writing of one period or another that doesn't *say* anything. One of our songs, actually a couple or three are not allowed to be done in some churches because of what they say. The words are too direct and some pastors don't want to hear those words and don't want their congregations to hear them regardless of the fact that many in the congregation are already hearing them outside the church and the church is quaintly silent about them. What a sermon! We love the classical sacred music as much as the next parson and person, but Lent is not a time for luxuries. It's a time for testing, a time for passion, a time for musical Gethsemanes and crucifixions. We can't imagine a "beautiful" or "gorgeous" song about the crucifixion. Excruciating, yes. Not to wallow in the guilt as some people may like to believe, but to remind us of the "pay off" to the fantastic "gift" we were given at Christmas, that living, fleshly child who so painfully gave this life so that we could rejoice, expensively, not cheaply; seriously, not wantonly; in exile and in community.

3. Sing and stage "I Wonder Why"

Throughout the season, Sunday after Sunday, or in one particular program or on Palm Sunday or during Holy Week, sing and stage with "living statues" our song "I Wonder Why?" (No. 46 in the *Avery & Marsh Songbook*). Use a soloist or the choir singing the stanzas as actors, made up of all ages and types in the congregation, assume the roles in the story. On each stanza relate the actors to a central cross that you may have in the church already or to a statuesque Jesus figure standing with arms painfully outstretched and head bowed as if on the cross. On each stanza have the actors take a simple standing position before the words are sung then move into position as the words are sung.

- Stanza 1: "I wonder why, I wonder why, If his disciples were like us here Why they all left him and ran in fear As the world did crucify, crucify him?" From their standing position actors simply become statues of people running, hiding their eyes from the Crucifixion, covering their faces with coats as if to avoid detection, moving out from the central cross toward the congregation and exits.
- Stanza 2: "I wonder why, I wonder why, If they were people like you and me Why they refused then to set him free, For the crowd yelled: 'Crucify, crucify him! ...' " Two actors on different sides point to the cross mockingly or with anger. Two other actors hold up hands as if shouting with hostility.

- Stanza 3: "I wonder why, I wonder why, If they were soldiers like boys we know, Why they all beat him and mocked him so Then went out to crucify, crucify him?" Two soldiers pantomime driving nails and freeze with hammer hand back and the other holding Jesus' arm against the cross. A third actor stands several feet away and salutes throughout the stanza.
- Stanza 4: "I wonder why, I wonder why, If they were leaders like those we trust, Why they were cruel and so unjust When they judged to crucify, crucify him?" Four actors, male and female, looking official and authoritative stand with folded arms, smug expressions, pointing to the cross as if ordering his death, or looking with an apologetic "what else could I do?" expression and wave of the hand.
- Last stanza: "I wonder why, I wonder why, We did not know him and love him then? Would we allow him to die again? Would the world still crucify, crucify him?" Have all the above statues take their places, or if there is not enough room, have representatives of each scene in place. Then let the preacher or another person simply point to the congregation, one at a time, as the stanza is sung, and freeze on the last repeated "I wonder why?"

Each stanza on each Sunday could be a Call to Prayer. Pray, then, for the group depicted by the statues and sung about in that stanza: disciples; the fickle public; military personnel who must obey orders; government and religious leaders given power over human life; all of us.

4. Try Advent music in Lent

Some music of ours is going to be helpful if you use the Lenten Old Testament reading, Jeremiah 31:31-34 (Revised Common Lectionary, Year B). These words were adapted by us and set as "Says the Lord," selection No. 3 from *Godsend*, our Advent cantata. It is set for baritone and soprano soloists and choir. We feel that in performance the mystery and awe of the prophetic statements come across quite well. It is also a nice thing to be able to take something from an Advent Cantata and find it appropriate for Lent. The Gospel reading for the same Sunday is John 12:20-33 and includes the words which we set as a Lenten Introit in *Hooray For God*, No. 2: "I, if I be lifted up...." It is for soloist and choir and has a big, dramatic ending.

5. Other selections from *Hooray for God*, No. 2

While looking through *Hooray For God*, No. 2, consider "On This Mountain" and try it for Easter. One year we formed a choir of people from our workshop and others who could sing and sight-read and we presented it at our final worship service. It was stunning (we thought). Since the popularity of space encounters and galactic confrontations, we also recommend from the same collection "O God of Space." Remember that the basses and tenors start on a falsetto *g*, the same actual sound as the women. The piece does not work if the lower voices sing it down an octave. The reaction of the young people in our congregation to it was: "What was that 'Star Trek' music that you sang at the beginning?" And they listened to the whole thing.

6. Put up an exhibit of popular songs

Let Lent be a time for serious examination of one's spiritual life, asking the questions of meaning and life that following Jesus entails. As a way to get at that, set up a display containing copies of sheet music with *questioning* titles showing. Some suggested titles are: *"What's It All About, Alfie," "Why Was I Born?," "Lost in the Stars," "Why?," "Should I or Shouldn't I?,"* etc. There are lots of collections of songs that would take just a short time to go through to find appropriate ones. (See more about the question theme in Idea #10 in "Other Ideas" below.)

Other Ideas

1. Explore and explain the traditions of Lent

In advance of Ash Wednesday, announce the season and its dates for your congregation, so they have a sense of what is coming. Don't assume everyone knows why there are forty days in Lent, or that Sundays don't count. (There is an important proclamation contained in the honoring of every Sunday as Easter Day.) Do a brief dissertation on ashes. Present a brief and understandable-by-all-ages history of the season of Lent in the life of the church. Not for academic reasons, not for hoity-toity liturgical sophistication, but because this history helps us understand the Gospel.

2. Emphasize the Christian lifestyle

Whatever the themes of your Lenten services, we suggest that you speak to the increasing interest in what we shall call the "Christian lifestyle." More and more church members are becoming open to the claims of God upon their personal lives — in work, in family life, in the use of leisure time, and upon their role as citizens of a world in ecological and economic crisis. It would be a sad thing if leaders of worship did not respond to this interest, and Lent is an obvious time to respond intensely.

In preaching and in praying during the season, and perhaps in the use of personal testimonies of a new kind, take up the use of sacrificial and responsible living, living in such a way that we do not intentionally victimize the people of the world by our self-indulgence. And make every effort to relate the scripture readings of the season to the daily lives of all members as explicitly and clearly as possible. (Yes, we know you try to do this all the time, but we church leaders often deceive ourselves about the actual relevance of what happens in worship to the nitty-gritty of the work-a-day-world.)

3. Use props

We are becoming more and more convinced that the use of *props* is helpful, even essential, for communication, beyond the simple reliance on words. One interesting approach to the Sundays of Lent, in preaching and worship, may be the use of a visual, holdable, passable symbol or prop on each Sunday. We know these work with children's sermons; the fact is that they work for all sermons, to help people remember, and to relate the Bible's teachings to real life.

4. Listen to how the underdogs worship

Sacrificing our own securities in worship and having a series of services in which we hear how the *underdog*, the *exile*, and the *have-nots* worship. Of course, there is the distinct possibility that what we get for our sacrifice is richer than what we have given up. Here's a list of some of the exiles as we see them: the American Indian, the African, the Oriental, the youth, the children, the women, the gay, the blacks, the Spanish.

Let's take the American Indian as an example. Do some research on how the American Indian worships God, their pantheistic God, and also Jesus Christ. What methods do they employ when they have not been influenced by the missionaries we sent them? Listen to the excitement/hypnotism of their indigenous music as compared to their singing of our old gospel songs. What did they

111

lose in the process? Get their prayers and read them. Learn a dance to have a group or the whole congregation perform. After getting these things together, put together a service of worship, the whole Indian thing. Is the kiss of peace the same as their passing the pipe of peace? What a terrible thing to do in the sanctuary! And, yet, that is what they did in their sanctuaries, large tents, and outdoors under the sky that they considered the tent of the world.

Then, the most remarkable thing: Read the scripture from the standpoint of the exile. Justo and Catherine Gonzalez, good friends and highly stimulating church historians, tell us to relook at the Good Samaritan story with ourselves, the comfortable, proper, on-top people, as the man beaten and lying in the ditch. And the Good Samaritan, nay, the good Apache, comes to us in our need. Wow! How's that for a sermon topic and viewpoint?

This same technique can be used for all the other exiles listed above. This could be an absolutely thrilling Lent and a time in which our sacrifice would be in continuing to come to worship weekly, knowing that the comforts we expect will not be there in the service, and instead there will be the challenge of listening to the exiles in the spirit of Jesus' passion.

5. List the martyrs

As a spoken Call to Worship or as an act of thanksgiving, list several martyrs from various times in history. Name the people and tell in a sentence or two how and when they died because of their beliefs. Do we not need occasional reminders of the seedbeds from which we sprang, and of the cost of our heritage?

6. Remember those who serve sacrificially in your church

The great Beatles' song "Eleanor Rigby" reminds us to look at the woman who cleans up the church after the gorgeous wedding. Who else? The people who have to babysit in the nursery during the worship service when they would rather be up in the sanctuary, perhaps because the paid babysitter didn't show up again. The kids who are made to come to worship and don't understand half of what is going on in the service and are put down when they behave like kids ordinarily do. The people who year after year work with the youth group and year after year are told that next year someone else will take over. The organist who plays week after week on an instrument that is inadequate, in poor shape, slow, etc., and who has musical tastes and standards. The singer in the choir who can read music, sing a difficult harmony part, etc., who sits by the singer who can't sing a harmony part, but year after year sings the melody an octave or two lower. The singer who sings the melody an octave lower because he can't sing a harmony part and is in the choir because his wife wants him there. The choir director who has to deal with both. Gosh, this list could go on and on and include almost everyone.

7. Have a conversation-sermon

Subject: "What do people (what did you?) *give up* to be a church member (or to be a Christian)?" Ask people, having warned them before the service about the question — or the week before, to share aloud in their pews. A second question: What did you get back to *replace* what was *given* up?

8. Have different voices read different parts in the Bible readings

This a simple method for letting the scriptures live. Where different characters appear in the passage being read in the service, let different members of the church, of appropriate age and sex, read the parts, with a day or two to "look it over." Make it an acting assignment with a simple strive for good, clear reading, with participants down front and the pastor or other leader reading the narrative lines.

9. Hand things around

When a chalice was given for our collection of chalices recently, Dick-the-pastor followed his impulse and passed it through the entire congregation so everyone could see the beautiful grain of the wood and the unusual shape. Another time, it was a picture relating to a theme of the service but too small for all to see up front. Another time it was an unusual symbol. Thus the sense of touch is involved in worship and each individual is included, his or her attention given importance. And the distraction, as people passed the item for twenty minutes or so, is quite minimal.

10. Create scrapbook-style exhibits

Set up a "scrapbook"-style series of exhibits and demonstrations in connection with worship. The point of the displays, whether mounted or passed or screened or acted out, is to consider the themes of *conflict* and *questions* for Lent, and the theme of *decisions* for Holy Week.

To illustrate *conflict*, try these:
- Find pictures of different kinds of "opposites." Using newspapers, magazines, and your own camera, get pictures showing old and young in opposition to each other, rich and poor, black and white, fat and thin, lazy and active, male and female, white collar worker and laborer, capitalists and communists, etc. While you are looking for these you may run across pictures of some of these opposing people who are reconciling themselves to each other, for instance, black and white shaking hands. Save these pictures for the Holy Week "Decision" section or the Easter "New Life" section. While looking for opposites it might be interesting to have a picture of two people, one of them crying and the other laughing and put a caption beneath it asking: "Are they both responding to the same thing?"
- Find pictures of obvious conflicts, like a few war pictures showing both sides. Don't leave out sports pictures of a karate couple, basketball players, and other sports figures. Then you may be able to find pictures of people who are being controlled by some inanimate object that may not be working properly or may be broken. For instance, somebody trying to fix a broken down car, somebody with a reel-to-reel tape recorder who is being strangled by miles of unwound tape, etc.

To illustrate *questions*, try these:
- Find pictures of people who are standing or looking quizzical, looking over a beach, or lying in a meadow and looking contemplative, looking out a window, and the like.
- It would be interesting to add headlines from newspapers or articles in which a pertinent question is being asked, explicitly or implicitly. An implicit example would be a headline about abortion. An explicit example would be a headline reading, "Should we be in control of life?"

To illustrate *decisions*, try these:
- Pictures of people getting married, being ordained as ministers, becoming American citizens, and so forth.

113

- Pictures of sports figures at decisive moments, like a tennis player looking at a ball but having not yet touched the ball with his racket, a basketball player getting ready to shoot a foul shot, etc.
- Pictures of a judge and jury, pictures of the President signing a bill, pictures of a doctor giving prescriptions, pictures of a confirmation class.
- Include pictures of people deciding whether to smoke or not, whether to drink or not, whether to take drugs or not, etc.

11. Perform deGhelderode dramas

The Wakefield Mystery plays and other medieval mysteries are full of dramas that are appropriate for both of these seasons. Search the catalogs, for they are full of short and full-length plays about the Holy Week experiences. One of the most exciting authors whose work we have done is Michel deGhelderode. His *Woman at the Tomb* is a shocking but very moving consideration of how all women who surrounded Jesus, though they see nothing in each other, eventually make it to Jesus' tomb. His full-length play *Barabbas* is a highly dramatic account of Jesus' crucifixion and Barabbas' own death. If full productions of these plays are impossible for you, do a reading or a study group on them. Copies of the plays can be purchased from Samuel French, Inc., 25 West 45th Street, New York, NY 10010 or 7623 Sunset Blvd., Hollywood, CA 90046, or www.samuelfrench.com.

12. Proclaim the Lenten message with a banner

Here is a statement that can be made into posters or emblazoned on banners: Confused? Convinced! Converted+. Remember the color of Lent is purple with either black or red for Good Friday.

13. Have groups receive the offering

For the six Sundays in Lent have people representing different organizations in the church take up the offering and have another member of the same group do the prayer following. Make it clear to the congregation that some of the money that is given each week goes for supporting and giving light and heat and space and equipment for various groups that have been represented. Do this dramatically if possible. For instance, have the oldest group in the congregation (in ours it would be the Lunch Bunch) take it up one week and the youngest people in church school do it the following week. On another occasion have members of the choir leave the choir loft and take it. In our church it would be quite unique and interesting to see members of the Presby Players drama group who are not members of our church taking up the offering, reminding them as well as the congregation that it's the First Presbyterian Church of Port Jervis that supports them.

14. Survey the congregation about decisions, and pray about them

Late in Lent, or perhaps on Palm Sunday in honor of Jesus' decision to go to Jerusalem and face the music, ask the congregation about the decisions they are facing. "What hard decisions have you faced recently, or are you facing now, for which you would like others to pray?" Or, if that's too hard and personal: "What do you think are the hardest decisions of life as you have experienced it?" Ask them to stand in the pews and identify them briefly. Then have a time of prayer, that our decisions may be faithful to God, that we may know God's will for our lives, that we may not hurt others by what we decide, that God may work through the mistakes we are bound to make. Perhaps you should read aloud in or before such a prayer the old hymn, based on words of Jeremiah, "Have Thine Own Way."

15. Entomb the light under a bushel basket

As Lent is the darkest season of the church year, we suggest a symbol: get an old-fashioned bushel basket and put a lamp or candle underneath it. You will remember in the Sermon on the Mount the quotation about not putting a light under a basket. We think that explaining the basket as a symbol of the tomb in which Jesus, the light of the world, was buried would be significant. In fact, the Call to Worship on each of the Sundays in Lent could include the placing of the basket over the lamp or candle by somebody from the congregation (rather than a staff person). If you do this, use people of different ages. It might be interesting to think about and then explain to the worshiping congregation that a child as well as an older person has different ways of entombing the light of truth.

16. Dramatize the wilderness temptations

One of the traditional readings for Lent is the story of Jesus' forty days in the wilderness, which included the temptations. Act this out. Have somebody playing the role of Christ wandering slowly around the sanctuary thinking, yawning, stretching, praying, and perhaps even reading from a scroll. All of this is to indicate the length of time he spent. (He definitely should not eat because it was a fasting time, too.) As he approaches a specific spot in the front of the sanctuary, have either a person or just a voice emerge to tempt Jesus with the first one of the temptations. This should be done very sneakily, very craftily, very oily. Have Jesus reject this temptation with the scripture's words and move on to another part of the sanctuary. And have another person or another voice tempt him. Do the same for the third temptation.

It's more interesting if we have three devils rather than one just tracking him down. On the temptation of bread, have some bread on the Communion table to point at. On the temptation to rule the world, indicate the congregation as followers of a political leader. On the temptation to throw himself down and be supported by angels, use a high place in the sanctuary to present this.

17. Dramatize the raising of Lazarus

Miracle stories that are pantomimed are immediately phony. They are dangerous to do. One way to act out this Lenten scripture is to have some people standing around waiting for the miracle that is taking place *out of our sight* as the scripture is read. Then have Lazarus appear, and if he can be covered with bandages, like an Egyptian mummy, it can be a thought-provoking experience. Eugene O'Neill wrote a play called *Lazarus Laughed* that is available in the collection of nine plays by Eugene O'Neill put out in the Modern Library Series. It's a very complex play, but it has a number of things that recommend it to worship leaders or a pantomimist. Just the idea of the appearing Lazarus laughing after coming to life is intriguing. This would be a very difficult play to put on, as it takes a cast of literally hundreds. But it should be read by people interpreting the passage — and perhaps in an informal play-reading night.

18. Dramatize the Transfiguration

Another Lenten reading that could be staged effectively is the story of Jesus' Transfiguration. It will need six people. As the story is read, let the Jesus figure go into the balcony or some other high place in the sanctuary. As you remember, everything suddenly gets white, so we suggest that the Jesus wear a robe that is a dark color on the outside and pure white on the inside. As the two other figures (Moses and Elijah) appear in white, have Jesus spread his arms out holding the cape open.

Obviously, he should be wearing all white underneath. The other three figures, the disciples who went with Jesus, should be wearing darker clothing and should remain some distance from the transfigured three. Use lights, glitter, whatever, to emphasize the blinding whiteness.

19. Participate in the story of the blind man

When you share the Gospel lection from John 9 (lectionary year A), simply have different individuals and groups read the several voices in the story. Stress the intense debate between Jesus and religious leaders.

20. Pray for those who won't come to worship

Specifically, pray for the indifferent — who don't care, who are untouched by the word; for the hostile — who have been "turned off" or hurt by Christians or have misunderstood the church's intentions; for the "cool" — those who are resisting with a facade of sophistication or self-sufficiency. In short, seek to understand in prayer the people who are not present in worship.

21. Organize a banner or poster night

Gather families or have an existing group make banners or posters setting forth and symbolizing key lines from the epistle lectionary passages for the season. Let the people read a passage in a contemporary translation and choose what they believe to be the key text. Let them design bold and eye-catching presentations of those words. Hang the banners or posters in the place of worship through the season, perhaps presenting the appropriate one following the Epistle reading each Sunday.

22. Explore blindness

As you consider the Lenten reading about the blind man, try (a) to identify with his experience, and (b) to understand the meaning of the story through experience.

Ask the congregation to close their eyes and walk around the room for two minutes, feeling their way as if blind. Or let half the people close their eyes and be led around by the other half, those sitting next to them — then trade roles in this "blind walk." Following this, let people explain how they felt and what they would probably miss most if they were blind. Then, ask the congregation to identify *other kinds of blindness* they have experienced in their own lives (not just criticizing others): What do you now understand about life that you didn't use to understand? What did you once ignore that you now think is important? Then, let people identify how God heals our various kinds of blindness.

23. Try snakes, not alive, but symbolically

The pericopes for the Fourth Sunday in lectionary year B include Numbers 21:4-9 wherein Moses is told to make a metal snake and put it on a pole, so that anyone who is bitten could look at it and be healed, and the Gospel of John 3:14-21 reiterates the story. Right! It is part of the lead in to the famous John 3:16 passage.

A few years ago Don came back from a trip to Greece and the Grecian Islands with a silver snake, jewelry-type, arm bracelet ... how do you describe it? Well, when you wear it, it looks like a snake is coiled up your arm. We are planning to borrow it back for a week to put on a pole as indicated in the scripture. Once again it will make the reading come to life and the children will enjoy it tremendously and perhaps even listen to the rest of the reading and understand what it's about.

The use of jewelry in biblical reading could be very effective. There are so many allusions to marble and jasper and other precious and semiprecious jewels and stones in the Bible, and having something to hand around to show the beauty and worth of these things anchors the use of symbol and metaphor. Thank God there are enough people in our congregation who are still trying to answer metaphorical questions! It keeps it from becoming too verbal and too one-sided.

24. Explain worship in the bulletin

Have a statement about the many moods of worship. On the first Sunday in Lent, have the whole article about Lent and one extra paragraph about the major mood of that specific day. If you try this, it is unnecessary to point out or to read it with and for them. Trust them to do it on their own. If you have a good artist in your church, invite the artist to draw something relating to each of the moods or use appropriate clip-art. These pictures will immediately attract people and initiate reading: Don't be so verbose that people stop reading.

25. Explore prayers of confession

What Prayers of Confession do you use in your worship — ones printed in a denominational book of worship? Prayers written by the pastor? Prayers from various sources? We find that the rather hurried, often mindless reading by congregations in unison Prayers of Confession, with their loaded and intense expressions of penitence, often obscure and archaic phrases and extravagant admissions of guilt — all in small print — is frequently less than a meaningful liturgical experience. Perhaps such prayers over a period of months and years have a cumulative effect, but that effect may itself be questionable, since we rarely talk about the role of guilt and forgiveness in our churches.

So we suggest that a few weeks ahead of Lent you organize some of your most sensitive members, a variety of ages and types of people, to study the possibilities in this part of worship. What works for them? What doesn't? What is the theological basis of including Acts of Confession, anyway? How can prayers about guilt and failure express the feelings of a diverse group of people? Look at several traditional prayers, look at some of the new worship materials available. Then, let the group prepare *new* Prayers of Confession for Lent or some other kinds of *Acts* of Confession other than prayers read from the program.

26. Pray about power

Lent reminds us that Jesus used his power not to save himself, but to do his Father's will. Have several members of your church prepare and lead prayers about various kinds of power in the world: A politician about political power or the power of governments; a business leader about the power of business and industry over people's lives; someone who works in media about the power of the media to shape the life of a society; a scientist about nuclear power; a military person about military power; someone else (a poor person? a rich person?) about the power of wealth, etc. Maybe you should open up the subject to the congregation: "What kinds of power concern you in the world right now? Whose wielding of power should be the subject of prayer?"

27. Make a list of victims

Have a big board or large pieces of newsprint or some surface that is both accessible to people and not unattractive in the place of worship, a surface that is in full view of the congregation through the Sunday service. Invite people through the weeks of Lent to write in that space with markers the identity of victims of injustice in the world — persons, groups, kinds of people, etc. Announce ahead of time that not all members will agree immediately with all parts of the list, but ask them to think about each one on the list before denouncing. Through the season, read the list as a Call to Prayer, or as part of a sermon, or between stanzas of the hymns about the suffering and death of Jesus. Pray for those on the list, specifically. Ask people to pray for them during the week.

28. List temptations

In the same form as No. 27 above, or in another way, have people list those things which they see as serious temptations for them — but not just sexual temptations or about cheating on taxes and other individual, private kinds! Ask them to identify temptations for governments, ethnic and racial groups, businesses, schools, churches, labor unions, groups of workers. Ask them to identify temptations peculiar to their jobs, their places in the family, their gender. Pray about those temptations. A heading for the list could be (across the board in big letters) "LEAD US NOT INTO ..."

29. Act out "The Grand Inquisitor"

Dostoevky's own retelling of the story of Jesus' temptation in the wilderness in *The Brothers Karamazov* is one of the more provocative literary interpretations ever published. Read it, tell it as a story in relation to a sermon on Lent's first Sunday, or — better yet — have it acted out simply by two good readers in your congregation. The implications for life in this world of power and oppression are obvious and interesting.

30. Display light in the art of Rembrandt

We remember a small alcove in the Alte Pinakothek Museum of Munich with awe. There were nine small etchings by Rembrandt showing events in the life of Christ (including the raising of Lazarus), which showed the master's amazing ability to illuminate. The use of light in these pictures is overwhelming, gripping. Copies of most of these particular etchings and other biblical pictures by Rembrandt are available in books and museum stores. Make a Lenten display, with signs calling attention to the role of light in his art.

31. Call for basic decisions about the Gospel

An aspect of Lenten lectionary readings are the themes of sin and salvation, of judgment and mercy, of call to repentance and of the offer of redemption. So this Lent can properly contain, in various forms, a call to basic decisions about the Gospel and its implications for the Church. Lent can be a time of evangelistic preaching, of strong proclamation of the eternal choices before all humanity. But avoid the clichés! (What sin? What *is* salvation, anyway? What do you *do* after you say, "I'm sorry, Lord"?)

32. Deal with the issues of questions and conflict

Lent has an undercurrent of *conflict*, especially as we near Good Friday, along with the rudely disturbing *questions* that Jesus presents to the world, questions which often turned people away. Perhaps Lent can be a time to face realistically and graciously the conflicts and potential conflicts between the church and the world and in your own congregation, recognizing the inevitability of some conflicts when we get down to the business of the kingdom. In preaching, in prayer, in music: Deal with this issue and the "flip-side" issue of personal and corporate reconciliation. How does God bring us back together? Can we, in fact, disagree and argue and struggle in the churches and still be together and work together and love each other? Regarding the Church's relation to the world, one of the most haunting texts in the Bible is "Beware when all people speak well of you." Is your church popular in town? Are you well thought of by everybody? Watch out!

33. Get outside the church walls

Most people in the world will not know it's Lent, or will just think of Lent as a time to give up candy — unless you do something about it. So put your rugged cross out on the church lawn. Hang a big banner in front of the church; circulate colorful and interesting announcements of events of the season in the community. Do your Lenten concerts in public places, not just in church. Rather than caroling just being a Christmastime thing, take the Gospel around in song during Lent, and not just during Holy Week. Send a group of singers out into the shopping mall on a flatbed truck to present songs of the season around a large cross; run a series of Lenten ads in the newspapers or on radio: thought-provoking commercials, not just announcements of hours of worship. Put a series of ads in the newspapers and on the radio containing some of the hard questions Jesus asked. Have your ecumenical Good Friday event out in the park, not just inside.

Worshiping During Holy Week

From the Christian viewpoint, Holy Week is the most important week of the year. If we begin the planning process early, the Worship Committee and/or representative members of our congregations can share in the creative anticipation of the week, with ideas growing out of imaginations and experiences of more people than just the professional staff of the church. Let it happen.

As you look ahead to Holy Week — to stories of Palm Sunday, the cleansing of the temple, conflicts with authorities, the Last Supper, Gethsemane, betrayals and trials, crucifixion and burial — consider the possibilities: Could it be that Holy Week can be for us the source of real comfort and profound security in a year of crisis and change, as most years end up being? Perhaps this year it is time to emphasize the Good News emerging from that fateful week more than the Bad News, the chastisement and the judgment. Not pie-in-the-sky Good News, not all-is-swell Good News, but the transforming and real Good News that —

God is for us,

Jesus is with us in our need and confusion,

God's love is a permanent and ultimate possession.

For example, it can be a week in which we trace how Jesus experiences all the hard and upsetting things we can experience: loneliness, frustration, injustice, the agony of decision, physical pain, loss of all things. Drama and readings and music and prayers can significantly illuminate his participation in our reality and then proclaim his triumph over human problems.

But, on the other hand, maybe we must be disturbed as we never have been before by the grim realities of human sin and social disorder in light of the events of that last week. Injustice is still a fact in the lives of millions, just as it was when Jesus faced Pilate and Herod and the crowd. Hypocrisy is still a common attribute of religious people, just as when Jesus was on trial before Caiaphas. Corruption is still part of government (you may have noticed), cruelty still characteristic of the masses, disloyalty still apparent among disciples. Maybe these things need to be looked at again, screamed about, repented from, in this year of social change.

Whatever themes emerge for your people, let Holy Week be a pilgrimage, a journey with Jesus. Communicate the concept of the week as a *week*, not just as Palm Sunday and Easter and "oh, yes, there's Communion on Thursday." Involve people in a series of daily readings or short services at the church or at home. Use the public media for daily presentations, commercially sponsored if necessary.

One final question: *What about Good Friday?* For some of you, Good Friday regularly contains a prescribed evening service "out of the book." But for others the options are open. Plan carefully: Ecumenical services? Morning and evening events? Noonday worship? A youth event? Three hours of silence, noon to three? An appropriate play? Whatever you do, include all ages, let observances be for people who work as well as retired folks, kids as well as adults. Let them be public, so the town will know it's Good Friday — outdoors, in a mall, somewhere visible. Let them be passionate, not pallid, not ho-hum, not passive. Even if you have a service "out of the book," let it scream, let it shout, let it weep, let it bleed.

A day-by-day observance

One year, Don bought a small acrylic bird feeder that he put on the front window of his office. It was held in place with one of those clear suction-cup hangers. Even when the feeder was full, and even when the birds were fighting each other over a choice bit of corn, when the sun hit it right, a small rainbow appeared on the upper left-hand wall that Don faced. It moved slowly across the wall and by closing time it gently disappeared. It was a glorious thing to behold. It was so great to know that whatever else happened in that office, and some sad things and some terrible things as well as many good things had happened, there would be a rainbow passing through, that sumptuous reminder of God's promise to Noah and therefore to all of us.

We mention this as we want to look forward with positiveness that beyond Lent and Holy Week there is Easter. And Holy Week has its terrible moments and its bright moments, and we know a rainbow depends on rain and sun simultaneously.

One major suggestion for Holy Week is *have one*. Many churches (actually, not too many) have services of worship of one kind or another each *day* of Holy Week. The closest we ever came to that was to have a thirty-minute organ and vocal concert around noon each day of the week one year, culminating in a three-hour service of silence and music on Good Friday. What we are suggesting for this year is to have a service that has readings, music, and prayers for each day so that the week really becomes special. Many Roman Catholic churches have early masses before working people have to start their jobs. This might be the best time for you. Others have masses in the evenings or those who want the time after work and before the busyness of the evening. Our lunchtime concerts, even though people were invited to bring their lunches with them while we furnished tea or coffee in the rear of the sanctuary, were sparsely attended. But then it takes a while to set up a tradition.

Since the readings for Holy Week are the same for all three years of the Revised Common Lectionary, we offer these suggestions for the reading that can be used any year. (If you just can't figure out a way to have daily events in Holy Week, use these ideas to stimulate thinking about other Lenten occasions as well as Maundy Thursday and Good Friday services you do have regularly.)

Monday

The Second Lesson is a marvelous one from Hebrews 9:11-15 which makes very clear the change from the sacrificial blood of animals to the blood of the Lamb of God, Jesus, the Christ. This can be dramatized, and perhaps it should be, to bring home the expense that God went to for us. We suggest you use some simple props: an old-looking dish, possibly wood, in which a dark liquid is put and have it labeled "blood of goats and calves." Have it on or near the Communion table or altar and have someone interpret/tell about the Old Testament method of throwing the blood on the altar to sanctify it. Have an urn with ashes, marked "ashes of a heifer," and throw them against the legs of the table. On the farther side of the table have bandages that have obviously been used on a bleeding person or clothing that would be about the same size as a lion cloth. Have someone, perhaps a different person, explain about the crucifixion of Jesus and point out the blood markings. In the center have the pastor standing with the communion pitcher and a chalice, and as he/she explains the symbolic transference of the blood of Jesus' sacrifice, have him/her pour some wine into the chalice. Point out that this is not to be gruesome but a reminder of things left from the primitive culture of our religious ancestors that have become symbolic or transferred into something else for our present-day worship.

The Gospel Lesson, John 12:1-11, tells of the anointing of Jesus' feet by Mary. Have a group of four (or more); Mary, Martha, Jesus, and Judas are essential. Pantomime the story as it is read slowly and emotionally by a lay reader. This can be done in historic costume or in contemporary dress. If done historically, get props that look the part; if contemporary, use some kind of modern-day perfume or cologne and make it strong enough so that people can smell it easily. After Jesus' statement have the actors freeze and the reader walk in front of the actors/pantomimists to read the concluding paragraph. At the end of that the people could come slowly out of "freeze" and go back to their pews. Follow these two scenes with a prayer and possibly Sidney Carter's song, "Said Judas to Mary" (or simply "Judas and Mary"). It is available in many hymnals and collections of songs for the church.

For the Old Testament readings (they are from Isaiah Monday, Tuesday, Wednesday, and Friday) pull out all the dramatic, prophetic stops. Have a man dressed in historical costume stand some place unusual, say the balcony or a corner in the rear of the sanctuary where he can be seen above the congregation, and have him spotlighted from beneath. This takes nothing more than a 300-watt white (or yellow or amber or any other appropriate color [perhaps change them as you get deeper into Holy Week]) set in front of and below the prophet. If the person can memorize the words, marvelous! If not, have someone read the words, some unseen person (preferably on microphone) in a most dramatic manner. The prophet can stand stock still as if in a form of ecstasy (yes, that's what happened to many of the prophets as they whipped themselves up into ecstatic states and then had their visions!), or he can move a little bit as new ideas are introduced. The prophets are getting short shrift these days, and may get even less in the next few years to come, so it is our duty to balance the Bible's message of grace with a reminder of the prophecy and the cost.

Tuesday

The Second Lesson, 1 Corinthians 1:18-31, can appropriately call for a scale, no, not a musical scale, but a set of balances. As the reader reads this complicated piece of scripture, have someone put weights on either scale, one labeled the Jews, the other Greeks. Figure out ways in which this balance or off-balance is tempered by the center section of the scales, the upright portion, which can be labeled, and which often looks like, "The Cross."

The Gospel, John 12:20-36, is complex but can be pantomimed with some work. You need a Philip, an Andrew, and a Jesus. We suggest turning the congregation into the crowd who wanted to see Jesus, so write their lines on the bulletin with cues so they know when to say them. As the reader — who is reading all the rest of the scripture and leading the congregation — gets to Jesus' answers, it would be a good idea to have some props for Jesus to use: some wheat that he can pull out of a pocket or sleeve depending on the type of costume used. Jesus should turn to face the congregation when the reader starts reading his answers and statements. Have Jesus look involved and aware that his difficult statements about being "lifted up" are hard for the listeners to comprehend. And have him leave quietly to hide.

The Old Testament Lesson is dealt with above and the same type of staging should be continued during the week.

Wednesday

The Second Lesson, Hebrews 12:1-3, is an interesting one for the use of props. You have gathered by now that each day will have the statue for *the Old Testament, props for the Second Lesson, and pantomime for the Gospel Lesson.* Get a large white sheet of paper or cardboard and with a *red* marker write a long list of specific sins that we know we (or surely someone else) are guilty of doing, saying, thinking. On the phrase, "the sin that clings so closely" turn a spotlight on this list. Then, however, read Romans 5:9, "now we have been justified by his blood." At that point, turn a *red* spotlight on the sheet and *all the sins will be wiped out!* If you can be more daring, pour red paint (water color, that is) looking very much like blood, over the sheet to accomplish the same thing. Try all of these suggestions in privacy before you do them in the public worship!

The Gospel Lesson, John 13:21-32, is one of the most dramatic of the week. You need a Judas and a couple of chief priests to pantomime the thirty pence sequence. Do this on one side of the chancel or front of the sanctuary. Then have Judas join Jesus and the other eleven disciples around the Communion table. Each disciple should come up to Jesus, who stands with a dish in his hands, and look him in the eye as the reader says: "Is it I?" Have the reader take just a bit of liberty with the scripture by repeating the sentence as each disciple comes up. (Verse 25 in the NRSV actually reads, "Lord, who is it?" but we suggest for this one verse you use the sharper wording from the parallel story in Matthew 26, where the RSV renders the question as "Is it I, Lord?" Matthew 26:22). Judas should, of course, be the last one. At the last line of the scripture all should freeze, each disciple having gone back to a place around the table, still wondering. Have Judas turn at the end and look out over the heads of the congregation, thinking: "What have I done? What am I doing?"

Thursday

Many of you probably have special services that you have been doing on Maundy Thursday through the years. If not, then we have some suggestions continuing in the pattern as set above.

The Old Testament Lesson, Exodus 12:1-14, is different in that the voice is God's speaking to Moses. Possibly have another figure representing Moses, looking quite different from Isaiah, who will just listen to God and react simply. Have the voice of God be heard on the loudspeaker system. If you have equipment to set up a number of speakers coming from various parts of the room, then toss God's message from one place after another. It is the story of the Passover!

The Second Lesson, 1 Corinthians 11:23-26, is Paul's statement of handing on the practice Lord's Supper. This passage includes the "Words of Institution" as most of us use them in Communion, so it is a very important passage. Have the reader open an envelope and read it as the letter that Paul sent, reading carefully and handling the chalice and the plate of bread as those words are mentioned.

The Gospel, John 13:1-17, 31b-35 is the familiar story of Jesus washing the feet of the disciples. This can be easily acted out as the reader reads the passage. It would probably be better understood if it were done in historical costume with the disciples acting tired and dirty before Jesus does his washing. This can be a very moving scene, and extremely so to those whose feet are being washed. Eventually, according to some church experiences, a whole congregation can do this to each other, the people being prepared before hand to deal with pantyhose situations. Think about it. There is nothing we do to each other as we visit that fills the same kind of friendly and loving and servant response as foot-washing.

Friday

Some churches still have a three-hour service from noon until three for their congregations and friends to participate in. Some do not. Here is a suggested morning or evening service, not three hours, but continuing the above pattern.

The Old Testament goes back to Isaiah again, 52:13—53:12. It is the moving passage about the prophecy of Jesus being wounded for our transgressions. Make sure that as you pick readers for all of the scriptural texts, you choose people (or someone) who can really get into the words. They are so dramatic that often we just read them calmly or flatly, and they are *imperative* to us as Christians.

For the Second Lesson, the lectionary provides two choices, Hebrews 10:16-25 or Hebrews 4:14-16; 5:7-9. For dramatic purposes, we suggest the latter. While it is a complicated one to do with props. The one thing that comes to our collective minds is to have some props of clothing and other things that high priests wear or carry that are very ornate. Have someone wearing/carrying them and at the appropriate words remove them and pick up something common and everyday to replace them. The passage reminds us that Jesus, though God's chosen high priest *a la* Melchizedek, suffered as a common man and therefore knows our experience.

The Gospel is the story of the trial and eventual crucifixion and burial as written in John 18:1—19:42. This is a long and involved passage but one which is familiar to all Christians. It will take a lot of people and a lot of rehearsing. As it is written it is almost like a script. Have your group of pantomimists (you will have one by this time) try the script on. Remember: Spoken words need to be slowed down somewhat to let the actors do what is being read, or at least to indicate what is being read.

Suggestion: when there is dialogue, let the actor freeze in a position that would be appropriate for the words he/she is saying and then move on the descriptive passages. This story can be equally effective in modern dress or historical costume. Use one person to be the Cross, standing straight with arms wide, on which Jesus pantomimes being crucified. Don't hold back on the harshness of the story; it is there and must not be forgotten.

Saturday

Although there are scheduled readings in the lectionary for this day, rather than dramatize them, we suggest you gather your congregation and have a service of Waiting. This can include silent prayers, individual prayers, open-eyed prayers, and corporate prayers dealing with the hopes and promises implied in the Resurrection for which you are all gathered to see in. Open-eyed prayers can be silent prayers as you look again at some of the props used during the week, slides of famous paintings, and etchings of Holy Week subjects and themes. We suggest *no music*. Music has a tendency to romanticize heavy moments or can turn them sentimental and that would be awful on this night of nights. If your service is at 11 or 11:30 at night, when midnight strikes, *then* should come the announcement that "He is risen! He is risen indeed!" It is not just at the rising of the sun that we are aware of the triumph over death. We have been aware of it for nearly 2,000 years.

So with readings as the center of the Holy Week services of worship, use hymns, prayers, special music. The services should be, perhaps, thirty minutes, not much longer, because so many people are centered on television show schedules, and there is the added excitement of early Easter shows and we all get so busy. But suggesting that people put aside half an hour a night for the most devastating week in human history may not be too much to ask. "Could you not watch with me for ..." Jesus said to his sleepy disciples. Let us update that and as followers of Jesus say a resounding: "YES!"

Using music during Holy Week

Comforting. Music can be so comforting. Perhaps this Holy Week the prelude and the offertory can be genuinely comforting to the congregation as they gather together to worship on Palm Sunday, Thursday evening for the Last Supper and Tenebrae, Good Friday at whatever service you may have, Saturday evening for a vigil. Then Easter Sunday the sound should be triumphant, with the comfort coming through in the excitement that as He is risen so we are risen.

Some specific ideas:

1. View things through Mary's memory

Don has written three of a series of organ pieces called "Mary Remembers" that include "Mary Remembers Palm Sunday," "Mary Remembers the Trial," and "Mary Remembers the Annunciation." Each makes interesting use of the organ and includes whispered words by the choir — and a brief, spoken introduction. We have discovered that the congregation listens better after they have heard someone point out what's different about this occasion — for instance with the title and dedication, if it's appropriate or unusual. (These are published by Proclamation Productions, Inc.)

2. Try these anthems

"Can Anybody Tell Me Why?" by J. Bert Carlson (Art Masters Studios, www.mpa.org/agency/23p.html) is an anthem we recommend. The words ask the question how God can love us so much that he did what he did for people who are still going around killing each other, hurting, scorning, and so forth. We suggest for a further impact to divide the choir into two groups, somewhat apart, so the congregation is hit, as it were, from all sides. Having divided them, then divide the lines between each group and the groups together, like a double choir.

Speaking of divided, Samuel Adler has a marvelous and hard anthem called "Division." It is for speaking chorus, singing chorus, and glockenspiel (Agape, www.agapemusic.com). It takes a long time to prepare it but the congregation is going to be overwhelmed when it is performed. It's not only about division, but will probably divide the congregation into those for it and those against it, and that will give you the opportunity to talk about the work! How does this fit under comfort? Well, both pieces remind us that there is strife in the world but in spite of it truth and God's love are in favor of people. Our differences are not abnormal; we can live with them and with each other. And there is comfort in living together.

Likewise, with another gorgeous anthem, "Questions" by Michael Cohen (Cobblehill Music, handled by Bourne, www.bourne.com). It has a haunting melody in a popish vein. It asks: Will the world have changed because of what we have done, or will it remain the same because we didn't do anything? "Soon we will not be young." The music is comforting, and the words are challenging, and the tension between the two is moving.

3. Invite people to listen to organ practice

Let people know when the organist is playing or even practicing, and invite them to come into the sanctuary and listen quietly. Keep the doors open at announced times for those of us who need rest and comfort so there will be this special place to go and read from the Bibles or hymnals in the racks, listen to some music (even recordings, maybe), pray and just be quiet and think. "Comfort ye my people."

Other ideas

1. Keep these "P" ideas in mind

- **Passion.** As you consider the passion of Christ in liturgical events of different kinds, do it all with passion. Feeling, concentration, conviction, intensity are appropriate to the story. This means, leaders, first prepare yourselves in prayer and meditation. It then means come on strong: Shout with the crowds, weep with the disciples, pray hard with Jesus in the garden, let your words and music rush when the story rushes to its climaxes, be silent when that's all there is left to do on Thursday and Friday. It also means let your feelings (and those of the choirs and congregations) out in the open. Let there be passion.

- **Publicity, Promotion.** Let the world know it's Holy Week, and not just time to get new clothes for Easter. In the press, on the air, on television: Communicate the scriptural content of the whole week. Announce all your services and other events, so people won't come on Easter without having experienced a little of what led up to it. A few daily sentences about the story in lots of white space in the paper may get through to someone who doesn't know much at all about the Savior.

- **Public.** Get outside to the masses, out of the church buildings where most people know the story and some of its meaning. Have a silent parade on Good Friday, with solemn banners and symbols of the Passion and posters telling why he died. Have a short ecumenical gathering in the city park on Palm Sunday after morning services — for waving of palms, one strong hymn, and prayers for your city, your particular Jerusalem. Invite the public officials. Have very short dramatizations of events of Jesus' week in a shopping mall, on the steps of City Hall — where people are. And concerts. Drape that big cross out on the front lawn with purple. Go public.

- **Personal decision.** In your Holy Week services and other events, call people to decisions about their lives. Some churches do this much too often, and with obvious manipulation. Many of our churches go to the other extreme, and never ever give people an opportunity to show they have decided something for God. You can best figure out appropriate ways this can be done in your church — whether by people just raising a hand, filling out a card, coming quietly to the Communion rail, telling a neighbor in the pew, standing up, saying it out loud, whatever. A simple act of confirmation and sharing, that all may marvel and rejoice and take courage.

2. Produce a Holy Week documentary

Every church has several people with video cameras, and probably some of them have a passion about taping action. Get a team of such persons to make a "documentary" of the scenes of Holy Week with a few actors as if the stories were happening in your town. Use the church or another church for the cleansing of the temple and for the scenes with the High Priests, the courthouse for the civil trials, the police station, a nearby woods for Gethsemane, a visible hilltop, a cemetery (with an open grave), etc. If they will cooperate, use the local ecclesiastical and public officials — the judge, the police, pastors. (They should cooperate if church people are also photographed as "bad guys" in the story — and there are no good guys but Jesus, and if they are not made to look foolish.) You may want to show only a side view or back view of Jesus, so people won't get hung up on his appearance or on the actor's rightness for the part. Show the program on Maundy Thursday or Good Friday.

3. Put Holy Week stories in the media

Use your creative writers in the church. Assign a team to prepare newspaper-style accounts of the several events of Holy Week. Publish a "newspaper" from your church, or buy space for them each day in the local paper so all the town can read them. Buy time for them to be presented on radio or television by people of the congregation. Yes, as if the week were happening here and now. If you are doing the documentary in No. 2 above, take some still shots at the same time for a full treatment in the press.

4. Hold a Tenebrae service

Many, many churches of various brands have a Tenebrae Service in Holy Week. If you don't, we recommend this traditional event as one of great educational and emotional content. It may appropriately be held on Thursday night, as a ceremony after Holy Communion, or on Friday. We call the event "The Service of Shadows," since "Tenebrae" (which means shadow or *darkness*) is not an easy word for kids to remember — and why not use a word you don't have to translate? Here's how we do it:

A. Seven candles in a row are lighted from a previously lighted "Christ Candle" — which was lighted on Christmas Eve. (Explain this as you begin.)

B. Sing "Were You There?" or another appropriate hymn.

C. Introduce the ceremony, explaining that it's from the fourth century, explaining the "Kyrie Eleison" as the oldest known Christian prayer, listing the "shadows" and saying any other things needed to enhance understanding.

D. Turn out all the lights. Seven church officers move into place behind the candles. Readers take their places.

E. The seven stories from scripture are read, with titles given. Here are the stories and the titles as we have learned and adapted the ceremony (abbreviate the stories as you see fit):
- The shadow of betrayal. Matthew 26:20-25
- The shadow of inner agony. Luke 22:40-44
- The shadow of loneliness. Matthew 26:40-45
- The shadow of desertion. Matthew 26:47-50, 55-56
- The shadow of accusation. Matthew 26:59-67
- The shadow of mockery. Mark 15:12-20
- The shadow of death. Luke 23:33-46

F. The pastor could serve as reader, but it is preferable to have the whole ceremony done by other church leaders. Use seven readers or just two, alternating. They should use little flashlights.

G. After each story, a different elder or church council member (from the line behind the candles) puts out one candle, saying the title ("The Shadow of Accusation," etc.), then leading the congregation in saying the "Kyrie" — "Lord, have mercy upon us; Christ, have mercy upon us; Lord, have mercy upon us."

H. After all seven candles are out and only the Christ Candle is burning, the pastor slowly and deliberately extinguishes the Christ Candle, saying, "It is finished."

I. A chime rings slowly 33 times, for the years of Jesus' life.

J. A doorway light is put on for people to leave in silence.

K. Let all be silent, except for the reading and the "Kyrie." Practice with the officers carefully, since all is done in near darkness. Let the putting out of candles be visible to all, done from behind. Use no programs.

5. Let laity speak about "What the cross of Jesus means to me"

During the week, or as a special Palm Sunday or Good Friday presentation, let four laypersons speak briefly on the meaning of the cross in their experience. Ask them well in advance for a carefully prepared, thoughtful, and illustrated speech. Ask them to explain all the clichés they borrow from historic comments about the cross.

6. Pray for prisoners

In times of intercession during the week, announce and lead prayers for the many kinds of prisoners in the world — in honor of Jesus-the-Prisoner. First of all, there are thousands and thousands of people imprisoned for religious and political beliefs in many nations. Second, there are ordinary criminals, many of them with no knowledge of alternatives to crime. Third, there are the occasional prisoners of your own community and county jails, kids or adults who "get in trouble" and need your church's ministry. What other kinds can your congregation think of? Ask them.

7. Have a debate

Ask some of your more articulate and opinionated members to prepare a formal debate regarding Jesus, on the proposition "Jesus is revolutionary and a threat to the social order." Let the two sides of the debate, with two or three members on each team, pretend to be people of his time — conservative disciples vs. members of the Sanhedrin or Pharisees, for instance. Perhaps a local speech and drama teacher or students involved in scholastic or collegiate debating would enjoy presenting this as a Holy Week sermon or special program.

8. Offer classic America sermons

Use a series of readings of sermons on the cross or the person of Christ by early American preachers — one presented each day during Holy Week at lunchtime, on the radio, or in a prominent place in the community. Look into the works of Jonathan Edwards, Phillips Brooks, present-day preachers, and heroes of your particular denomination.

9. Serve a special symbolic meal on Maundy Thursday

This idea comes from Grace United Methodist Church of Williamston, South Carolina, to whom we offer strong thanks. Try a public luncheon, a sacrificial meal of sorts, resembling a meal in ancient Palestine — with cheese, olives, grapes, and other fruits and vegetables mentioned in the scriptures and a simple meat salad. Put these foods on a large table with a seven-branch candelabra in the center, so people can help themselves during the hours of the meal.

Have symbols all around the room. The folks in Williamston had palm branches strung from fishing line on all the walls; they displayed large dice, whip, blindfold, ladder, money bag, sword, rope, crown of thorns, hammer and nails. These hung on the walls. There should be a large cross with the INRI sign on it. Draping the entrance door with red and black cloth adds to the specialness of the place and a feeling of history. On each table: a candle surrounded with nails and thorns. Ask people to eat in silence.

Background music might be combined with readings of the Passion story from the Gospels or with "newscasts" from the record "The Greatest Week in History," released some years ago by the Mennonite Church, descriptions of Holy Week events in modern news form. Another, nearby part of the church building might be open and appropriately lighted for private prayer after the luncheon.

10. Plan some alternatives to the "seven last words" on Good Friday

It is possible that we have overused Jesus' words from the cross for preaching on Good Friday. If you have a three-hour service, try a different theme one year. Build sermons, anthems, hymns, and dramatic readings around "Personalities of the Passion" (the several major characters in the story), or episodes in the Passion narrative, with the theme "The Way of the Cross" (Gethsemane, Betrayal, The Trials, The Road to Calvary, etc.).

11. Sing songs from a flatbed truck

In keeping with our probably repetitious emphasis on getting out of doors to the public, we suggest that, just as you go caroling at Christmas time, you send out the choirs and youth groups to the shopping malls and stores to sing the songs of Holy Week. You can probably find a flatbed truck for the purpose. Put a large, rustic cross on the truck, around which the singers can stand. Use the spirituals and other strong, direct songs about the stories of the suffering, death, and resurrection of Jesus.

12. Have the people read the stories of the week

On Palm Sunday list for your congregation the stories pertinent to each day of Holy Week from the Gospels, and invite them to read the stories in family groups at home. As money allows, you might even have the stories printed in the newspaper and read on the radio.

13. Use Maundy Thursday as a time to speak encouragement

During your Maundy Thursday Communion service or after the church supper that precedes it (if you are doing that), invite the folks to speak to each other, ceremoniously and in Christian love, moving from their places to go to particular people to whom they wish to speak. Suggest that there may be words of affection, of hope, of encouragement, of challenge, of loving and constructive criticism, of thanks; or there may be a Bible verse of special importance to share. Also suggest that those who have no such words to offer may simply pray for specific other persons in the church family during this time. Let leaders of the church be prepared to set an example and initiate the reverent communication as they see fit.

Worshiping During Easter

The Season of Easter, "the Great Fifty Days," begins on Easter Sunday, and continues until Pentecost, with Ascension Sunday on the seventh and last Sunday before Pentecost. Do celebrate the whole season (also called Eastertide) and not just that one special Easter Sunday with Sundays following as merely springtime Sundays of diminishing importance. Claim the season to develop important themes, to let the many meanings of the Resurrection unfold and to build toward Pentecost, "the Day of the Spirit," and "the Birthday of the Church."

We suggest for the Season of Easter the concentration on a theme idea or concept, and we do so for a very particular reason. Easter is, in Christian proclamation, the key event of human history. Yet we often get the impression that few Christians have any profound understanding of its meaning. It continues for most people to be primarily about life after death, and has very little to do with the here and now. Eastertide as a seven-week season has singular importance in the church year if only for the reason that we need that time to spell out the implications of the Resurrection: Its vindication of Jesus' teachings, its judgment upon human pride and injustice, its reversal of his agonizing death, its proclamation of his rule over human history, etc.

Themes and approaches

1. Resurrection Faith

First, those of you who are guided by the Revised Common Lectionary, the ecumenical calendar of scripture readings, will note that for this season only, during all three years of the lectionary cycle, readings from the book of Acts replace the Old Testament as the First Lesson. Also, while the Epistle readings vary with the three years, the Gospel readings are from John every Sunday all three years, except for the third Sunday of Easter in Years A and B.

With this concentration of readings from Acts and John, we suggest a theme for the season: "Resurrection Faith." While the two books are quite different in mood and style, you can emphasize the *dynamic* and active life and growth of the church with Acts and the profound and unique nature of *belief* in the fourth Gospel. What is faith? How can we believe today as the first Christians believed? What was the source of the early church's vitality and power? What is the relation of faith and freedom, the difference between faith and dogma? Must doctrine *divide* Christians? And how can we communicate our faith to others? These are some of the questions that may arise in preaching, in prayers, in selection of music, and in other parts of worship during the season if you take up these lectionary sequences.

Of course, the Epistle readings each year can be used in complementary fashion to the Resurrection Faith theme. For example, the readings in Year A, from First Peter, help to spell out the *meaning of the Christian community.*

One more word about John. Because of the tendency of people to think of Easter only in after-death terms, the exposition, not only in sermons but also in prayers and in music, of the season's Gospel lessons from John must be done with particular care, as containing guidelines for a Christian lifestyle. If nothing else happens in the Great Fifty Days other than the serious consideration of those Johannine texts, the season will have been important — as such consideration points people toward how to live a new life.

131

2. Victory and Vindication

A theme related to the lectionary, but also to other scriptures identified with Easter, is that of *Victory*. For us, one of the central meanings of the Resurrection is in Christ's victory as *Vindication* of his teachings, his way of life, and his presentation of God. Jesus was victorious over enemies by surrendering himself, by suffering and dying for them and for the world. And his victory establishes the supremacy of his way over all other ways of living. What does this mean for the style of the congregation in the community? It may mean, at least, that we should pray in Eastertide for boldness and confidence before the powers that be.

A second meaning of Christ's victory, one amplified in the lections from John, is that of triumph over death. The Christian congregation's considerations of death should be frequent and profound, and Eastertide offers a good opportunity. During the season, pray about death, sing about death, preach about death, discuss death — as a key to our theology for life. Why were those apostles in Acts apparently unafraid of death? What is a mature belief about eternal life? How does our attitude about death affect our living and doing? Can people in your church live without fear? Can terminal suffering be redeemed by Christ somehow?

3. "We Are the Easter People!"

We gather that this phrase, which has emerged from our carol "Every Morning is Easter Morning," has come to be of some importance to people around the world, and it relates to the lectionary passages of the season from Acts. The phrase stresses two ideas that emerge from the Acts readings. First, it speaks of the growth of a community as a result of the Resurrection. (Professor John Knox used to say that the only visible result of Jesus' resurrection is the church.) In the Acts of the Apostles, the church grows as a response to the news of Jesus' rising, news contained in the early speeches from that book. Have the whole congregation read Acts during the season. Study its story of the first "Easter People." To gather, to worship, and to work together as "Easter People" is to be an affirmative, joyful, and lively community. Let the Sundays of Eastertide be designed for such growth.

A second aspect of this phrase is its stress on "The Good News." Preachers, make sure that every sermon of the season — no, every sermon of every season — contains in some form the essential Good News, not just bad news. Examine every sermon you prepare to make sure it has such content. Moreover, let's try in this season to determine precisely what the Good News is in a world fraught with complex problems. Perhaps the whole church staff should try to write in a few sentences what exactly the Good News is to them — beyond easy religious phrases and traditional formulations. Perhaps the congregation should do the same thing. One obvious implication is that our physical selves are affirmed and set free. Therefore, worship in Eastertide appropriately contains forms of physical, bodily action as well as listening, speaking, and singing.

To put across a theme such as "We Are The Easter People," use all the means possible at your disposal. Don't overestimate the attention of your congregation to slogans or symbols; let there be holy bombardment of the senses. Use slogan-buttons; people old and young like to wear them. Use big symbols and words mounted in the place of worship. Use the symbols suggested for "redemption" in "Other ideas" section below. Sing our song mentioned above or others related to whatever theme you may choose. Relate the theme to season-long family and individual Bible reading. Use it in your newsletters.

4. Rebirth

Here's a theme to consider in liturgy (music, prayers, sermons, silences) and in study related to liturgy. Rebirth — because Easter is about a new kind of life, free, joyful, and guided by new directives. Rebirth — because the call to decision is an essential element in the Christian faith, the call away from the past to a new future. Rebirth — because the symbolism of Easter is that dramatic, the message that radical, the possibilities that profound.

First, this theme emerges as we focus at Easter on the *sacrament of baptism,* as they did in ancient times. Schedule baptisms, infant (if your church does that kind of thing!) and adult, on Easter Sunday morning. The meaning of the sacrament in the Bible is primarily twofold: We are washed, as with water; we die and rise again, as by drowning and coming up. The sixth chapter of Paul's "Letter to the Romans" relates baptism and Easter for all time, and moves us beyond the folklore and superficial meanings of the day and season. Baptism compels our personal participation in Jesus' dying and rising, once and for all and over and over again.

Second, the theme of rebirth, as illuminated by baptism, suggests that Easter is a time for *decision.* We suggested in our Holy Week chapter that Holy Week might contain opportunities for people to make public decisions about their lives. Perhaps Easter, with its multitudes of people coming to worship, is even a more proper time. Yes, it would be startling for those coming in Easter finery to do their annual nod to God to find themselves called to decision, offered the chance to leave the past behind and make a new start on life with new goals. But, after all, that's a rather essential part of Christianity. Being "born again" has too long been left as subject matter for the revivalists and fundamentalists. It needs clear and rational explanation, it needs an affirmative meaning (beyond the context of guilt and "old time religion"). Easter may be just the time.

Let leaders of worship (not just the professional staff) offer a call to commitment on Easter Sunday. Invite people to register their decisions in some simple but obvious and important way. Don't just suggest people "go home and be different" or "try to come next week"; let them respond NOW. Then the themes of the Rebirth of Our Church (with new goals of mission and outreach and knowledge of the faith) and the Rebirth of the Nation (with new national priorities of justice and care) can be continuing concerns of the "Great *Fifty* Days."

5. The RE prefix

RE is the prefix that means *again* ... another chance ... a REsurrection. And so we make REcommendations for the Season of Easter.

- REconsider. Basic things. What is your church about? Does it have a direction? Is it a direction that is consistent with biblical suggestions? For instance, does it really feed the poor? or just the membership? Does it spend time and money on mission? or just repaint the building? Does it deal with huge issues like death, divorce, human relationships, suffering? or just comforts? What is your life about? Have you wasted time in REpeating things you never bothered to examine? Do you RElate? Have you had a RElapse REgarding your New Year's REsolutions? Now is the time to REgain control!

- REstore. Basic things. Energy. Sense of humor as well as direction. Examine your fund of memories, abilities, limitations, strengths. Start thinking about REtiring with things you can do, with money to support you, and people to share with.

- REdiscover. The strength of your marriage or relationship. Your friends. Your family (now hear this, pastors!) Your choir. Your choir director. Your organist. Your vacation time. Your job. Your avocations. (Somebody once asked Don what he did for fun, hobbies. He REalized he didn't do anything that was different from his work, so he REthought and took a Batik course.) Your town. Your church, both the people and the building. Your worth.

- REfrain. From overeating. Overdrinking. Overworking. Overexercising. Overexpecting. Overdemanding. Overlooking. Overhearing. And REfrain from cynicism, especially on Easter Sunday. The anticipated big crowds of Easter Sunday constitute a God-given opportunity, a challenge for your creativity and prayer. Work on ways to break through the indifference, lack of understanding and superficiality of those crowds and their Easter observance. They come with needs, possibilities, and questions. Don't just be snide and critical.
- REturn. Borrowed books and records. Favor for favor. Ugliness with kindness. Borrowed money. To your old stomping grounds. To your favorite vacation spot. To your favorite book or author. Your thanks to God. And to man and woman. To the Holy Land, if at all possible.
- REapply. Take a course in Bible study, even if it's on a book that doesn't interest you or support you. Get back to reading the Bible. Attend all rehearsals and meetings you're committed to. Think through your pledge. Try night school.
- REvive. Your wildest dreams and hopes and longings and expectations for your life. Your daily schedule (no, that's REvise, perhaps). Your congregation. Your town. Your family. Exercise.
- REload. Your camera. Your CD player. Your schedule with REconsidered things. Your battery. Your imagination. Your memory bank (you are what you REmember ... Build memories). The ice tray and your copy machine.
- REsume. Living. Loving. Playing. Praying. Worshiping. REspirating.

6. Heroes of the faith

People who analyze the contemporary scene often mention the absence of heroes. Especially in this era of disillusionment and the debunking of myth, a period marked by political scandal, failure of old systems and even the humanizing of sports figures, there are signs that people are desperate for heroes.

Three times in our small church we have had a series of sermons and services on "Heroes of the Faith." These series have been among the most interesting things that have happened here, bringing history alive, involving the imaginations of all ages, broadening our liturgical and musical experience, and providing new heroic images for Christian living. Consider the idea for a five-, six-, or seven-week series, between Easter and Pentecost.

- **The concept:** In the series, each service contains the words, music, and otherwise-stated witness of a great Christian of the past. And the sermon presents the context and outlines of the person's life, proclaiming the Christian faith as clarified, illuminated, and dramatized in that life. In other words, this is not just a series of lectures about dead people, with preparatory music and prayers. As much as possible, select calls to worship, prayers, ascriptions of praise, benedictions, and parts of the sermon from the writings of the great person, announcing the source as they happen. At least let themes of the service's parts be suggested by the burning concerns and characteristics of that person. If words by the hero have been set to music, as hymns, solos or anthems, use that music. Or choose music from the period, country, or tradition he or she represents; e.g., German chorales, English Psalters, colonial American hymns, spirituals, Gregorian chant — all through the service (just this one week, Mrs. Jones) for a real exposure. Early in the service, of course, you will want to introduce the person briefly, with dates and place and why you're giving such honor and attention. Plan the series well ahead, employing the "history buffs," artists, dramatists (for biographical scenes and readings), audio-visual experts, and, of course, musicians — all helping to plan the services.

- **Music throughout the series:** You will immediately think of hymns on the "Heroes" theme — "Faith of Our Fathers" and Bach's setting of "Now Praise We Great and Famous Men" (if you can get beyond the sexist lyrics) and "For All the Saints" and Kent Schneider's "There's A Church Within Us." Our paired Introit and Dismissal, "Lord, Is It I?" and "Send Me" from the booklet *Hooray for God*, worked effectively to begin and end each service the last time we had such a series. And "The Great Parade" provided a dramatic bit of musical continuity. We sang the whole song to begin and end the series and used instrumental settings of the theme occasionally. The whole festival service of "The Great Parade" would probably be an appropriate finale for the series (available from Proclamation Productions). Check this.

- **Symbols:** With careful planning, the "Heroes of the Faith" can be made more memorable and the educational value of the series enhanced, by the selection of a symbolic prop for each figure. Each week in our church, a new symbol met the people's eyes as they entered the church, one more prop added to those of previous weeks in the series, all placed before and around a big, rustic cross. Big symbols, visible to all, as dramatic and interesting as possible. For example? See below.

- **Pass a torch:** Perhaps the most exciting part of one "Heroes" series for us consisted of the passing of a real torch in a short ceremony before each sermon. An older man or woman brought a burning torch from the back of the church to hand to a younger member who brought it to a holder in front of the assembled symbols for that series. As this was done, slowly, carefully, with a flourish, the organ played or the choir sang the chorus of "The Great Parade." A brief word of explanation introduced this ceremony each week, such as:

  "Down through the centuries, the Good News of God's love and justice and peace is passed, like a torch, from generation to generation. People of all nations and races, times and places, have borne this Word and witness to this time and people — to us.

  The torch (using Sterno) continued burning to the end of the service.

- **How about scripture?** In our experience, the study of Christian biographies and writings of earlier Christians brings new light to particular passages and themes of the Bible. But in the suggestions below, no Bible readings are listed, because each person or committee will respond differently, finding different texts coming to mind or jumping from the pages of the biographies or writings. For those who are obliged to read and preach on assigned texts each week, this series may be impossible. But maybe not. Maybe the texts of the day will suggest the person from history. Maybe the service can include separate considerations of a pericope and a biography (on the premise that God didn't stop acting at the end of the first century). Think about it.

- **The seven services:** Here are general and token suggestions for seven services, including three twentieth-century heroes of the faith. You should notice immediately that this list is inadequate in one certain way: It includes no women. This is because these seven examples are probably the best from our three series, because God did not "raise our consciousness" about the role of women in history until the last of the three series, and because (let this be a challenge for us all) the material about Christian women in history is itself woefully inadequate and hard to find.

A. **Peter, the Apostle.** *Symbolic prop:* A large fish net, draped visibly, and used in the sermon to dramatize Peter's life as a "fisher of people." *Reading:* To review Peter's story, print up the key passages about Peter — his call to follow, his recognition of Jesus as Messiah at Caesarea Philippi, his denial, his reinstatement after the resurrection, and the beginning of his sermon on Pentecost — a brief synopsis of each. Use them as a responsive reading, with the people reading Peter's own words. *Ideas for music:* Sidney Carter's song "Bitter Was the Night," our "The Cock Begins to Crow" (from *More, More, More*) and the strong hymn, found in several recent hymnbooks and suitable for choir, "They Cast Their Nets in Galilee."

B. **Francis of Assisi, 1182-1226.** *Symbol:* A tattered burlap robe, simulating a monk's simple garment, with a rope belt. *Readings and music:* The hymn "All Creatures of Our God and King" with words based on words of Francis; the "Canticle of the Sun" as a responsive reading; the "Prayer of St. Francis" ("Lord, make me an instrument of thy peace") as a unison prayer and/or in an anthem setting (of which there are several).

C. **John Knox, fifteenth-century Scottish reformer.** *Symbol:* A brass trumpet, since he has been called "God's Trumpet," loudly and boldly proclaiming God's Word in the face of tyranny. *Music:* Throughout the service, hymn-settings of texts from the Scottish Psalter as found in most hymnals, and the great and appropriate hymn "March On, O Soul, with Strength." *Readings:* Look for Knox's own sermons and the "Scots Confession" which he collaborated on and which is in the Presbyterian *Book Of Confessions*.

D. **Johann Sebastian Bach, 1685-1750.** *Symbol:* A copy of the Mass in B minor, or some other major composition, on an antique or brass music stand. *Readings:* Don't miss reading from Bach's collected letters or other fragments about his Christian belief. *Music:* Obviously, the best thing to do is use his music throughout the service, and with a variety of instruments and groups.

E. **Reinhold Niebuhr.** *Symbol:* A morning newspaper with a sword, symbolizing the Word of God, sticking through it. *Music:* Though you may want to use the English hymn "O God of Earth and Altar," a service full of purely American music would be interesting, including a revivalist song to represent R.N.'s cultural background. *Readings:* A great prayer of confession of Niebuhr's found in *Prayers For Services* by Morgan Phelps Noyes; passages from *Leaves From The Notebook Of A Tamed Cynic*. (Don't be afraid to have a provocative Call to Worship or to have a staged reading of the diary-like passages from *Leaves*.)

F. **Pope John XXIII.** *Symbol:* A window in its frame, which you borrow in a display stand from a construction firm or lumber company; open it at the beginning of the sermon, for John was said to have "opened the window, and the world flew in." *Readings:* Passages from *Pacem In Terris* and other papal pronouncements. *Music:* Settings of parts of the Mass and/or some of the new songs coming from post-Vatican Council Catholicism.

G. **Dietrich Bonhoeffer.** *Symbol:* A noose, since he was hanged by the Nazis in 1945, and since we need to be reminded that even in our own time some people are dying for their faith. *Readings:* Poetry and prayers and personal meditations in *Prisoners For God (Letters And Papers From Prison)*; also parts of *Cost Of Discipleship*. *Music:* Traditional German hymns on which he grew up; also our setting of his words from *Cost Of Discipleship* for tenor, soprano, and choir — "When Christ Calls a Man."

Possible themes: Peter as a forgiven and transformed common man; the poverty of Francis, or his joy in living; the courage of Knox; or faith and politics; the heart-full devotion of Bach; Niebuhr's passion for social justice and love in the real world; Pope John's ecumenical spirit and compassion for suffering people; Bonhoeffer's struggle with God's will and his willingness to die for Christ.

Dance Easter

"Dance, dance, wherever you may be." So starts the chorus in what was the most popular hymn of the '70s, "The Lord of the Dance," words by Sydney Carter to a nineteenth-century Shaker tune, "The Gift to be Simple." Since the Shaker song was a hymn describing specific movements for the worshiper to do and stating the proper place to do them, it was not as far a cry as some may think to use the old Colonial tune for the new words. Most of all, the new song reminded Christians who are aware of history and who recognize that they are in the great march (a form of dance) of Christendom through the centuries that there used to be other methods of worshiping. Perhaps this Easter is the time to reinstate them. Renewal! Easter!

Even some conservative denominations, which for a long time looked askance at dance (though there is no biblical reference that condemns dance as a form of praise and communication), now encourage people of all ages to take courses in sacred dance and even to have groups in their churches. And we have discovered in our travels congregations who sing only medium-well but are able to dance well-done. And many people who cannot carry a tune can move in rhythm (just as, sadly, there are many singers with a poor sense of rhythm, body-wide and note-wise ... not to mention organists — and remember, Don, is one!). People who cannot read a note of music or a word of English can and will move when invited and encouraged to do so. We are grateful, and said so in a litany of gratitude in one of our services of worship, to have had a congregation that was willing to move and to dance since Mr. and Mrs. Ko, from Taiwan, spoke no English and could only participate when we did something physical.

So it is Easter; so let us dance! According to *Alternate Celebrations Catalogue*, 4th Edition, Easter vigils and particularly sunrise services date back to a time when people thought the sun danced when it rose, and they would gather near water so they could see more clearly the sun "dancing" on the waves. So, since we are part of nature, let's see where and how we can do it.

Take the hymn "Jesus Christ is Risen Today" or "Christ the Lord is Risen Today," the one with the "Alleluia" after each phrase of words. Here is a simple step to teach the congregation: On the "Alleluia" step Left, Right, Left and hop on the Left then Right, Left, Right and hop on the Right. Do this on the "Alleluia" only or you will collapse before the hymn is through. This is a step that is very easy to do in the pews, where some worshipers will feel safer, or out in the aisles. It can be done with the whole congregation singing the hymn from the hymnals; or let the choir sing the words and the congregation just dance and sing "alleluia." If you have a dance choir or a group of people who dance easily, let them choreograph movements to do during the words that are sung by the choir (if they do it while the congregation sings, no one will see them if they need or want to be seen). Don't be shy about it. Once the members of the congregation have been invited to dance and they know you mean it, they may go full force, and it will be a glorious thing to behold.

One thing: Allow for non-participation. When you try something new or something that involves unusual activity on the part of all the people, always allow for people who don't want to participate. Invite, don't demand. Suggest, don't insist. In any congregation, there may be people in great sadness, in emotional stress, in a phase of self-consciousness. Be kind to them. And let each service include moments of ministry to those in need, even if the main theme of the service is joyful celebration.

Easter symbols

1. Redeem the symbol — the Easter egg

Rather than just fighting or ignoring the ostensibly secular or "heathen" traditions related to festival times, perhaps we would do better to use them, transform them and, in some cases, find their ancient religious meanings. The Easter egg comes from very ancient sources, including the myths of creation in several cultures — myths which described a cosmogonic egg as the source of the universe. In other cultures, the egg obviously stood for powers of regeneration and rebirth, especially at springtime. Then, many centuries ago, Christians saw in the egg a symbol of the tomb of Christ and of all human beings, from which we break forth in a springtime of the spirit, bursting the walls by the power of God.

Use the symbol. Let it be a symbol of the possibility of new life in Jesus Christ. Invite individuals and families of the church to decorate eggs and to bring them to worship on Easter Day to exchange as gifts with one another. But let the decorations be with Christian symbols and words, including other symbols of Jesus and his resurrection. Have artists of your church prepare and mimeograph sketches and explanations of many such symbols from which egg decorators can choose. And somehow let the wider community know of this possible interpretation of the Easter egg so that Easter egg hunts may all remind people of the resurrection, even though they may be sponsored by the Kiwanis Club or the community and not the church.

2. Use the symbol — a sprout or seedling

In his excellent little book, *The Year of the Lord* (Concordia Publishing House: St. Louis, 1967), Theodore Kleinhans notes that in Naples there was the Easter tradition of giving a seedling of wheat to each person who came to worship on Resurrection Day. If you can't get a seedling of wheat, perhaps a seed or sprout of another kind would do — other forms of new life of this kind have been used in Mediterranean countries. They all can remind us of the New Testament teaching, that a grain of wheat must first be buried and die before it can sprout and grow. In the service, interpret this text and the symbol with an opportunity for people to share "signs of new life" they see in their own experience and in current church life and in the world.

3. Redeem the symbol — the Easter parade

Well, it's not a symbol but a symbolic act of the "Heathen world": The showing off of new clothes on the city street on Easter Day. Can you think of another kind of Easter parade that would claim public attention and point beyond our American preoccupation with clothes and glamour and money? Invite other churches in your neighborhood to join your congregation to march a few blocks with banners and Bibles displayed prominently and Easter songs sung lustily for all to see and hear. Invite people to join in the parade as you go, a "Parade of the Easter People." This will obviously take some interchurch planning and should receive some advance publicity and some news coverage, so that Monday's newspapers could show this different kind of Easter parade as well as the styles revealed on Fifth Avenue in honor of other gods.

4. Symbolize Easter with sunshine

Stars were a symbol we suggested for Epiphany; crosses of all kinds for Lent. For Easter have artistic depictions of the sun rising and shining. You can use gold foil, you can us gold paint, orange cardboard, papier-mâché, all kinds of materials. The symbol also lends itself to mural painting. The sunrise always suggests a new day, an open future, hope, change, growth. It also suggests an affirmative understanding of God. Put a large, glorious sunrise before the congregation for the season, another over the door by which they leave worship.

5. Try this whale of a symbol

The whale (or "big fish") has long been a symbol of resurrection, partly because of Jesus' reference to the "sign of Jonah," possibly a reference to his resurrection. (Jonah emerged, reborn, after three days, with a new sense of mission, etc.) The whale is a delightful kind of symbol, one to be enjoyed by all ages. Invite people to draw or paint or carve or bake or mold or wear all kinds of whales. This ties in nicely with the growing concern for the preservation of the whale as a fellow creature of remarkable intelligence, family devotion, and beauty.

Other ideas

1. Pray before the big Easter celebrations

Leaders, in a quiet and solitary place, pray and listen for God, before facing the big and challenging crowds. Don't forget. Don't forget. (Yes, this is for the music leaders and educators, too. Not just the preachers.) Don't forget.

2. Let fellowship happen

On Easter Sunday assert the continuing fellowship of the church more, not less. Make it obvious to one-time worshipers that there is community and friendship and love in this church, something they may need and desire for their lives. Include them in this fellowship by asking people to greet each other during the service; by sharing leadership with a variety of lay people, young and old; with a "coffee hour" before or after; by making all parts of worship personal, rather than just pompous and eloquent and loud.

3. Roll the stone

In the Mark 16:1-8 version of the first Easter morning the women ask of each other, "Who will roll away the stone for us from the entrance to the tomb?" For many people there is a stone, a very large stone, blocking their entry into the church. This stone is made up of disbelief in a physical resurrection, hopelessness in and for the world in general, cynicism, doubting that there is any good in human beings, and the like. Such people quite often are interested in conversation with believers, from curiosity as well as often from a desire to believe. In conversation they usually come on strong with the historical reasons for doubting, anatomical reasons, psychological reasons, and a whole gamut of "layers of stone." Often, eventually someone rolls that stone from the entrance. It may be the most surprising one; not the first person who started talking to them, but the person who took up when the first person gave up. Don knows. He was there. And luckily or providentially or through the Spirit he has been on both sides of those conversations.

Now, a scene can be improvised by clever actors, or written by a clever writer or a listening committee, on this very situation. It would become part of the sermon: the three women asking the question. And also answering with some of the fears that they have: (1) He didn't do all that he promised to do. (2) I don't want to be disappointed. (3) What if he is still there? (4) How could he get out? (5) No one is going to believe this. Such questions and then some practical thinking on how three ordinary women are going to move that rock: "You're stronger than we are, you start ... put your shoulder down low and lift up ... all together ... no, someone needs to lead or direct or drive ... lean your back into it ... etc."

Now all of these statements have a counterpart in answering and dealing with the originally stated problem. "The strongest in faith start the conversation; think earth and world and how it can be lifted up, even by you; three of us believe and listen to us, take my hand, that's a start; come into the church and then search from inside not from outside, etc." And in many cases, lo and behold, the stone, the very large stone, has already rolled back. We suggest you try this with a small group, your drama group, a youth group, a college group, any group that is made up of supportive people. They may do it as part of their ongoing programs. Then after they have tried it, use it in the Easter service. There may be those visiting with friends who will have their stones rolled back or at least a wedge for the next person or service to work with.

4. Create continuity with series

There are many ways of establishing continuity through the services of the season: A series of prayers — for this church, for the nation, for personal faith, by particular representatives of the congregation; a series of new hymns, or old hymns considered in new ways; a series of sermons or the sharing by preachers of the lections for the season in advance; what else? Such continuity involves the congregation more totally in the experience of worship.

5. Read John's Gospel

Since all but one of Sunday's Gospel readings during the seven Sundays of Easter are from the fourth Gospel, if you do follow the lectionary, invite the whole congregation to make the reading of that book a project for the fifty-day season. Provide background papers and other guidance to the Gospel, or if you have not chosen your adult Bible study for the spring, let John be the book studied by a group or several groups. This is a way to get to a new depth in experience of the scriptures, as worship and study relate for the congregation.

6. Sing Easter hymns all through the season

It seems a shame to celebrate our Master's resurrection in song only one or two Sundays a year. What more important and blessed fact and idea can we sing about? Let the people of your church know that Easter is every Sunday by beginning each service or somehow including in each hour of worship an Easter hymn or carol — all season long! Not only are there some stirring Easter hymns that we rarely sing from our hymnals, but there are some strong and singable newer songs about the Resurrection in many songbooks now available. You might introduce some of these less familiar songs during group meetings on other days of the weeks before you ask folks to sing them on Sunday, and don't forget to practice them with the choirs.

7. Hear a doctor's testimony about death

Perhaps you have in your congregation a physician whose faith is mature and deep. Invite such a man or woman to share his or her faith about the reality of death, telling if possible of ways to claim God's help in the face of death. Give the physician lots of time to think about this and be

140

ready to discuss the matter at length, to open up the subject. And if you are thinking that many doctors would be quite unwilling to discuss the subject, you are probably right. But times are changing in this area of thought among people in the medical community.

If you don't have a doctor in the church, or if you don't think your particular physician-member would do it, invite a thoughtful and articulate nurse to speak. Many nurses are actually closer to patients during long illness than many doctors.

8. Share an Easter meal

We have so many dinners at our churches and yet for us the idea of an Easter Banquet never crossed our minds. We're slow! But what an idea! Instead of celebrating in word and music (and hopefully some dancing, pantomiming, etc.) only in the sanctuary and then going our separate ways home, imagine it spilling over and culminating in a meal in the really crowded dining room and even spilling over into other rooms. A covered dish meal, of course, people furnishing for those who cannot bring. We remember one Christmas when a recently separated man whose family had left town tried to get breakfast in Port Jervis. There was no place open! Not even at the local inn! And he had to eat his Christmas dinner alone. The following year as Christmas approached he reminded us of his dilemma and suggested that some of the church people might like to gather at the church building to have a Christmas dinner to which the single and other alone people would be invited. No one offered to be in charge of this. We did our tiny bit by having him and some of the lonely over to our house, but that isn't what he had in mind. What he had in mind sounds much more like this Easter idea. "What in the world is lovelier than laughter after a meal, rich in proteins and carbohydrates and low in sodium, starches, sugar and fats? ... And this could be the beginning of the Easter season series of programs for explicit help, such as "Framing and Maintaining a Simpler Life."

9. Try this poetic dialog

Included here is a delightful poetic dialog by Dave Steele built around Psalm 150. We did it in our church with a reader reading the Psalm from the lectern and the other voice coming over the loudspeakers as if it were coming from somewhere in the congregation. Of course, we followed it with our Sacred Dancers, upper middle class notwithstanding! There are lots more like it in a collection called *God Must Have a Sense of Humor: He made Aardvarks and Orangutans and Me!* by Dave Steele.

> PRAISE THE LORD!
> Man never was intended, surely,
> To come to church so doggoned early;
> Yet, here I am beneath this steeple
> Gathered with God's dozin' people.
> Just look at us! ... I might have guessed ...
> We all could use a lot more rest.
> Perhaps this morn we'll be so blessed.
> PRAISE GOD IN HIS SANCTUARY!
> PRAISE HIM IN HIS MIGHTY FIRMAMENT!
> Good! ... He's going to read a psalm.
> I love them, for they seem so calm.

I'll join the other people here
And let my mind slip out of gear.
PRAISE HIM FOR HIS MIGHTY DEEDS!
PRAISE HIM ACCORDING TO HIS EXCEEDING GREATNESS!
The Jones' are late ... They'll have to wait.
(My word, it's hard to concentrate!)
PRAISE HIM WITH TRUMPET SOUND!
I've come to find some peace and ease
And so, Dear Lord, no trumpets, please!
Well, I recall, that dreadful noise
Committed by those Beazley boys
Who tooted here last Eastertide
And gave me thoughts of homicide.
PRAISE HIM WITH LUTE AND HARP!
Lutes and harps ... That's much more wise!
And I'll lean back and close my eyes ...
PRAISE HIM WITH TIMBREL AND DANCE!
Do you suppose there's any chance
That someone will get up and dance?
Oh, no one here would be so crass!
Thank God we're upper middle class!
PRAISE HIM WITH STRINGS AND PIPE!
PRAISE HIM WITH SOUNDING CYMBALS!
What?
PRAISE HIM WITH SOUNDING CYMBALS! (CRASH!)
One more like that, for heaven's sake,
And we will all be wide awake.
PRAISE HIM WITH LOUD CRASHING CYMBALS! (CRASH! CRASH!)
Well, Lord, I guess to each one here
Your point is now completely clear.
You seem to feel your drowsy sheep
Can't worship well while half asleep.
We thought you were more tenderhearted.
But now we're up ... So let's get started!
LET EVERYTHING THAT BREATHES PRAISE THE LORD!
PRAISE THE LORD!

10. Another idea for Psalm 150

During Eastertide, explore the possibilities of Psalm 150, Sunday after Sunday. Assign it to a creative group. Sing hymns based on it, and anthem settings for various-aged choirs. Have a dancer or team of dancers respond to it, line by line. Have a dancer lead the congregation in physical responses to it — simple ones in the pews and aisles. And, of course, read it. In fact, PRACTICE reading it in unison or responsively with the congregation, to achieve the spirit and drama of the words. (Practice? Yes, before the service or in the service; it's short. Try it and see how much more meaningful readings can become for everybody.) And, of course, have the instruments named actually present and responding, uniting after the last "Praise the Lord!" for a glorious explosion of sound.

11. Shoot pictures of laughter

For Easter Sunday or later in the season, assign to all the photographers in the church the task of taking pictures of people laughing. Have them print them, enlarge them if possible, even up to poster size. Even make it a kind of contest, for the most interesting picture or for the widest assortment of kinds and ages of people caught in genuine, unposed laughter — or smiles. Then put the pictures up all around the church building, especially where you worship. The slogan for the project: Psalm 126, verse 2: "How we laughed; how we sang for joy!"

12. Dramatize Emmaus

To experience the excitement and down-deep joy of the Resurrection, ask a couple of people to improvise (without extensive rehearsal, but with time to think) a short scene in a service. Let them be the two disciples who walked with the risen Master to Emmaus, starting the scene, just after Jesus has left them, with one saying: "When did you know it was he?" Assign them ahead of time to explain in the scene how they feel, what they are going to do now, and how they will explain to other people about the presence of Jesus. Stop the scene as soon as the audience has been able to get into the emotional situation with the actors. Have the actors freeze in position, then ask (or have the pastor ask): "What would you feel in their situation? What do you feel about the risen Jesus? What would you say? What can you say now? What difference would his presence make in your own dining room, your own family?" And perhaps others could come up to start the scene again or continue from that point.

13. Ask "What's new — or could be?"

A time of sharing. Ask the congregation to think (as part of a sermon, or a time of praise and thanksgiving, or any other appropriate part of your church's service) of what new thing each of them could do during the Season of Easter to make their life more significant, more useful for God, more full of love and the peace of God. "What will you do? What would you like to do, if you can? What do you need to do, to attain 'fullness of life'?" Ask the congregation then to turn into groups of three or four, probably not with members of a family together — or maybe so! — and to share these aspirations and hopes and desires in a few moments of conversation, each taking a turn or opting just to listen to the others. Then sing an Easter hymn or a Gloria Patri in gratitude for new possibilities.

14. Use a variety of styles

We push this idea often, but it is especially important when you have lots of people who aren't usually "church folks" and you need to involve them and reach them. Plan to have a variety of musical styles represented in the service, and even a variety of styles of literature. Bach, rock, folk, Romantic, old, new — all kinds of music for the wide variety of tastes present, all kinds of perceptions of the reality of the resurrection. And prayers that are stately, terse, eloquent, poignant, ancient, contemporary — all kinds, read by different people. *And point out the variety*, rejoicing in the scope of the Spirit's inspiration.

15. Have a call to worship of "Easter voices"

To open your Easter Sunday service, have two people read the words of the Resurrection story — one the narration and another the words of the angel, from Matthew 28 or Luke 24 or Mark 16, in a dramatic style, from *behind the congregation*. (Following the Prelude, and a simple "Let us celebrate!" from the pastor in the chancel, voices from behind the people will demand attention and represent the coming of the story through the centuries to us.) If you use Mark's version, a third voice could speak the words of the women at the tomb. Respond immediately to this reading with the opening of the first, fervent hymn of celebration.

16. Try this on Easter Day and every time you celebrate baptism

"I am baptized!" The renewal of our baptismal covenants should have great meaning for the congregation, and is highly appropriate for Resurrection Day. We also use it after every celebration of baptism. The first few times, give the historic background as follows: "Somewhere we read that Martin Luther, the great reformer of the sixteenth century, did this. When he woke up in the morning in those turbulent times of history and needed reminding of his identity and purpose — just as we do on many mornings of our lives, he would put his hand on his head to recall how a priest put water on his head in baptism. And he would say '*Baptizatus sum!*' (the Latin words meaning 'I am baptized!')" Then, leading the people in the gesture and responsive proclamation, let the pastor say: "Let all who are baptized, put your hand on your head, recalling how water was poured on your head or how you were gently lowered into the water, and repeat after me:

 'I am baptized!'
 'I am chosen!'
 'I am a child of God!'
 'I belong to Jesus Christ!'
 'Amen!' "

17. Have a time for good news

During the "Great Fifty Days" take time each Sunday, in the portion of your service allocated to words and songs of praise, for "Good News" from the congregation. Ask two persons each week to be ready to share a news article or description of an event that shows God at work in the world. Follow this time of sharing with a Psalm or a hymn or a "Gloria Patri" or some other appropriate offering of gratitude. If you have bulletins, simply list this as "Time for Good News." One time, let others share good news spontaneously by standing and telling the congregation or by speaking with their neighbors in the pews. Another idea: Make a display of the news articles of good news in the back of your meeting place.

18. Let people explain their offerings of flowers

Especially in small churches, it should be possible to let those bringing flowers for the celebration of the Resurrection bring them forward themselves and announce the memory each flower represents. This could happen as the first thing in the service, before the prelude, or early in the service, after the opening hymn and prayer. Have your "flower chairperson" up front to show where the flower can be placed to build the arrangement desired. Then let the whole congregation stand to sing in honor of Christ's victory and the precious memories the flowers represent.

19. Trump guilt with Easter

As a celebration of the possibility of rebirth, invite the congregation to write on a large piece of paper (handed out as they arrive) a particular mistake, sin, problem, or experience of alienation from the past, one which has continued to bother them through the months or years, a "hang-up." Then, at a point in the service, have everyone stand and hold up this paper (without having to let others see it) and dramatically tear it up and offer the torn pieces in baskets passed among the pews, as an Easter hymn is played. Let the leader of worship proclaim the forgiving grace of God and the words of 2 Corinthians: "If anyone is in Christ, he is a new creation. The old is gone, the new has come!" Explain this ceremony as practice, an acting out of what must and can happen in our minds and hearts, since "nothing can separate us from the love of God" — not even our worst sins of the past.

We suggest this liturgical act because there seem to be many, many people who cannot fully accept God's grace for their personal lives, people who are "hung up" on past failures and sins. Give the folks time to prepare for this and think about it in the service. It may make a big difference for some people.

20. Tell stories of rebirth

On each of the Sundays of the "Great Fifty," let a story of conversion or of dramatic change in a person's life be told along with (before? after?) the readings of scripture. The stories may be of some great figure in history, of some great person of the present (known or unknown to the public), or by someone about himself or herself, a member of the staff and congregation. Keep them brief, unsentimental, strong, and clear: Examples of the power of the Gospel in people's personal lives.

21. Encourage laity to tell "How I've changed my mind"

For two or three Sundays of the season invite people to prepare short statements about how their thinking about life, about God, about the church has changed in ten years. (There was a series of articles on this theme in *Christian Century* several years ago.) The point of all this might be that God continues to teach us new truth and we can continue to grow in wisdom and understanding.

22. Dramatize the primitive church

One of the passages suggested for reading in the lectionary on the Fourth Sunday of Easter in Year A is Acts 2:42ff, in which the early church is shown as people sharing their possessions, their food, their fellowship. Can you figure out a way to stage this simply in a service? Have people gather around a Communion table or elsewhere before the congregation, bringing different possessions or food to offer the group, telling how much money they got for how much they sold that they may now share with the others, sharing information about threats of persecution, etc. Maybe just a three-minute scene, just enough to show the radical nature of the early church community, following the readings of the scripture.

23. Pray for the pioneers and the skeptics

Especially during Eastertide, pray for those who introduce new ideas, new insights, and new challenges to society and risk persecution — the pioneers of modern times. Some may be scientists, some scholars, some artists and musicians, some novelists, some politicians, some theologians and preachers, some leaders of movements. Also pray for the Thomases of today, the skeptics, those who question what other people more readily accept. Some may question out of insecurity, some may have doubts because of earlier disillusionments, some may be avoiding commitment, and some may be simply wiser than other people, able to keep their heads while others are losing theirs. Pray for openness of mind to pioneers and skeptics on the part of Christians.

24. Worship with this responsive act of praise, including words from the Psalms

An Offering Of Praise

The Lord is risen!

THE LORD IS RISEN INDEED!

All you tyrants of the world, persecutors and oppressors of the weak — beware! Watch out! But victims of the world, you slaves, and you that suffer and have no freedom — be glad! Rejoice!

THE LORD IS RISEN INDEED! "BY HIS OWN POWER AND HOLY STRENGTH, HE HAS WON THE VICTORY!"

All you rich and powerful, comfortable and secure in what you have — beware! Watch out! But you that are poor, you weak people, outcasts and poor, rejected ones — be glad! Rejoice!

THE LORD IS RISEN INDEED! "THE GODS OF THE NATIONS ARE IDOLS THAT CRUMBLE, BUT THE LORD RULES THE WORLD."

All you pompous ones, smug in your religion and filled with pride, cold-hearted in your piety — beware! Watch out! But you that are humble and meek before God, you that hunger for goodness and long for God's mercy — be glad! Rejoice!

THE LORD IS RISEN INDEED! "TRUST IN THE LORD WHO LOVES RIGHTEOUS-NESS, ALL WHO FEAR HIM. HE HELPS YOU AND PROTECTS YOU."

All you that lie, who deny the truth and destroy what is good, and holy — beware! Watch out! But you that are faithful and loyal, who struggle to serve the truth — be glad! Rejoice!

THE LORD IS RISEN INDEED! "LIGHT SHINES IN THE DARKNESS FOR GOOD PEOPLE, FOR THE KIND, THE MERCIFUL AND FOR THE JUST."

Behold, the Lord has won the victory — over sin and death and all powers of evil! So let us all be glad! Let all the earth turn and rejoice!

THE LORD IS RISEN INDEED! ALLELUIA!

25. Share signs of victory

On the Sundays of Eastertide, invite people to share signs of God's victorious action in their lives. Invite two people to be prepared to come forward and speak briefly and then invite others, no more than one or two, to speak spontaneously from the congregation. Tell them to be specific and to honor the assignment, speaking not of other kinds of gifts from God but particularly of triumphs over evil, sickness, patterns of self-destruction, division, and death.

26. Give testimonies about God's triumphs

After the reading of scriptures about Jesus' resurrection, as part of the sermon or in preparation for it, or as an offering of praise, let people tell of God's triumphs. Be specific: Invite people to stand in their places and tell, in a few words or sentences, how they have seen good triumph over evil in recent days or years, or how they have seen truth triumph (or outlast) falsehood, or love prevail over hate. Ask them to give specific examples. You may wish to intersperse their testimonies with stanzas of a triumphant Easter hymn. Now give the people TIME to think, since we are not used to sharing good news, only bad news, and don't give up quickly if no one volunteers immediately. Hang in there; wait.

27. Witness to renewal in your town

Another kind of testimony is the identification of signs of new life in a village, city, or town. Invite people to stand and share such evidence of new life — among people, institutions, businesses, groups — as possible signs of God's power to bring the dead and dying to new life. (Yes: "possible signs," since we cannot confidently assume that our judgments are God's judgments; but we must boldly give thanks and claim God's grace about such matters.)

Worshiping During Pentecost

And so we reach the final season of our church year, number three of the BIG 3.

In Advent Jesus was coming, was *announced,* was promised. And we were all of us at one time coming, on the way, announced noticeably in our mothers' pregnancies. During Christmas Jesus was *resting,* storing energy, building muscles. And we were reminded that not only did we also go through that process, but also now as adults we need to face the importance of resting, sleeping, time off, and time away to re-store. Epiphany was Jesus' season of *growing,* stretching the muscles, finding out who he was, making decisions. And indeed we must have our epiphanies too, our times throughout our lives when we must grow, when we must reach out, when we must experiment with new ideas and new concepts and new things. Growing pains and leads quite naturally to movement. So Lent was Jesus' time for *moving,* hurrying to do the work that was necessary, the work he had decided he had to do. Likewise we reach the point when we act on our decisions, on our knowledge of who we are. And Jesus had to be *dying.* So we meet death. We are dying a little bit each day, many kinds of death. Possibly the worst kind of death for us is the death of the spirit — or the death of the Spirit.

But then Jesus started *breathing* again. This is something we don't know anything about for ourselves. Will we breathe again? Is the afterlife a time and space in which we may have breath again? Here, at this point in the cycle, Jesus leaves us behind experientially. And then sometime later he leaves us altogether in physical form. He said he would not leave us entirely alone and that it was a good thing that he would not be around. And sure enough in Pentecost we take over. The Holy Spirit descends on us and now the rest of the trip is "you and me, babe!" So we have three words for Pentecost: *infiltrating, inflaming,* and *inspiring.*

Infiltrate is defined as "to pass, enter, or join surreptitiously." And so it was, and so it is. The Holy Spirit entered secretly, amazingly, when we were not expecting the Spirit in ourselves and certainly not in others. And then the manifestations took over and surprised us all. The wind, the hovering flames, the actions were most noticeable! And then began the movement when all the people who had received the Holy Spirit, start telling others about it. And for years this was done surreptitiously. It had to be because there was the risk of death. Now, many of us are still doing it surreptitiously, perhaps because, though the fear of death is no longer there, the fear of embarrassment is. Perhaps we are embarrassed by the fervor of some of our sisters and brothers as they infiltrate.

Which brings us to the next word: *inflame.* The flames fluttering over the heads of the believers was obviously a positive sign, an exciting sign. And the flames were eventually transferred into hearts of people. But the word "inflamed" has both positive and negative connotations. "To arouse to strong emotion. To produce or be affected by inflammation" are two definitions of the word. And inflammation means "localized heat, redness, swelling, and pain as a result of irritation, injury, or infection." And some years we go through very upsetting, sensitive periods when even congregations are inflamed and inflame each other as they irritate each other, injure each other, and infect each other. The Holy Spirit is being used instead of using us, to divide people, to label and separate people, to set the approved against the disapproved. The Holy Spirit works at the foot of the cross and at the opening of the empty tomb, the two places where all who claim Christ's claim on them must meet as equals. The Holy Spirit does not work as a thing separated from the rest of the cycle from Advent through Easter. The Holy Spirit as symbolized by the Heavenly Dove must have two wings to fly in any direction other than in a circle.

149

And this moves us to our final word: *inspire*: "To animate the mind or emotions of. To stimulate and influence. To elicit; create. To inhale." (All definitions are from the *American Heritage Dictionary of the English Language*.) What a marvelous word! Can anything be more appropriate to the Holy Spirit? The Holy Spirit infiltrates us and animates our minds and emotions, brings fresh, new breath to us. It's like Easter, like Jesus was at Easter, a man, a person, with new breath. The breath of life, of joy, of salvation, of dignity, of worth. And with this Spirit inflaming us we move out to stimulate and influence others with this joyous new life. A life that is a togetherness with God and with each other, not a separateness from God and from other each. It is our joy to elicit, to bring to light God's truth. It is our privilege to create, to make, to mold, to shape, to design, to lift up, to nurture, to embrace. What a season is this Pentecost! A time to love, to gather, to share, to fly! The last of the big three: Christmas! Easter! Pentecost!

Before we move on, let us remind you of some of the traditions and obvious ideas for this season. Red is the color, in honor of the fire of the Spirit, so invite the members to wear as much red as possible. The renewal of baptisms and confirmation is as appropriate for this day as for Easter. In earlier epochs, the dropping and scattering of red rose petals (for the tongues of fire) and the blowing of trumpets (for the wind) highlighted the day's celebrations, as did the releasing of a dove (as a symbol of the Spirit). Before literacy was widespread, the dramatization of the Acts 2 story was done with flair and imagination — a good idea for our word-saturated culture now, and for congregations where Pentecost is a rather new idea. Pentecost is a day, of course, but in some churches it continues more or less as a season all the way to Advent. As a season, it also gives time for homiletical and liturgical consideration of the meaning of the Holy Spirit, of the doctrine of the Trinity, of the meaning and purpose of the Church as created on Pentecost, and the teachings of Jesus as ways to fulfill our identity as the people of God.

The Holy Spirit

We suggest *The church of the Spirit* as a theme for this season. And beyond, or deeper, than the stereotypical notions of Pentecostal or "charismatic" experiences we suggest two possible biblical passages developing that title or slogan: The "Fruits of the Spirit" and "The Gifts of the Spirit."

- **The fruits of the Spirit** (or "harvest" or "what the Spirit produces" in other translations) are listed in Paul's letter to the Galatians, chapter 5, the final verses: love, joy, peace, patience, kindness, goodness, faithfulness, humility, and self-control. Ambiguously, Paul speaks of these as gifts or products of the Spirit's coming, but also suggests that we must work at them, concentrate on having them and doing them rather than the works of the "flesh" or "human nature." *How about building a series of nine services around the nine fruits?* Choose appropriate hymns and anthems, plan related expressions of social concern, preach on each of them, one by one.
- **The gifts of the Spirit** are the subject of Paul's first letter to the Corinthians, chapter 12. The opening of the chapter is a marvelous text about the ministry of the whole church with its diversity of talents and responsibilities. The "gifts" include ability to speak with wisdom, ability to speak with knowledge, faith, power to heal, power to work miracles, preaching, ability to discern different gifts, and tongues. To build a series around this list may be more difficult and even stressful for the preacher and other leaders, but the possibilities are certainly intriguing. And of course chapter 13 holds up love as the greatest gift.

- **The names of the church** present a third possibility for your services after Pentecost: Take one of the Bible's terms of identification of the church each Sunday for several Sundays: The body of Christ, the household of faith, the people of God, the new Israel, et al. There is a strong and useful litany in the Presbyterian Worshipbook using such names, and this list as well as your Bible "wordbooks" can supplement your own knowledge. And there are an increasing number of songs and anthems relevant to this theme (and not all of them are written by Avery and Marsh!). Ultimately, this theme can serve to point your congregation beyond itself, not only to the rich history of the church but also to its own mission in the world and to its own future as a community of faith.

The "birthday of the church"

Remember that Pentecost, marking the coming of the Spirit to waiting disciples fifty days after Easter, is the "birthday of the Church." Among the "birthday" themes of the day, lest you forget, are these emerging from Acts 2:
- The communication of the Gospel in the languages of the world
- The beginning of the church as a force and fellowship among the nations
- Motivation and inspiration from God as an answer to prayer and waiting
- The gathering of the new fellowship, formed through baptism and later nourished at the Table; visions and dreams as gifts of God to his people, identified in Peter's Pentecost sermon
- The transformation of ordinary people into powerful agents of world change by the Spirit
- The preaching of the Resurrection (also in Peter's address) as a confirmation of Jesus' life and works

Pentecost and mission

Mission is another possible theme for Pentecost, though this is what the churches should be thinking about and praying about all the time. We need to constantly reaffirm that the coming of the Spirit in the New Testament is not just a "new high" for the disciples, not just an ecstatic experience which is an end in itself, not just a vertical, God-and-I kind of thing, but always the start of *action in the world*. The Spirit communicates — outward, drives people out, guides and directs for service. So often our churches are eager for good feeling, happy experiences, fellowship of an often frivolous variety. And today it is quite normal to take the Holy Spirit's name in vain, identifying the Spirit with all warm and vigorous good will.

Moreover, the word "mission" still has old fashioned meaning for lots of average church members, representing something certain other people do out there somewhere, not what all Christians do wherever they are. Immersion in the Acts narratives, prayers about what the congregation is doing that is of the same nature as events in Acts, hymns and anthems and dramatizations about the work of God among and through us — all might lead to a deeper sense of mission for the congregation. And continuing prayer (along with those waiting disciples in Acts 2:1) to know "What do we do now, Lord?" may lead to new Pentecosts.

Dreams and visions

"This is what I will do in the last days, God says: I will pour out my Spirit on everyone. Your sons and daughters will proclaim my message; your young men will see visions, and your old men will have dreams." Acts 2 presents Peter's message on that memorable Pentecost Day and gives us the theme for our consideration of Pentecost any year.

Since it is nearly 2,000 years since that memorable Pentecost, it is time that we, the church, got specific about our dreams and visions. Perhaps a time should be set up for the young people to express their visions of a world that would be closer to the heavenly kingdom. Justice for all would be high on the priority list. Having heard their visions, invite the old people to dream dreams about the same prospect. Having heard those, combine the two and present them to the congregation at large at a worship service. Then, in this service of consideration and commitment, start working on the agenda for your church. Make a list of the things that need to be done in your church alone, and set up meetings and committees for study and development of an agenda. Then start working on them, individually and as groups.

Having tried to improve things in your own church, now turn the same energy out into the closer marketplace. By that we mean the places where your congregation works and plays. Talk to those in charge of the schedule and priorities in your field of work and see how the changes that are being made in your church can be worked out there. From the closer marketplace go to the larger marketplace and then the world. This is a huge task that the church has to deal with or stop merely talking about. With the flames hovering over our heads, the flames that bear our names and our names alone, we need to go out into the world not only teaching and preaching but *practicing* what Jesus has told us. A good study of theology would be helpful because Pentecost is the time for penitence and deliberation and then doing. As the sports people say: "Move it!"

Using music during the Pentecost season

1. Encourage three other kinds of musical language

Pentecost seems a time when the advantage music has over other means of communicating is most obvious. To those of us who do not speak in tongues but appreciate it and recognize it as a valid gift of the Holy Spirit the next best thing is music. Music without words quite often needs interpretation, just as speaking in tongues does. Music is often surprising, almost always emotional, sometimes ecstatic, often gets us to moving in dance movements and eventually out into the world to share it with others. The same can be said of speaking in tongues. Many of us cannot speak in tongues. Many of us cannot sing either, but almost everybody can hum, whistle, or la-la. So we suggest you consider the possibilities of these three kinds of musical language.

- **Humming.** An off-Broadway show some years ago started off with the entire cast lying on their backs on the floor. They started humming, a variety of pitches, not just the same note. They got louder and louder and louder. As they continued humming louder they rose to their feet and moved as close to each other as they could. When the humming finally reached a noise so loud that almost nobody could stand it, the actors made an explosive sound and all leaped back crashing to the floor. This was a memorable and fantastic moment simulating the American bombing of Vietnam. Horrible, electrifying, unforgettable, and all of it done with just a hum.

The congregation sits quietly humming the Negro spiritual, "Were You There?" And let's not forget it's a spiritual, and let's not forget it's black. What could be going on while this humming is happening? The offering could be taken up with the pastor reminding us of Jesus' offering to us of himself on the cross. A small group of people could be pantomiming the Crucifixion. The appropriate people could be passing out the Communion elements. Or the humming could be done just by itself.

Ask yourselves: When do I find myself humming? When do I hum to myself? When do I hum with others? When do I hum with the television? Or with a CD? Or the radio? Why do I hum? Where do I hum? What can I offer with my humming?

- **Whistling.** As we have traveled around the country inviting people to whistle on some of our songs as well as many traditional hymns and carols, we have discovered that whistling is almost a lost art. (How many of you remember the radio show, *The Whistler*? See what we mean?) We have discovered that many people who can't carry a tune and who have been told so by loving neighbors who say to them, "Please don't sing," think they can or know they can whistle. So invite them to whistle. We suggest you might try this first at a church dinner but eventually get it up in the sanctuary, "Where God is," as the little girl was heard to say. Many old hymns and carols can get a new rhythmic life if the congregation whistles through the first verse instead of just hearing the organist play through it. It's possible to discover that a song we have been singing slower and slower really sounds much better at a bright tempo that whistling encourages. Check the above and ask yourselves the same questions about whistling as you did about humming. One of Disney's most popular songs was "Whistle While You Work." We suggest you try this. If you have a large staff, all occupying the same room, we suggest you organize this whistling so they are all doing the same tune. Rather than risking the chance of everybody going berserk.

- **La-la-ing.** What do you do with those poor little kids in the worship service who, with great struggles, hold the heavy hymnals and pretend to read along with the adults? Poor dears, they are trying so hard to fake a foreign language, mouthing sounds one beat late. What to do? Invite everybody to la-la-la. And the kids will sing along joyously and loudly and constantly and feel that they are an important part of the worshiping congregation. In learning a new hymn, Don, rather than involve the congregation in both words and music at the same time, has everybody la-la the first verse. This is a faster way to learn not only the tune, but the spirit of the hymn as well. A further suggestion is to have the congregation sing a verse of a hymn, traditional or new, and then follow it with a la-la verse done very quietly so they can savor the lyrics of the verse they have just sung. Hymns go so fast sometimes, whether done slowly or quietly, that the words just slip right by us.

Variations on la-la-ing are the following:

To simulate brass sounds try pa-pa-ing.

To simulate reed sounds try ma-ma-ing or na-na-ing.

To simulate muted brass sounds try wa-wa-ing.

To simulate sheep in the shepherd's flock risk baa-baa-ing.

Chances are, the congregation will not sleep through the musical portions of the service if you try these things. Happy M-M, Happy WA, Happy HA HA HA!

2. Risk different sounds

We have seen so many church bulletins and posters of church programs and flyers of a season of church music that are so limited that they do nothing but "The Messiah" and Faure and Mendelssohn. The indication to us is that the choir or the choir director is limited to one type of sound and their congregation is limited to believe that is what good church music is. How sad! We recently listened to the recording of Duke Ellington's "Second Sacred Service" and were completely overwhelmed by a Scandinavian singer with a fantastic range who can sing gloriously, operatically, and also with a pop sound, including Scat singing, and "dead center" on pitch. She risks. And her joy and faith and trust illuminate and embellish her risk taking, and we listeners receive the beautiful message from her. Don has his children's choir, the Genesis Singers, make all kinds of sounds from belting a la Judy Garland to imitating wobbly, operatic soloists, from flute-like coloratura to whispered microphone sounds. There is the hope and belief that eventually the young singers will be able to have a variety of sounds at their command and then will choose the appropriate sound for each piece they sing. The message is always the same: eventual Good News. The methods can be so different. Let us rejoice in all of them.

3. Read hymns aloud

There are a number of hymns that the congregation is familiar with and which we can make more meaningful by simply reading them aloud. We do this once in a while, inviting the congregation to read a verse before they sing it. Our suggestion here is a bit different. Find some good readers, really good ones, the kind who get leads in plays in your town, actors, people who can wax dramatic and really color words. Have one such person read the words of, say "Spirit Divine, Attend Our Prayers." It should not be read with a singsong meter as if it is being fit to the music, but read as a poem or dramatic statement. Have the person practice on a microphone if you have one. It is a marvelous feeling to know that everyone in the room can hear what is being done! You might use this as the call to worship. Then later in the service sing the hymn. The following Sunday perhaps, the organist or pianist can play a prelude on the hymn tune, the congregation having been reminded of the words in the bulletin or hymnal.

After the first Sunday, divide the presentations of reading versus sung hymns so that once in a while we hear great words in one service and then sing them in another. Point out the legacy or hymn texts by using them more than once and in a variety of ways. Perhaps you have dancers who could interpret the words or dance to the music without the words being read. Perhaps you have banner makers who can apply their skills to visualizing these hymns. Pantomime the actions described in the hymns. Have the congregation share a symbolic movement with each other. It is a glorious sight to behold when a large congregation raises their arms together in praising God. It is also a very natural thing to do. Go through your own hymnal and find the hymns that are best known. If you have evening worship services make use of lights. The red lights can symbolize the flames of the hovering Holy Spirit as the words are read. There are many possibilities. Discover some of them.

4. Praise God with instruments

Get a number of instrumentalists standing in various parts of the sanctuary. Have one start the opening phrase of the known hymn tune at a certain tempo. Suddenly let another instrument burst forth from another part of the room with the same tune in a different tempo. Add a third. A fourth. A fifth. Let the cacophony continue for a moment then on a given signal, all start again in unison, playing together and making the hair on our heads rise like tongues of fire hovering there!

5. Let Pentecost flow from the organ

This is the day to let the organ shine: to whisper, to blow, to build to a huge crescendo, etc. A good organist can make the hair rise! The story of Pentecost lends itself to improvisations on a "strange hum" in the air, a sound like a wind, and the cacophony. One year we took one large, really large wooden pipe out of the organ and when we wanted the sound of a "great wind," the organist let go on that key and it practically blew the choir out of the loft. Somebody said afterward: "Love lofted me!" and he was immediately struck by lightning, which gave us ideas for staging Annanias and his wife! But we are suggesting that you, organist, much maligned, get to the console and start improvising on the above three themes. As the youth say: "Have a blast!"

6. Use these four Pentecost songs

In our series of books we have four specific songs for Pentecost: "If There Is a Holy Spirit" (*Hymns Hot and Carols Cool*), "Happy Birthday" (*More, More, More*), "What Makes the Wind Blow?" (*Alive and Singing*), and "We Are the Church" (*Songs for the Easter People*).

"If There Is a Holy Spirit" has been arranged for SATB by Don McAfee. We think it is a marvelous arrangement. He has used some exciting chords and countermelodies. The piano or organ part has a strong life of its own and the ending is quite something.

"What Makes the Wind Blow?" is available in a number of settings. First there is a lovely, lush choral arrangement SATB by Carlton Young. He has done some very interesting stretching of the rhythms, which makes the whimsicality of the wind quite obvious. Then he has arranged it again for medium voice solo and piano. It starts off like the choral arrangement then takes a different turn with a lovely, soft, high ending. Then we have a vocal solo arrangement that we ourselves have done. The piano part is rather difficult but we think it adds up to a semi-art song treatment. Each of the three verses has a different type of accompaniment bringing out the mood of the lyrics. In this version there is one place you get to use the middle pedal on your piano! Joy, joy, joy!

"We Are the Church" has been arranged for two-part choir, soloists, congregation and organ/ piano by Carlton Young. Not only is it a fun arrangement but it has two extra dividends: arrangements for Bb instruments, C instruments and bass instruments; and stick figure drawings (with word descriptions underneath) of the movements we have worked out for the chorus.

"Make Joy visible!" said Dick once, and we do it now at every opportunity.

7. Try Elmer's Glue

In our Book No. 6 there is "The Holy Spirit and Elmer's Glue" which can be sung by congregations, family groups, the church school, sharing groups, particularly as they work on problem solving or artistic projects. This book also contains "Different is Beautiful" which has turned out to be a very popular song. We also have a solo arrangement with piano accompaniment, and a fun picture on the cover. This song is good for any time, but Pentecost is a particularly appropriate time since that is the day the diverse groups suddenly understood each other and accepted each other.

8. Sing these songs

Three other songs of ours can find a new context and a new life in the season of Pentecost: "Love Them Now," "O Let's Get On," and "Sing Love Songs." "Love Them Now" is available in a number of forms. It is in our collection *Songs for the Search* and is also written up as a sermon with improvised scenes or stories. Then we have a solo arrangement that we did ourselves that has a counter-melody under the chorus and just chords for the verses so the singer can be as free as possible. Aside from these there is a choral version arranged by Carlton Young for choir, congregation with optional solos. This has the added advantage of a page that can be reproduced for the congregation. Sam (that's Carlton Young's other name) has also arranged this for solo voice. "O Let's Get On" is in *More, More, More*, and John Wilson has made an exciting choral arrangement for SATB that has an almost country and western flavor.

A final song that can be used appropriately for Pentecost is "Sing Love Songs" from *Alive and Singing*. All three of these songs remind us who we are and suggest that we get moving to share the Good News of Easter, quickly, honestly, and openly.

Other ideas

1. Drape the church in red

For Pentecost Sunday, or for several Sundays of the season, drape the church doors with red cloth, outside and inside. Another possibility: Small red and orange pennants, triangle-shaped ones, hanging on string or wire across sidewalks or entrances or streets — the kind used at the opening of new gas stations. Why? To impress people in a memorable way of what Pentecost is about. Focus on the story of "tongues of fire."

2. Talk about the Holy Spirit

The biblical teachings and words are interesting and stimulating for Christians; and the average church member, while she has heard of the "Charismatic Movement" and such things, probably doesn't really know much about the biblical doctrine of the Spirit. Take time to teach, to define, to act out the meanings.

Consider the spirit of your congregation. The spirit, the feelings, the teamwork, the way of working together, the mood as people gather for worship and meetings. Leaders, you think about it. Give the people an opportunity to pray and talk and think about it — but not too introspectively, not too selfishly. Professor John Knox used to explain the Holy Spirit as the *esprit d'corps* of the primitive church. Consider that idea. Is your spirit actually "holy"?

Give attention to the praying of the congregation. Plan ahead for ways to encourage prayer among your members by what you do on Sundays. Plan for deepening the Sunday-service prayers, for involving people profoundly, vigorously, corporately in prayers of adoration, intercession, confession, and commitment. Think about it: Do members of your church really pray during the week? Do they know to pray for each other? On Sunday mornings do people just sit passively listening or listening randomly to the pastor's praying? Do they really care about what's being prayed about? Do the prayers offered during the service express what they feel and know — or just what some present or dead writer of prayers felt and knew? Remember: The Spirit came to praying disciples. That wasn't just a coincidence.

3. Have a conversation sermon on "spirit"

Let the preacher stand near the people and ask them, "What are the occasions of 'spirit' you can think of?" (Team spirit, group spirit, individual ecstasy, all kinds — as we ordinarily use the word.) Then ask, "Can you think of occasions of 'spirit' that had evil results?" (An example, crowd spirit in Nazi Germany, lynch mobs.) Third question: "How can we tell the difference? When is 'spirit' to be identified as 'Holy Spirit'?" The text for this search can be Paul's "Test the spirits."

4. Listen to the breathing

As a kind of "Call to Worship" or introduction to a time of prayer, invite the congregation to be very still and listen to their own breathing. Then guide their thoughts: *We breathe because we are alive ... and to stay alive. We breathe in the air we need, and breathe out — all in our own rhythms, individual and unique. The Spirit is like breath, like wind, which can fill us and give us life and vigor. Sit straight, close your eyes, and breathe slowly, deeply, as if you are breathing in the Holy Spirit of God. Relax as you exhale, then breathe in deeply ... O God, Holy Spirit, fill our lives and give us peace and strength, the power of the risen, breathing Jesus Christ....* Like that, taking time, allowing time for listening and resting at the threshold of prayer.

5. Enliven Pentecost as "a day for wind and fire"

Try a Sunday afternoon conference and celebration. Pushing the symbols of wind and fire helps people find out what Pentecost really was and is. Try it. Gather Christians of all kinds in your city and area to focus on the Holy Spirit and the "birthday of the church" and the church's mission on Pentecost. Unite both the more conventional church members and the charismatics in depth by focusing for the day on the meaning of the church and on all the "gifts of the Spirit" as presented in the New Testament.

Here is a suggested schedule:

3:30   Registration, with flame-shaped name tags.
4:00   Workshop: Songs about the Spirit; reading and dramatizations of scripture about the Spirit; sharing with partners and in discussion actual different techniques for communicating the Good News.
5:30   Dinner and diversions (banner-making, training in drama, small-group activities, more about music, making paper airplanes, etc.)
7:00   Worship: A service celebrating the birthday of the church using some of the techniques and new songs tried at the workshop.
8:30   Good-byes, following the throwing of white dove-like paper airplanes.

And try this in the program: (a) Have everybody bring *musical instruments* to use in the musical times, even with the traditional hymns. As they arrive, aim them to tune with organ and/or piano, then to sit near that instrument and to play along all through the program (not waiting to be invited). (b) *A birthday cake.* You wouldn't believe the size it takes to feed 300 people, as we did one year! "Come, Wind and Fire" or some other slogan might be iced on the cake. (c) *Buttons.* Slogan buttons can be given to all attending to wear home and keep as message-souvenirs of the event. Let them also bear a scriptural theme. You can have them made specially at a low cost.

6. Celebrate the birthday of the church three ways

First, *celebrate the mission you're doing now* — with posters, banners. Have a parade of big posters or of simple banners made by different church groups. Have each poster or banner bear the name or simple description of a mission project your church is actively involved in or supports through the denomination. Lots of them, if you can figure it out. For example, list all the colleges and seminaries of your denomination, since your mission giving probably helps pay for them. Name hospitals and their location, inner city centers of ministry, radio programs owned by the denomination, etc. Have this parade encircle the congregation, as an old mission hymn is played, like "O Zion, Haste." And call out the names and places loudly as each is brought into the parade.

157

Second, *honor the mission that created your church.* How did your church get founded? Where did people come from to start your church? Who were they? Have a Sunday, or a part of a service, honoring this precious history — so people will know that the Gospel didn't originate with us, that we are not existing as a church because of any qualifications or achievement of our own. "Mission" is not just us going out to heathen "them," but is what made US aware of God's grace in the first place.

Third, *make an offering of missionary intentions.* At the end of the Pentecost Sunday service, or some other time during the Sundays after Pentecost, invite members to write down names of people they will visit, phone, write to, and in other ways attempt to communicate with about Jesus Christ and the Good News. Have them make two copies of this list or a single name and put one copy in a special offering. Dedicate the offering with earnest prayers and songs for the guidance of the Spirit, for the ability to communicate.

7. Consider the people gathered in your "Jerusalem"

The Spirit gave apostles the power to communicate in languages of many different kinds of people gathered in Jerusalem for the Jewish festival. This story could provide a background and point of departure for a consideration of your city. Use a sermon period, a study group, or a continuing time of prayer in a sequence of Sundays to consider: What different languages are spoken here, and is anyone preaching and praying and talking to people about the Gospel in those languages? What different kinds of people — rich, poor, socially active, lonely and inactive, wild and adventurous — are there in conspicuous groups around town, and how is the church relating to them? What groups are there that are formed around interests and skills, according to ages? Are your services appealing to them? Is the church's schedule of activities of interest to them? What new "tongues" must be tried to communicate?

8. Hold a Pentecost candlelight service

We all have our thrilling candlelight services in late Advent or Christmas Eve commemorating the occasion when Light came into the world through the birth of Jesus. Since in our church the "Christ Candle" was put out on Maundy Thursday in the "Tenebrae" ("Service of Shadows") and relighted on Easter when Jesus triumphs over death, how about a Pentecost Candlelight service? After all, the tongues of flame are one of the richest symbols of the Holy Spirit, so why not make use of this in a daytime or evening service that includes the lighting of candles for everyone? Do it the same way you did your Christmas Eve service and point out the relationship of Jesus, the Light, being passed on to all the world, as well as reminding all of the "fire of the Spirit," the glow of God's love within and among us. Use red candles, or a combination of red, yellow, orange among the people.

9. Symbolize Trinity Sunday

If you do observe Trinity Sunday, don't just talk and intellectualize about it. Have a Sunday school class or adult group or volunteer group prepare all the symbols they can learn about for display: Symbols of the Trinity and the "three persons" and their relationship. Decorate the whole church building with them, march them in during a processional hymn, prepare small ones to pin on people.

10. Allow for the breeze

As you plan your summer (we are saying to ourselves as well as to all you faithful readers), allow for time for silence, for wandering and wondering in solitude — away from spouse and family, for charitable self-evaluation. In short, for the wind of the Spirit, which sometimes comes like a soft, cool, refreshing breeze to lift our faces to new horizons. Don't forget. Solitude. Time. The Spirit.

11. Wear red

Red is the color of Pentecost, so wear red dresses, red shirts, red pants, red jackets, red hose, red shoes, red ties, red scarves, red hair (if you are determined to use red dye anyway), red socks, red belts, whatever.

12. Wear white

But we just said wear red! Ah, yes, but the English traditionally wear white robes on Pentecost, which is why they call it Whitsunday. White is the color for joy, and is also symbolic of purity (appropriate to Pentecost confirmations). So if you want to stand out in the crowd of red, wear white and tell everybody why you are doing it so they won't think you are just trying to be different.

13. Invite the birds

One year a pigeon flew into the open window in our sanctuary and we had a terrible time getting her out. He (we had no time to discover the sexual identity of said bird) swooped around cooing with fright as a couple of adults tried to focus him on the open window and all the rest of us kids laughed with glee. We are reminded of this happening as we approach Pentecost. There is an old tradition of bringing doves to worship on Pentecost, in honor of the Holy Spirit. Perhaps in your community someone raises doves or pigeons. If so, invite them to bring the birds to church to remind us of one of the great symbols of Pentecost. Let the birds be placed somewhere through the hour where they can be heard cooing and fluttering.

14. Schedule baptisms

Next to Easter, Pentecost is the most natural and exciting day for people to join the church family. If you remember the first Christian Pentecost, 3,000 were baptized according to the story in Acts. In most of our churches, 3,000 is not a possibility, but even one is glorious.

15. Physicalize joy

In many Christian countries through the years, Pentecost Sunday, indeed the whole week after the day itself, was a time of games and fairs and decorations. So what better way to physicalize "utmost Joy" than to go as a church group and play tennis and hit the ball as high as the Heavenly Dove could fly while wearing white clothes trimmed with red? If tennis is not your bag, try bad-minton with a gorgeous shuttle-cock, now called a birdie (did they know about the Heavenly Dove?), or even hit fly balls with a bat or throw the discus or Frisbee or whatever. Don't just sit home and watch somebody else do them on television. Let the Spirit move you. Out.

16. Display flames

In all of the church buildings put flames large and small for Pentecost Sunday and maybe Sundays that follow. Construction paper, cloth, all kinds of materials, glued, hanging, tacked, painted, etc. Emphasize the day's holy significance by giving each person who comes to worship a little red and gold flame of construction paper or cardboard to pin on their lapel.

You can also make this a project from your Sunday school. Using a pattern about ten inches high, have the kids cut out flames from heavy paper or cardboard and color them with crayons. Then they can hang them on invisible thread (so invisible we always have trouble finding it) from a high pole suspended horizontally in the church. Hoist the flames up during the Sunday school hour on Pentecost Sunday, hanging above the chancel, fluttering in the breeze in all shades of red, orange, purple, and yellow. A suggestion about the flames' color: After the coloring with crayons, paint them over with black India ink for a burning look, and color both sides of the cardboard, since they should move above the people's heads. Experiment before involving the children.

17. Share dreams

In response to the proclamation of Joel quoted by Peter in Acts 2, invite the congregation to stand up and tell or write out "This is my dream" about the world, about their church, about themselves as Christians. Similarly, invite the youth group to respond to "Your young people shall prophesy" by prophesying. Not in the sense of predicting, but in the biblical sense of proclaiming, speaking forth for God. Ask the kids, "What do you have to proclaim, to denounce, to challenge the rest of the church about?" Read their responses to these questions in a service and print them up for a newsletter under the quotation from Joel. Do a similar thing in response to the "Your old people will dream dreams" line: What do the old folks in your church have to proclaim to the young people? Ask them. Repeat their answers in a service.

18. Get brassy

It is one of the old traditions to have trumpets play during the telling of the story from Acts 2 to represent the wind of the spirit. (If you don't have trumpets, probably trombones would do! or some of the windier stops on the organ, as a last resort.)

19. Go to a hilltop for Ascension Sunday

Do it on Sunday morning if you have a hill nearby, or at a special evening service or with a group of stalwart members at another time — on Ascension Sunday or on Ascension Day (forty days after Easter). Tell the story of the Master's departure on the top of a hill, beneath the glory of the spring sky. Stress at the story's end the fact that the disciples remain here on the earth to represent him, having to go down from the mountain to the waiting world. But stress also the belief that our Friend and Savior rules heaven and earth, beyond our ability to limit him.

20. March in "The Great Parade"

"The Great Parade" is a festival service, an educational celebration. It includes a roll call of Christian heroes from history, trumpet fanfares, drum rolls, and a parade song. The presentation can be a whole service or just the "sermon period." It involves the whole congregation. It has been done in small churches and with groups of several thousand.

21. Make a "fruitful" mobile

Have a group make a large mobile (ten or twenty feet across or whatever fits your worship space) of the "fruits of the Spirit" listed in Galatians 5. Use symbols and/or words for each of the "fruits," made out of whatever material seems appropriate. Hang the mobile over the congregation, or somewhere else it can be seen during the services after Pentecost. If you have a sermon series on the "fruits," you might add one each Sunday, the symbol for that quality or characteristic of the Christian life under consideration. The center of the mobile might be the flame or dove to represent the Spirit, or the down-reaching hand of God superimposed on a large flame — or vice versa. A good project for group of artists in your church?

22. Explore the variety of languages

As a conversation-sermon, or in some other form of response to the Pentecost story in Acts, ask: What languages are available to us for communicating the Good News? There are, of course, spoken languages — those known by missionaries representing our churches and in translations of the Bible and other printed materials. What other languages? What languages does the body speak? Touching is a language — either tender and loving communication or cruel and rough. Facial expressions are a language — how do we look to other people who don't know God's love? Giving money, food, or other gifts is a kind of language — how well do we speak it as a church? What other languages are there? "What language can I borrow to thank Thee, dearest Friend?" as the poet of "O Sacred Head Now Wounded" asked.

23. Try a seesaw as a symbol for Pentecost

As we read through the lessons for that very long season, we are struck by the fact that the people of God go so often from high to low in their relationship to God. Also, in a number of the readings there is the call to return to God, to get back on a high with God, to claim God's control over their lives. So we thought of the seesaw and the marvelous feelings children (of God or otherwise) have when they are on the end that is high up in the air. We also remembered the corresponding low feelings on the other side. As we contemplated on this symbol we thought it really showed quite obviously where we were with God. If your church is used to having children's sermons and you have the space for it, it would be a really interesting focal point to have a seesaw in the sanctuary. Now before you look askance or worry about what other people might think of it, remember what Jesus said: "Unless you come as a child." The seesaw can also be used by the adults as a barometer of where they are at the moment with God. It might be a place to check each week to see how things are going. Am I up or down? Am I high or low? Is my flame burning brightly or dimly? Where am I?

24. Have a red-letter day

Now think about this as you read it, and think about it again afterward. Many of the things suggested in this chapter are surprising or elicit "You're kidding!" responses. But remember what was said about the believers on that day: "They must be drunk!" Well, this Red Letter Day idea is unusual but can be the sermon with props and congregational participation. It takes some risking and some listening. And the preacher puts it all together and makes sermonic points.

As the people enter, each person is given a red letter. You need nine shades of red and with the variety of reds in different packs of construction paper it is possible to do this, particularly when you include maroon and burgundy and red-orange, etc. Here is the list of letters you need; you choose the colors:

    EOLV in one color
    OYJ in another
    AEECP in a third

AEEICNPT In a fourth
EIDKNNSS in a fifth
EOODGNSS in a sixth
AEIUFFHLNSST in a seventh
IIUYHLMT in an eighth
EOOCFLLNRST in a ninth

As the sermon starts the congregation is told to search out other people holding letters of the same *shade of red*. (The ushers can be called on to help those who are color blind.) When they get together they have to spell out the word that their letters spell. You, as leader, know that they are the nine fruits of the Holy Spirit. Some words will be spelled out very quickly: Joy and Love. As you notice what is happening, and do look, talk to those who are finished. "Your word was easy to spell. Is it easy to sustain while others are taking longer, etc." When all of the words are completed have a person in each group call out the word.

The things you say as they are trying to figure out the words are part of the sermon and as you continue let it be relevant to the experience they have just gone through. Example: "Did you lose patience while trying to spell the word? Have you lost patience with the Word some time? Have you been patient with those around you?" etc.

As a conclusion perhaps: "Since the Holy Spirit moves in mysterious ways, perhaps you got the word that you need to examine or work on most. If you think so, write it down on a piece of red paper or the back of the letter you got, and take it home with you. Put it where you can see it often and let it work for you. Patience on the refrigerator door may mean: Think it over; should you be nibbling? Patience on the television may mean: Listen to the news differently. Patience on the mirror may mean: Stop fretting; God loves you. Patience on your desk top may mean: Give him time to think and to grow up. Perhaps it would be a good idea to move the sign around. Each day put it in a different place, in another room, on a different person. The fruits of the Spirit are not the same as the gifts of the Spirit. The gifts are free; the fruits need nurturing. Let this season be a fruitful one for you — one red letter day after another."

25. Share the signs of the Spirit

During the Sundays after Pentecost, have, as a special Liturgy of Gratitude or as part of a sermon, a time for people to identify "Signs of the Holy Spirit" in their lives or in the wider world. There are two ways to do this: (a) Have people stand in their places and tell everyone, with the congregation responding after each statement (with an antiphon of praise). (b) Have people form groups of three in their places and think and talk together, with a doxology or hymn following. Don't rush it, but don't take too long either. Keep this a rather formal act of worship, not just a time for chitchat. Perhaps the reading of Galatians 5:22 should precede the invitation to share.

26. Interweave a Pentecost hymn and news flashes about mission

Have the congregation sing a hymn like "O Spirit of the living God, in all thy plentitude of grace," and between the stanzas have people rise to read a bit of current information about a mission enterprise in the world as if reading a news item on the television. Include news about a far away church — Africa, India; include something about Christian work in another part of the U.S.A. or Canada; include something about the church's work in your own town, preferably ecumenical action. Other hymn possibilities: "O Zion, haste," "Jesus shall reign where'er the sun."

27. Delay Pentecost when Memorial Day conflicts

Some years, the Sunday that occurs fifty days after Easter, is the same weekend as Memorial Day. When that happened in our church in Port Jervis, we marked the event rather calmly that day, because many of our folks were preoccupied with Memorial Day weekend travels and gatherings. Then we pulled out the stops with confirmations, Communion, red clothing, special music, and all the rest on *the following Sunday*. This adjustment may offend some of our readers, but we felt that we didn't want to sacrifice such a great celebration to our legalism about the calendar — and we couldn't really change Memorial Day's date. (And that civil holiday is probably an important respite and emphasis for lots of people.) Think about it ahead of time.

From *The Avery And Marsh Songbook*

We Are The Church

Richard Avery and Donald Marsh

From *The Avery And Marsh Songbook*

Every Morning Is Easter Morning

Dedicated to Kathryn Wright

Richard Avery and Donald Marsh

ENDING:

167

Passed Thru The Waters

Richard Avery and Donald Marsh

168

I Wonder Why

A Lenten Song

Richard Avery and Donald Marsh

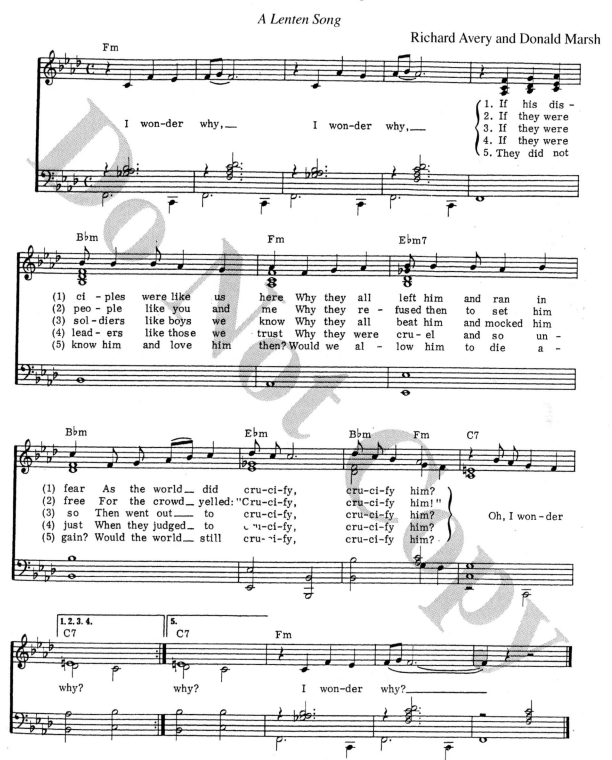

My God Breaks Down Walls

Based on Ephesians 2:14

Richard Avery and Donald Marsh

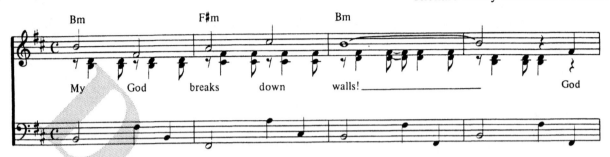

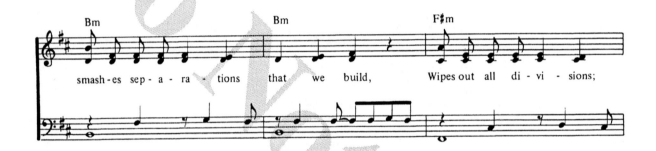

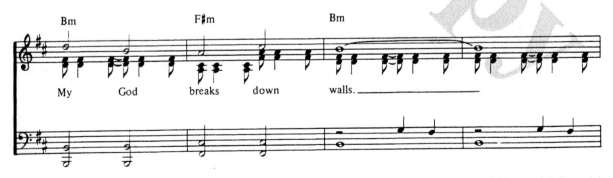

Ready, Lord!

A song of commitment to the mission of Jesus

Richard Avery and Donald Marsh

From *The Second Avery And Marsh Songbook*

The Spirit Of The Lord

"Our Purpose" *(Luke 4:16-20)*

Richard Avery and Donald Marsh

Use as a final hymn, as a statement of the church's purpose.

New Hopes, Old Dreams

A Hymn for Eastertide or Any Time

In honor of the 100th Anniversary of the
First Presbyterian Church of Brighton, Colorado

Richard Avery and Donald Marsh

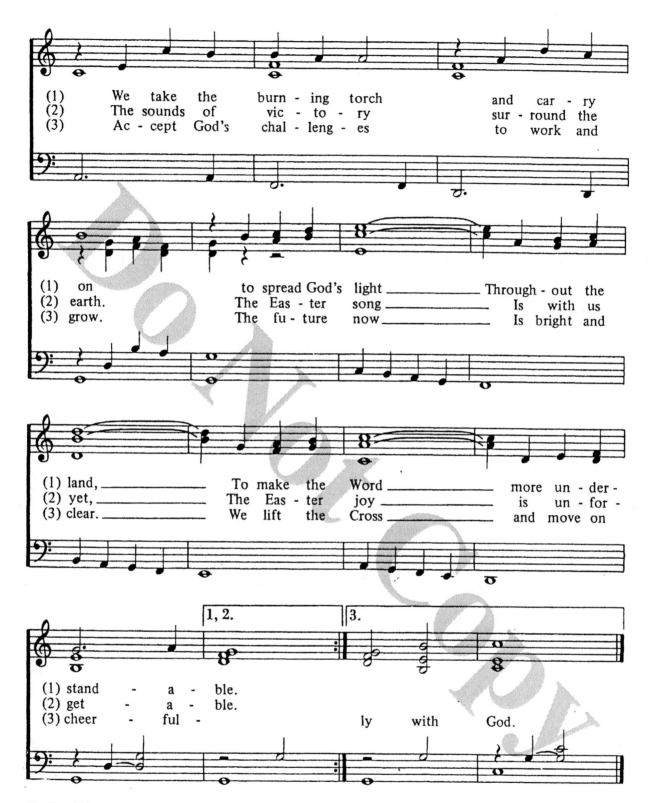

Peace I Give To You

John 14:27

Richard Avery and Donald Marsh

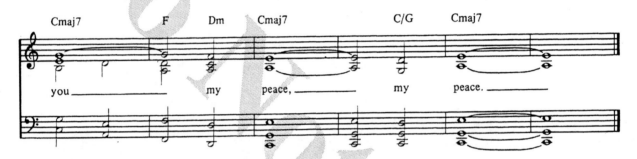

Follow The Star

A gathering song for Epiphany

Richard Avery and Donald Marsh

Fol-low the star! Fol-low the star! and some-day in its pres-ence you'll find out who you are. Learn how to see. Learn what to do. Then you'll learn the things that God has planned for you. So fol-low the star! Fol-low the star! and some-day in its pres-ence you'll find out who you are.

Jesus Stands With Open Arms

A gathering song

Richard Avery and Donald Marsh

Tell The Children

Richard Avery and Donald Marsh

Learn it well, write it down, tell the chil-dren. Put it on stage, put it in song, tell the chil-dren. Age to age, pass it a-long to the child-ren's chil-dren! The sa-cred sto-ry, what God has done, the love and glo-ry. — To ev-'ry-one, pass it on, tell the chil-dren.

Thy Kingdom Come

Richard Avery and Donald Marsh